# ZOINKS!

## THE SPOOKY FOLKLORE BEHIND SCOOBY DOO

**MARK NORMAN**

OAK TREE BOOKS

CHIN BEARD BOOKS

*ZOINKS!*
Published in 2024 by
**Chinbeard Books**

in association with
**Oak Tree Books**
oaktreebooks.uk

Text Copyright © 2024 Mark Norman
Illustrations © Copyright 2024 Rhi Wynter
Editor: Barnaby Eaton-Jones

The right of Mark Norman to be identified as the author of this work has been asserted in accordance with the Copyright, Designs and Patents Act 1988.

All rights reserved. No reproduction, copy or transmission of this publication may be made without express prior written permission. No paragraph of this publication may be reproduced, copied or transmitted except with express prior written permission or in accordance with the provisions of the Copyright Act 1956 (as amended). Any person who commits any unauthorised act in relation to this publication may be liable to criminal prosecution and civil claims for damage.

The views and opinions expressed herein belong to the author and do not necessarily reflect those of Chinbeard Books or Oak tree Books.

*To Fred, Daphne, Velma, Shaggy and Scooby
and all those who have portrayed them.*

# CONTENTS

Foreword . . . . . . . . . . . . . . . . . . . . .v
Preface . . . . . . . . . . . . . . . . . . . . . vii

Chapter One . . . . . . . . . . . . . . . . . . . .1
Chapter Two . . . . . . . . . . . . . . . . . . . 14
Chapter Three . . . . . . . . . . . . . . . . . . 28
Chapter Four . . . . . . . . . . . . . . . . . . . 49
Chapter Five . . . . . . . . . . . . . . . . . . . 73
Chapter Six . . . . . . . . . . . . . . . . . . . 92
Chapter Seven . . . . . . . . . . . . . . . . . .111

Afterword . . . . . . . . . . . . . . . . . . . .130
Appendix . . . . . . . . . . . . . . . . . . . .133
Acknowledgements . . . . . . . . . . . . . . . .155
About The Author . . . . . . . . . . . . . . . .157

# FOREWORD

Scooby Doo is the gift that keeps giving and I almost missed it.

When I was asked by head of Warner Brothers Animation Sam Register if I'd be interested in pitching ideas for a new, scarier and modern take on the iconic Hanna Barbera property, I initially turned him down. I was very familiar with the show, which had been around from before I was born. I knew it had a huge fanbase and had found its way into the very fabric of our culture as a gateway into horror for younger kids. Despite all that, I was not a big fan. Yes, I had watched it as a kid, but as an adult – and huge horror fan – it was just too young for me. Beyond the original, I had never really liked most of the spin-offs that I'd seen (full disclosure, I hadn't seen many of them). To me, passing on something I could not be passionate about was the right call. But Sam was persuasive. He told me that he would give me a chance to make a Scooby Doo show that would not only allow me – and fellow producers Tony Cervone and Spike Brandt – to create something we wanted to watch, but we could also make it truly scary for the first time. It wouldn't be easy, but if we could convince the WB brass of our vision, he'd give us a green light. That was the carrot, and I bit.

As I said, I had never delved much deeper than the original incarnation. Something, though, had made that version – *Scooby Doo Where Are You!* – resonate in our culture for over 50 years and I needed to figure out what that "something" was if I was going to be successful in creating a new generation of fans. This was where I came to a realization that I have held on to ever since...

Horror stories are just children's stories for adults.

Many of the same concepts from horror – the unknown, the fantastical, hidden and symbolic meaning in the actions of the antagonist, greater understanding of self at the end of the journey – are hallmarks of the great children's stories. *The Three Little Pigs*, *Hansel and Gretel*, *Snow White* are horror stories told from a child's perspective. Scooby Doo taps into that notion, the key of which being that none of the monsters are ultimately real. Like all good children's stories – most of which have their origins in folklore – the monsters are manifestations of fear and trauma. Being alone in the dark, getting lost in a strange place, fear of people different than you. Tapping into these primal fears, used to such great effect in folklore, has always been the key to Scooby Doo's success. The audience identifies with the Scooby gang because on some level the mysteries they are trying to solve tap into that fear and trauma. And the fact that at the end of each episode the monster/fear/trauma is revealed to not be real – but in fact an imposter that can be defeated and stopped – is the key to the series' success. The unmasking is catharsis.

Would kids get this? Probably not. At least not intellectually, but for myself and Tony it opened the door. We'd found our way in.

We pored over the original materials for *Scooby Doo Where Are You!*, and then began looking for new pieces of folklore we could adapt (such as the legend of the Hodag from Wisconsin, and the Summerian stories about the Anunnaki which featured heavily in our second season and our overarching series storyline). Of course, if we'd had a book like this one, it would have made our job much easier. We wanted the stories to resonate with the children and adults watching (there were a lot of adults watching as I would find out later). Many of the episode ideas came out of looking for fears and anxieties that would afflict our lead characters. The process then began to find a suitable monster to illustrate that fear. Having a book like this that would have done that legwork for us would have been invaluable.

It has been more than a decade now since writing any stories for Scooby Doo, but there is not a month that goes by that I don't read an article about the show. Scooby and his four human mystery-solving pals have permeated the consciousness of the world. That is not an exaggeration. There is not a country I have travelled to where the show is not known. That kind of cultural integration, in my opinion, is born out of a universal recognition of the stories we – and all the other incarnations of the show – told. Somewhere in the childhoods of all the children who watched is a story they heard, or a piece of folklore told around a campfire, that resonated and stuck with them. Fifty years and counting later, Scooby Doo is a piece of modern folklore that can be added to the history that came before it. I feel very fortunate to have played a small part in carrying on the tradition.

**Mitch Watson**
*Showrunner/Co-Creator/Head Writer*
***Scooby Doo: Mystery Incorporated***

# PREFACE

We all know the premise. A building, person or community is being terrorised by something not-of-this-world. Maybe it's a ghost, or a cryptid of some kind. It might be connected to that age-old legend of the recluse in the castle. Or it could be a being from another dimension.

Or maybe, it might just have been that creepy old fairground owner covering up some nefarious deed being committed under cover of darkness? And he would have gotten away with it to… if it wasn't for those meddling kids. And their talking dog.

Fred, Daphne, Velma, Shaggy and, of course, Scooby-Doo have been investigating spooky goings on for more than fifty years now. And they look good on it too. All that running and screaming is obviously beneficial to the health.

From its debut in 1969 through to the present day, the Scooby Doo franchise in all of its various iterations has always drawn heavily on real-world folklore and legend. From Season 1 Episode 1 where the Black Knight's armour miraculously comes to life to much more modern concepts surrounding the Nibiru Cataclysm in *Scooby-Doo! Mystery Incorporated* (2012), many of the show's stories have either referenced or directly dealt with folklore from around the globe.

In this book, the first to look directly at how Scooby-Doo sits within our real-life cultural background in this way, you can learn about the folklore, myths and legends that inspired so many of the gang's adventures and how it compares to the way that it is represented on the show. And surprisingly, more than a little about how Mystery Incorporated have generated urban legends and folklore within our own world. Jinkies!

# CHAPTER ONE

## COLLEGES AND CANNABIS
Scooby-Doo legends in the real world

## Development

Before we split up and look for clues into the real-world folklore that appears within Scooby-Doo, we should also note that the Scoobyverse has an effect upon our own environment too. Over the years, a number of myths and legends have sprung up around the programme. The lives of the Mystery Incorporated gang have also fed into what is now established pop culture.

We should begin at the beginning, with a look at how the institution that is Scooby-Doo came into being.

It was the assassination of United States Senator Robert F. Kennedy Jr in 1968, the year before *Scooby Doo Where Are You!*[1] first hit the screens, that kick-started the development of the show. Kennedy, a presidential candidate at the time, had just taken victory in the Californian primary when he was shot a number of times by 22-year-old Sirhan Sirhan. He died a day later.

1968 was a year of great unrest in America and, as often happens at such times, tensions spilled over into the media. In particular, children's television came under the spotlight. Lyndon Johnson was still in the White House, although he had decided not to seek re-election, and it was his administration that issued demands that the danger that depictions of cartoon violence posed to easily influenced children be addressed.

Parent groups, acting as unofficial watchdogs, began to protest against these programmes off the back of the Johnson edict. Leading the assault was

---

[1] Eagle-eyed reader will notice the lack of a hyphen in the middle of Scooby's name at this point. The first two seasons of *Where Are You!* broadcast in 1969 and 1970 clearly show the name as being unhyphenated. This makes perfect sense as Doo is the family name, with Scooby being a contraction of his full first name Scoobert. The next iteration of the show, Season 1 of *The New Scooby-Doo Movies* introduced the hyphen, which has been part of the name ever since. Even though it makes no sense in terms of naming conventions, the 'correct' spelling of the name post-1970 is therefore Scooby-Doo.

the group Action for Children's Television (ACT), which was newly formed and had first been looking into the syndicated show *Romper Room* – a vehicle for marketing associated toys. They turned their attention to these Saturday morning shows, many of which were from the Hanna-Barbera stable. Programmes such as *The Herculoids, Space Ghost* and the Marvel Comics-based *Fantastic Four* soon fell under the spotlight. Many were cancelled.

The request for programming that led to what would ultimately become the Scooby-Doo we know and love came from the CBS executive Fred Silverman. He had already found success (and the approval of the pressure groups) with *The Archie Show*. Music featured heavily in this programme; the song 'Sugar Sugar' came from the show and became a hit, reaching number one in the American Billboard charts in 1969 and staying there for four weeks. It was to become a hit once again twelve months later for soul singer Wilson Pickett. Based on the success of *The Archies*' original, Silverman asked Hanna-Barbera to develop a show about a teenage rock band who solved mysteries when they weren't performing.

William Hanna and Joseph Barbera had enjoyed successful careers at Metro-Goldwyn-Mayer before breaking away and forming their own studio, which became essentially responsible for creating the half-hour cartoon format for television at that time. Before this, cartoons were mostly 'shorts' of just a few minutes in length. In their time, the producers earned seven Oscars and eight Emmys, and were immortalised on the Walk of Fame in Hollywood. They also brought us most of the much-loved cartoon characters of the twentieth century, including the Flintstones, Captain Caveman, Dick Dastardly and Muttley, as well as the Mystery Incorporated gang.

It was to writers Joe Ruby and Ken Spears that Joe Barbera turned to realise Silverman's request. Also brought onto the project was character designer Iwao Takamoto, who had previously worked at Disney on films such as *Cinderella*, *Sleeping Beauty* and (appropriately for the new project) *Lady and the Tramp*.

The Scooby Doo format passed through a couple of iterations before it settled onto the final design that we see now. The first pitch was rejected by the station as being too scary looking for young viewers, at which point the decision was taken by Fred Silverman to concentrate on the comedic elements of the show. He tasked Joe Ruby and Ken Spears, along with Hanna and Barbera and their team, to rework the pitch and the rock band concept was dropped. Scooby himself was once a sheepdog. Ruby and Spears had originally written him as the Great Dane that we see now, but Joe Ruby became concerned that he would look too similar to the popular newspaper comic character *Marmaduke* and at the last minute he was changed to a sheepdog. Fred Silverman rejected this and he reverted back to his original design.

Scooby was not alone in having alterations to his design; the main characters all underwent changes from the original pitch. Starting life as Geoff, Kelly,

Linda and W.W., in the last version of the show, they were renamed to Fred, Daphne, Velma and "Shaggy" respectively. Their canine companion was named 'Too Much' up until the eleventh hour when this was changed.

There is one well-established story that tells how Scooby got his name. That is, on an overnight flight to a meeting, Silverman listened to the Frank Sinatra song *Strangers in the Night*. Sinatra's vocal improvisation at the end of the track allegedly provided the inspiration for the new name and the repackaged pitch was taken to CBS executives, where this time it was approved and *Scooby Doo Where Are You!* went into production.

In a 2002 blog post, comic book and television writer Mark Evanier (who has written for the show in the past) disputes this, suggesting that a far more likely source was the 1963 hit *Denise* by doo-wop band Randy and the Rainbows. This very catchy number had, and still has, a great deal of airplay and features in its refrain the oft-repeated line "I'm in love with you, Denise, Scooby Doo". Evanier's theory is that this is a stronger contender for the main name, with Sinatra's scat still contributing the 'Dooby' element to the catchphrase "Scooby Dooby Doo".

There is a further twist in this tale (or should it be 'tail'?). In his 2009 book *Iwao Takamoto: My Life with a Thousand Characters*, the legendary designer and producer notes that although Fred Silverman always swore by the story that he got the inspiration from listening to Sinatra on a plane journey, Takamoto knew for certain that there was a design in the Hanna Barbera archives from the early 1960s for a dog named 'Scooby'. The animal looked nothing like the Scooby-Doo who was to appear in the long-running franchise, but the name was certainly already to be found somewhere in the studio's past.

There is, incidentally, no good reason given as to why the title of the original series *Scooby Doo Where Are You!* does not end with a question mark.

## The Gang

In the main characters of Scooby Doo, the gang themselves, we find a number of stereotypes. To view this from a folklorist's angle, we might see Mystery Incorporated as archetypal characters. Folklore is full of archetypes. These are universal images or symbols that appear throughout all cultures in their art, their literature and their mythologies. Because they are universal, archetypes may be read the same way in any culture and hence the viewer will always ascribe a similar meaning to their interpretation. This sets them aside from most other symbols or motifs in a culture, which are essentially meaningless until the members of a particular cultural group ascribe meaning to them through their own beliefs and norms.

These are what we might consider to be the main stereotypes of the Mystery Incorporated gang in their original incarnation for *Scooby Doo Where*

*Are You!* (most of them being highly reflective of the era in which the show was conceived):

**FRED:** If anyone may be seen as the unofficial leader of the gang, then it is Fred Jones. He is represented by a white, middle-class male – powerfully built and generally brave (certainly representative of the patriarchal society that was still in place in the late 1960s). In American college terms, he would be considered as a sporty 'jock', but this is not carried through into his choice of fashion of white jumper, blue trousers and ever-present orange ascot. Indeed, in later iterations of the show such as *Scooby-Doo Mystery Incorporated* we see him picked on by his sportier peers. Fred demonstrates the rational thinking and level-headed sceptical qualities needed for the leader of a respected group of paranormal investigators. Originally named Geoff during the conceptual stage, with Harvey and Ronnie also having been mooted as suggestions, his final name was fixed by Fred Silverman.

**DAPHNE:** Daphne Blake provides the looks in the gang, if not the physical skills to go with them (at least not in the original series). In early seasons she was portrayed as, and known as, 'danger-prone' because of her propensity for blundering into difficulty. Although it was never suggested that she was stupid, Daphne was somewhat ditzy – a stereotype of the time that is somewhat more problematic now. Fortunately, as the characters developed for later iterations, her role was reimagined and she became a much stronger character; this reflected the changes in society of the time. Daphne learned self-defence and would often apply those skills when the gang was under threat. In the direct-to-DVD animated movie, *Scooby-Doo! and the Samurai Sword,* the gang have travelled to Tokyo where Daphne is competing in a prestigious martial arts tournament. Daphne's family is very wealthy, but she chooses to make her own way in the world rather than living off of their success. There is a rumour that the Blake family funded the setting up of Mystery Incorporated and bought the Mystery Machine, their iconic van, but this idea is not canonical. The rumour comes from information in an eight-part special *Scooby-Doo: Behind the Scenes* which was included on a VHS video release of *Scooby-Doo's Original Mysteries* from Warner Home Video in 2002. However, this content was made by a third-party company with its own script concepts. If the suggestion was canon, then we would not see the characters looking for work as we do at various points over the years.

**VELMA:** With her thick-rimmed glasses, short hair and turtleneck sweater, Velma Dinkley's stereotypical appearance matches her role as the intelligent, geeky member of the team – responsible for solving most of the clues and questioning anything remotely supernatural or unscientific. Velma has a younger sister named Madelyn, an obscure character who only appears in two of the later animated movies. In the direct-to-video *Scooby-Doo! Abracadabra-Doo* (2010), Madelyn demonstrates that – despite her logical approach – Velma has always been fond of a mystery, suggesting that she was "born with a mystery book in her hand". In the *Scooby-Doo: Mystery Incorporated* franchise we learn that Velma's parents, Angie and Dale Dinkley, run the Crystal Cove Spook Museum, which exhibits many of the costumes used by villains in the early seasons of the show. Angie Dinkley is a firm believer in the supernatural and has an extensive magical reference library. Despite their differing views on the subject of the paranormal, Velma consults her mother to learn more about gnomes in Season 1 Chapter 8,[2] 'The Grasp of the Gnome'.

**SHAGGY:** Best known by his nickname, Shaggy's birth name is Norville Rogers; a fact that was not learned until 1988 when producer and director Tom Ruegger developed the prequel spin-off *A Pup Named Scooby-Doo*. Ruegger states that he came up with the name Norville as a tribute to silent film comedian Oliver Hardy whose middle name was Norvell. Shaggy is the

---

[2]. Whilst most versions of the show call their individual programmes 'episodes', the *Mystery Incorporated* iteration chose to use the term 'chapter' instead, in order to reflect the fact that there was a season-wide story arc which each individual story contributed to and developed.

owner of Scooby Doo and the two share similar character traits, both having voracious appetites and a default position of cowardice when any threat is apparent. Shaggy spent a brief period as a vegetarian at the insistence of the original voice actor Casey Kasem, who was a vegan himself, but these days his diet takes in pretty much anything once again. In different versions of the show, Shaggy has had a romantic relationship with both Velma (which we will explore in a moment) and also her younger sister Madelyn.

**SCOOBY:** Technically speaking, Scooby is Shaggy's pet, although at times it is unclear who really controls who. He is partially anthropomorphic (see below) but most unusually has the ability to speak, which nobody around him ever seems to question. We learn over the years that the Doo family is quite substantial. Scooby has three brothers, Skippy-, Yabba – and Howdy-Doo and one sister, Ruby-Doo (who is mother to the much-maligned Scrappy-Doo). We also know of five cousins, two uncles and, going back further than Scooby's grandfather (Grandpa Scooby) and great-grandfather (Great-Grandpa Scooby), two further ancestors. Yankee Doodle Doo was owned by an ancestor of Shaggy's, McBaggy Rogers. The pair arrived in America on the Mayflower with the other pilgrims in 1620. Scooby's oldest ancestor is featured in Season 4 of *A Pup Named Scooby-Doo*. Missing Link Doo is a skeleton whose name would suggest that the point at which the Doo family developed anthropomorphic features was way back in pre-history.

## Scooby Myths in the Real World

We acknowledged at the beginning of this chapter that in the fifty-plus years that Scoob and the gang have been investigating myths and mysteries, they have also given rise to a few legends themselves in our world. So, let's explore some of the main ones that you may have come across – some well known and some less so.

### Velma is a Lesbian

Although Velma has had a few male potential love interests over time, in some more recent versions of the show it started to be suggested that she was gay. There had been speculation for some time that Velma was a lesbian and some have argued that there is some queer coding in the early versions of the show, such as Velma's un-feminine fashion and lack of interest in other characters, but nothing had ever been stated definitively. The idea had originally started as a myth therefore, but gained traction through her close relationship with the character of Marcie Fleach, nicknamed 'Hot Dog Water' in *Scooby-Doo! Mystery Incorporated* (2010 – 2013). The final episode of the second season has

Marcie affectionately saying, "that's my girl" about Velma, planting the seed of Velma's sexuality in a canonical perspective.

In 2020, gay Velma was confirmed as canon from two sources, negating the urban folklore that sprang up around her. The first of these sources was supervising producer of *Scooby-Doo! Mystery Incorporated*, Tony Cervone, who Instagrammed an image of Velma and Marcie in front of a Pride flag. In an interview with the website Buzzfeed, Cervone clarified that Velma was not bisexual (a misapprehension due to her ill-fated relationship with Shaggy) but was written to be gay.

"We always planned on Velma acting a little off and out of character while she was dating Shaggy, because that relationship was wrong for her and she had unspoken difficulty with the why. I don't think Marcie and Velma had to act on their feelings during the main timeline but, post reset, they are a couple… this was our intention."

Screenwriter James Gunn, who had written the live action *Scooby-Doo* (2002), subsequently spoke out on the social media platform formally known as Twitter (now 'X') to say that he had written Velma as gay in the first draft script. But the studio (Warner Bros) insisted on making changes to that – in the version that was filmed – any hint as to her sexuality was purely ambiguous (being then cut to nothing in the final release). In the sequel *Scooby-Doo 2: Monsters Unleashed* (2004), Velma has a boyfriend in the shape of the curator of the Coolsonian Criminology Museum, Patrick Wisely – the part being played by Seth Green.

There had even been a filmed kiss between Daphne (Sarah Michelle Gellar) and Velma (Linda Cardellini) in the original live action movie, part of the body-swapping scene in the woods. The two characters were struggling to re-align their souls when trying to restore normality, with the kiss being the solution to the problem. The scene was removed after a test screening in Sacramento where a small number of parents had complained – ironically completing a circle where parental complaints in 1968 had led to the creation of Scooby-Doo in the first place.

## The Five College Consortium Myth

A persistent myth tells that the five main characters who make up Mystery Incorporated are designed to represent the five colleges that make up the consortium of educational institutions in the Connecticut River Pioneer Valley of Western Massachusetts. The idea behind this story is that the traits of each of the Scooby-Doo characters sum up the typical student from each of the five establishments who cooperate in the consortium.

**Preppy, sporty Fred:** Amherst College, a private liberal arts college founded in 1821

**Thin, upper-class Daphne:** Mount Holyoke College, historically a women's college founded in 1837

**Lovable party animal Scooby:** University of Massachusetts (UMass) Amherst, a public research university founded in 1863

**Nerdy book lover Velma:** Smith College, a private women's college opened in 1875

**Beatnik Shaggy:** Hampshire College, opened in 1970 as an experiment into alternative education

Whilst a nice story, it is untrue. Yet there are a couple of particular clues that might lead us to this assumption. Firstly, as can be seen in the college summaries above, Hampshire College did not open until 1970, whereas Season 1 of *Scooby Doo Where Are You!* aired in 1969. The second clue is so obvious that you don't need Velma to explain it to you. In *My Life with a Thousand Characters*, Iwao Takamoto debunks the rumour himself with his ignorance of the American college system, stating:

"There is no truth in it. In fact, until all this came up, I don't think I could have named five colleges in the Boston area, let alone been familiar enough with them to copy their style. Besides, the Scooby gang are high school kids, not college kids."

It is worth noting that, strictly speaking, only four of the gang are high school age. Although Scooby's age is rarely mentioned, official notes in a magazine that accompanied the 2002 movie stated that Scooby was seven, which would put him in primary school (elementary school for US readers). Alternatively, he is 49 in human years, which would mean an adult education class or similar.

The reason that the Five College Consortium myth sticks around is because the characters seem to resonate with people. If you stop and think for a moment to consider why, then you realise that, actually, these character stereotypes are familiar in other ways too. We have already learned that Mystery Incorporated are based on a sitcom, and these are stereotypical sitcom characters: the leader, the brainy one, the attractive one and the bungling comedy sidekick. Go back even further into comedy history and you will find the exact same formula within the Commedia dell'arte:

**Il Capitano** – the self-appointed captain, or leader

**Innamoratori** – upper-class lovers (*both of others and themselves*)

**Vecchi** – scholarly, sensible characters

**Zanni** – the clowns

Seems familiar, doesn't it? You can apply it to many groups of characters in films or television shows: *Fawlty Towers*, *Blackadder*, *The Rocky Horror Picture Show*; they all use varying collections of Commedia characters as their base. These character themes are hard-wired into Western storytelling, so you recognise them instantly and associate yourself with them without even thinking about it. You become part of the gang.

It looks possible that there was something of a knowing nod to the myth of the Five College Consortium in *Scooby-Doo Mystery Incorporated*, Season 1 Episode 12. This episode, 'The Shrieking Madness', parodies famous writer H.P. Lovecraft with the character of Professor Hatecraft. As part of the episode, the gang visit Darrow University fraternities and compare them in preparation for their future college attendance. Fred is sent by his father to Mu Gamma Tau fraternity, where Fred Jones Snr is still so revered that some consider him to be a myth himself. Whilst the fraternity does have the same sporty associations as Amherst College in the Consortium legend, there was unfortunately never a Greek frat house of the same name, the closest match being Alpha Tau Gamma which is actually found at UMass rather than Amherst itself. Daphne is sent to a building that was provided by her own parents, the "Blake Family Centre for Self-Named Buildings". This probably says more about her parallels with her Commedia dell'arte character than with Mount Holyoke however.

In fact, this whole idea is a pure coincidence. Writer Adam Beechen, who penned the episode, admitted when asked about the idea for this book that "to be honest, this is the first I've heard of the Five College Consortium". Working as a freelancer who was credited for only three episodes of the season, Adam actually had relatively little knowledge about any over-arching plots or legend references that would come up in the final run of episodes.

## The Drug Myth

Some of the urban myths about the characters in Scooby-Doo are taken up in later iterations of the show and adopted in order to turn them into something canonical, such as the confirmation of Velma's sexuality in more recent years. On other occasions, the original myth is recognised by the writers and nods to it are included in the show without any direct confirmation of its intent to be seen as canon. This is the case with the obvious, and vehemently denied by the creators, drug reference myth associated with Shaggy being a bit of a stoner.

The drug references were never intended, but it is easy to see how they came about. For a start, Scooby and Shaggy constantly have the munchies. Shaggy has the look, vocal pattern and general demeanour of someone with more than a little weed in their back pocket. His propensity for using the word 'like' in his sentences is commented on unfavourably by the caricatured version of writer Harlan Ellison in the previously mentioned episode 'The Shrieking Madness', and – during their ill-fated relationship in the same season of *Scooby-Doo: Mystery Incorporated* – Velma tries to cure Shaggy of his annoying vocal tic by making him wear a rubber band on his wrist which she snaps every time he says it.

Scooby and Shaggy both have an effect not unlike getting high from their consumption of Scooby Snacks. Sometimes branded as 'Scooby Snax', these are small biscuits that are often used as bribes by the other members of the gang to encourage Scooby and Shaggy to act as bait and lure a foe into one of Fred's traps. The snack made its first appearance in the first season of the 1988 prequel concept *A Pup Named Scooby-Doo*, where all the characters are small children who run their own detective agency from a treehouse. In the first episode of Season 1, 'A Bicycle Built for Boo' (as well as in the opening titles for this version of the show), it is established that eating a Scooby Snack gives Scooby the energy of a rocket. In fact, because the style of the animation in *Pup* is very much of the *Tom and Jerry* school, we actually see Scoob turn into a rocket shape.

In the real world, it is no great surprise that a dog will be very excited at the prospect of a few treats, and William Hanna and Joseph Barbera had used this idea previously with their character of the dog Snuffles from *Quick Draw McGraw* in the late 1950s. Hanna stated that he imagined a Scooby Snack to be something like a caramel cookie, although in different versions of the show a number of flavours are mentioned.

The idea that the snack makes one compliant and full of energy has naturally led to the name being adopted in popular drug culture in a variety of ways. Capsules made from the psychedelic mushroom *psilocybe cubensis* mixed with other plant-based ingredients are nicknamed after the snack, whose name is also found as a slang term for meth – a drug that gives a fast high and is often associated with exhilaration or increased agitation. Conversely, the song *Scooby Snacks* – recorded by the group Fun Lovin' Criminals in 1996 – was said by their lead singer Huey Morgan to refer to Valium, a benzodiazepine that is valued by many for its calming properties despite being highly addictive.

Later iterations of the show, which had slightly more leeway in terms of censorship, would sometimes make fun of this particular myth. The first live action movie, *Scooby-Doo* (2002), has an early scene with the Mystery Machine parked at the beach. Smoke escapes from the sunroof and groaning voices can be heard inside. "Talk about toasted," slurs Shaggy. Him and Scooby are cooking burgers in the back of the van, but it is obvious what you are supposed to think. In another scene, sat next to a blonde girl on a plane, Shaggy learns that they both love Scooby Snacks. He asks her name and she tells him that it is Mary Jane. "Like, that is my favourite name," he says. As a slang term for marijuana, the term 'Mary Jane' entered into usage sometime in the early twentieth century, certainly being committed to print in a *Daily Express* newspaper article about the drug in October 1928.

The live action movie was full of such sideways references and jokes. Sadly, not all of them made it to the screen; the desire for a PG certificate sent many sequences to the cutting room floor. This meant that, as well as not seeing the kiss between Daphne and Velma already noted, Fred was also never seen going into Daphne's bedroom to protect her overnight, taking his toothbrush with him.

## Speech and Popular Culture

Every long-running series has a catchphrase or two that emerges over the years, and Scooby-Doo is no different. Phrases such as 'meddling kids', 'jeepers', 'zoinks' and 'jinkies' are all in common use within pop culture thanks to their repeated use on the show. In most cases, their origins lie elsewhere. Where do these phrases come from, and how have they been adopted and influenced our culture today?

In the case of Velma's go-to exclamation of 'jinkies', the erstwhile Professor Hatecraft chides her during her visit to Darrow University, telling her that "Jinkies is not a real word". Many other people would agree with him. But in fact, this expression of surprise was in existence at least thirty years prior to the creation of Scooby-Doo. The *Courier-Northerner* newspaper, published by Central Michigan University, published a letter to staff in the July 29th edition for the year 1939 that begins:

> "Dear Hal, Vade and staff: By jinkies, on my next pass day I will surely stop and see that 178 foot wheelbase fire truck."

The fact that early occurrences of the term are generally in the form 'by jinkies' suggests that it may have its roots in the creation of a non-blasphemous version of 'by Jove'.

Euphemistic alterations such as this are known linguistically as 'minced oaths'. Other examples include words such as 'shoot', 'gosh' or 'darn'. Substitutions or mis-spellings are made for words that are considered to be blasphemous, profane or inappropriate in some other way. Daphne's use of 'jeepers' is the same thing. Coming into use in the United States in the second half of the 1920s, jeepers was a euphemism for Jesus and, by extension, jeepers creepers was used for Jesus Christ. The Disney character of Jiminy Cricket finds his name coming from the same linguistic root.

The first link between the phrase and the types of experiences often investigated by Scooby and the gang comes about in a 1939 Looney Tunes short cartoon directed by Robert Clampett. In *Jeepers Creepers* police office Porky Pig is called to investigate strange goings-on at a mysterious-looking house, the dispatcher warning him to be careful as the location may have ghosts. The house is indeed haunted by a white-sheet ghost (more of them later in the book) who scares Porky from the property.

In the case of Shaggy, his oft-used exclamation of 'zoinks', after which this book is titled, was most definitely created for him, as there is no etymology that places it in popular culture before he first uttered it. It is possible, however, that the writers coined the phrase from the pre-existing word 'zoiks', which was an exclamation that was in use prior to the creation of the cartoon. It is likely that, once again, this is a minced oath with zoiks being a shortening of the archaic term 'gadzooks'. First recorded in the English language around the year 1652, the exclamation gadzooks came about by the contracting of the phrase 'God's hooks', relating to the crucifixion nails used to hang Christ on the cross in the Biblical story. In the world of children's television, many people from the United Kingdom will associate the phrase gadzooks with the jester ghost Timothy Claypole, played for many years by Michael Staniforth in the Bob Block series *Rentaghost* on the BBC. Claypole's other common phrase 'odds bodkins' is again a minced oath, meaning 'God's little body'. The members of Action for Children's Television back in the 1960s would undoubtedly have been delighted to find so much hidden religion in the new Scooby-Doo world.

The themes of Scooby-Doo and the use of the word 'zoinks' were taken up later when one of the Moshi Monsters was named Zoinks and was found to reside in Goosebump Manor.

Through repetition, the phrase used by the unmasked villain in so many episodes of Scooby-Doo, "I would have gotten away with it too, if it weren't for you meddling kids" (or a variation thereon) has become a trope that crops up in many other programmes as a sort of uncredited homage to the original and, at times, also becomes a parody of itself within Scooby-Doo as well. In *Scooby-Doo and the Witch's Ghost*, goth girl group the Hex Girls perform a number called 'Meddling Kids'. In 2017, author Edgar Cantero published the comedy-horror novel *Meddling Kids*. In this story, a group of adults who, as children, had formed the 'Blyton Summer Detective Club' to investigate mysteries in the school holidays, come back together to look again at a case with undertones from the Lovecraftian mythos of Cthulhu which had affected them badly in their youth.

The 'Blyton Summer Detective Club' directly references the popular children's author Enid Blyton and her *Famous Five* mystery series. Cantero's group was indeed made up of two boys, two girls and a dog and the parallels with Mystery Incorporated here should also be obvious. The blonde leader of Blyton's original Five is a less sporty Fred, tomboy George can only be Velma, the younger boy Dick has comedic undertones – a more subtle version of Shaggy (he is often pretty hungry too), and the more timid Anne can be seen in Daphne. Timmy the dog completes the picture. The Commedia dell'arte informs the make-up in the background once again.

When it comes to adding an element of language to our own, Shaggy is not the only one who can claim a trophy. Scooby has done exactly the same thing with his unique pattern of speech. We all know that Scooby has a habit of adding extra 'r' sounds to his words. Whilst this is an invented phonological disorder, there is some basis in language that it sits on. R-like sounds in phonetics are called rhotic consonants. They are difficult to describe but in different languages they might manifest in things such as rolled or guttural r's. There is an accepted speech condition known as rhotacism that sees one consonant being changed to a rhotic consonant in a particular situation. The late UK singer Cilla Black's Liverpool dialect was a good example of this, with the phrase 'lot of' being changed to 'lorra'. Scooby does this as well on occasion, such as when pronouncing Shaggy's name as 'Raggy'.

However, where Scooby's speech impediment is invented is in the *addition* of the 'r' sound to words, for example when he says "Ruh-Roh", Scooby is the only creature who exhibits this speech disorder. But, in 2014, Steven Long of Marquette University's Speech Pathology and Audiology Department diagnosed Scooby's condition as 'rhotic replacement'. So now there is a disorder, named in the real world by experts, that is only exhibited by one dog. And a cartoon one at that. As humans, interestingly, we tend to subtract sounds from patterns of speech when we have an impediment rather than adding to them. Children, for instance, tend to de-rhotacise their speech – the opposite of Scooby-Doo.

Some adults do it, too.

"Be vewy vewy quiet. Wabbit twacks".

With that, we shall leave behind the influences which Scooby and the Gang have had on us here in the real world, and look at the ways in which our own myths, legends and folklore are represented in Coolsville, Crystal Cove, or wherever in the Scoobyverse the mysteries take us. Let's climb aboard the Mystery Machine and head for Chapter Two…

# CHAPTER TWO
## LANDSCAPE AND THE GOTHIC

There can be no doubt that, from its very first episode, Scooby-Doo has placed at least one paw very firmly into the Gothic camp. This is apparent even from the first few seconds of the iconic title sequence, designed by Bill Perez and executed by Robert Schaefer, as a single bat flutters past a spooky-looking old house in the nighttime mist. It is then quickly followed by a whole cloud of fluttering bats! Later iterations of the show naturally used many different title designs (some of which were as psychedelic as the urban myth drug references), but when the show returned to its roots – with the more recent *Scooby-Doo and Guess Who?* – the titles followed suit; this time with the bats flying past an old castle, lit by a giant full moon to rival any supermoon.

But what is 'Gothic'? A brief definition would probably be useful before we examine the style in more detail. As a mode of fiction, Gothic literature has its roots in the eighteenth century with Horace Walpole's 1764 novel *The Castle of Otranto*, a medieval political tale full of supernatural adventure and foreboding. The Gothic writing style is often marked out by a sense of mystery, horror and gloom set in a dark and eerie landscape. Gothicists prefer to use the term 'mode' over 'genre' when describing Gothic fiction, precisely because it is a way of telling stories rather than a set of tropes to be included within them. Gothic literature takes its name from the architectural style that emerged in the Middle Ages. Evolving from earlier Romanesque work, and originally known as 'Opus Francigenum' or 'French Work', Gothic architecture gained the name that we know today in the sixteenth century. Its medieval stylings include vaulting, arches, tall and thin walls and the iconic flying buttresses that were necessary for adding increased support to the structures. Ornate Gothic stone buildings soon became intrinsically linked with the emerging horror literature.

Scooby-Doo utilises the Gothic in a number of ways. Design is a very obvious one. Haunted mansions, crumbling castles and creepy forests abound. And whether the gang is out and about or at home (which is either Coolsville in many versions or Crystal Cove – The Hauntedest Place on Earth in *Scooby-*

*Doo: Mystery Incorporated*), some things remain the same. A thunderstorm could be along at any time. It is often a dark and stormy night. In Season 1 Episode 11 of *Where Are You!*, 'A Gaggle of Galloping Ghosts', a lightning bolt strikes Franken Castle even though there isn't a cloud in the sky. And the moon is always full.[3]

In both mythology and folklore, as well as in the Gothic, the full moon carries a lot of significance. Hippocrates linked the moon to madness: "One who is seized with terror, fright and madness during the night is visited by the goddess of the moon." For many hundreds of years, links were made between lunacy, crime, suicide and the phases of the moon. The gravitational pull theory posited that as a high percentage of the human body was made up of water, then it would undergo the same sorts of effects that the moon has on the Earth's tides. Anecdotal evidence amongst doctors, nurses, mental health orderlies and the police has often suggested a close link between the full moon and madness-induced trauma. Over three-quarters of those polled in a 1995 study on the subject believed that this was the case.

Much modern scientific work on the subject has led to the myth of a causal link being fairly robustly debunked, but this has done little to quash the anecdotal stories to the contrary. This is of no great surprise when there is such a long period of superstition and folklore behind it.

Many cultures ascribed an association with death to the moon, the full moon being the zenith after which the moon begins to shrink and disappear, before emerging once again as a new moon in a cycle of death and rebirth. In early Hindu beliefs, the souls of the dead would go to the moon for this very reason, from where they could be reborn. Many ancient Greeks also saw the moon as the home of the dead.

This link between the full moon and death undoubtedly fed into beliefs that it could have an adverse effect on a person's sanity. Japanese priests believed that the moon deity had the power to see the future, but they would divine by examining the reflection of the celestial body in a mirror, because to stare directly at it would be to invite madness. The English philosopher Roger Bacon wrote in the thirteenth century that a number of people had died because they had not taken precautions to protect themselves from the moon's rays. Many people at this time would not sleep in the moonlight for this reason.

In Season 2 Episode 3 of *Be Cool, Scooby-Doo!*, 'Renn Scare', the ghostly jester, notes that the impending devastation will take place under such a moon in the first of his rhyming couplets:

---

[3]. Well… nearly always. Ironically, in the episode 'A Scooby-Doo Halloween' (in Season 2 of *What's New Scooby-Doo?*), the moon is clearly shown as a crescent at the start of the episode, which takes place on the night before Halloween. Fortunately, by the next night – Halloween itself – it has miraculously become a full moon. Because the rules must apply.

> "Make your plans, decorate this room
> All you do is guild your tomb
> At this feast under pale full moon
> You shall meet untimely doom"

In more recent times, links have been made through literature between the moon and two monsters who have appeared on a number of occasions in episodes of Scooby-Doo: werewolves, and Mr Hyde – the criminal alter-ego of Dr Jekyll in the novella penned by Robert Louis Stevenson.

The story of the *Strange Case of Dr Jekyll and Mr Hyde*, first published in 1886, will be familiar to most. It tells of the investigation of a series of incidents that seem to take place between Dr Henry Jekyll and a criminal named Edward Hyde, before revealing that the two are in fact the same person. Jekyll has formulated a chemical potion that transforms him into the evil Hyde, allowing him to experience the darker sides of his persona which would never otherwise come out. Numerous film adaptations have been made of the story, with one of the most famous being released in 1931 and earning an Academy Award for lead actor Fredric March.

An interesting urban legend seems to have been created surrounding the madness from the full moon and the story of Jekyll and Hyde in 1982. The Readers Digest *Into the Unknown* encyclopaedia suggested that there was an actual Victorian murder trial that provided the inspiration for the story. The author of the entry wrote that

> "In a 19th century homicide trial, so the story goes, Charles Hyde, the defendant, pleaded innocence on the grounds that the new and full moons regularly drove him mad. Hyde supposedly lost his case but achieved an immortality of sorts; Robert Louis Stevenson may have used him as a model for Dr Jekyll's murderous alter ego."

The story has been repeated on a number of occasions, including in an article on the BBC News website, but with no corroborating detail. This is because there appears to be none to be found. Most likely is that the author of this piece was misled by an actual trial from 1953 in Cornwall where a man named Charles Hyde used 'moon madness' as an excuse for stealing from a house.

Hyde was known generally as a good man. He was a husband, a father and a hard worker. But, as his wife allegedly testified, "he gets this Moon trouble, acting very strangely and going off for a week at a time". A year after the burglary trial, Charles Hyde was back in court after having been charged with breaking probation. Just before a full moon he had quit his job and travelled 1,300 miles to France to join the Foreign Legion. He was discharged on medical grounds but ended up back in court after stealing a wallet and cheque

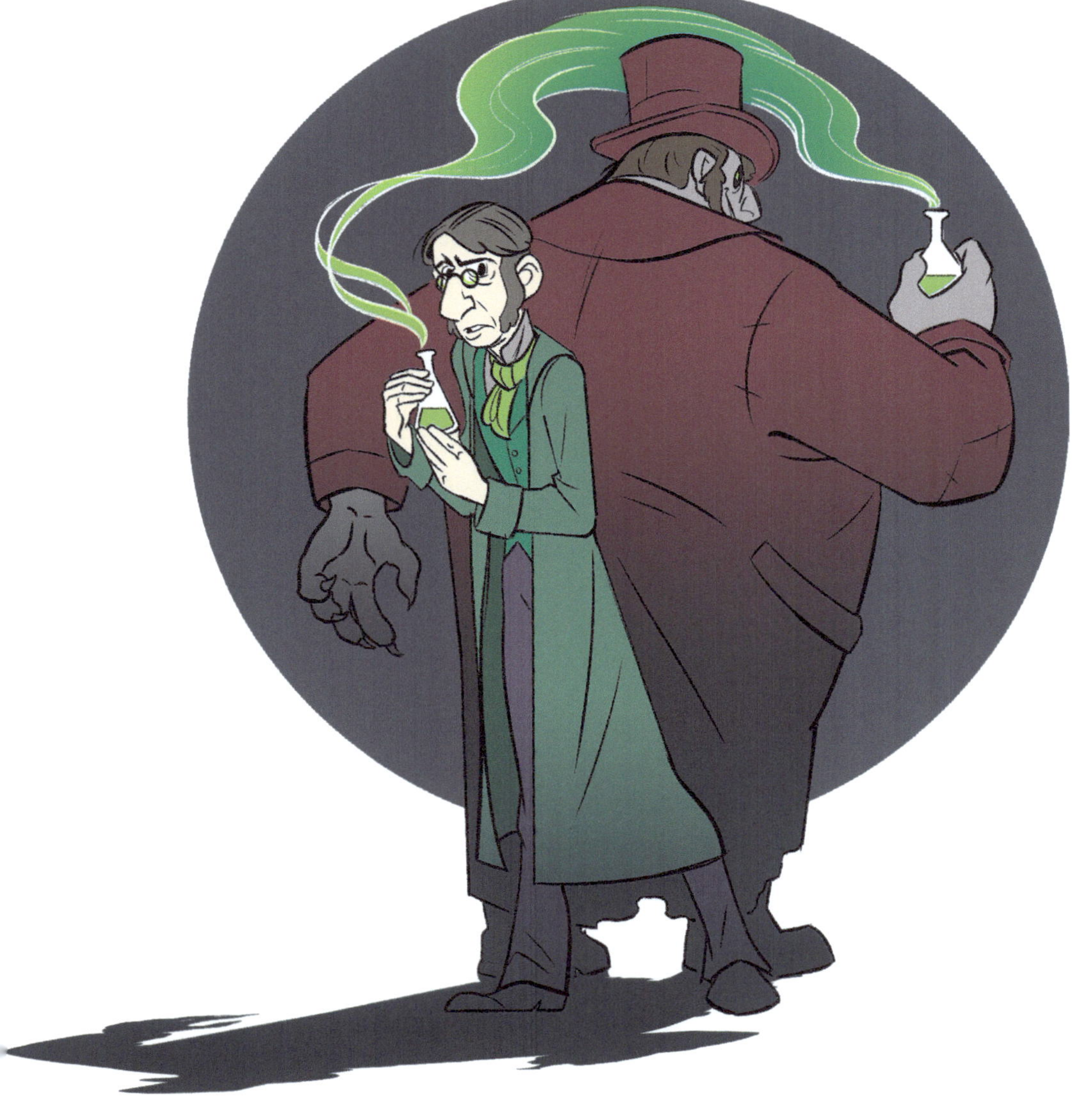

book from his brother-in-law's house. His plea of 'moon madness' did not work this time and he was sentenced to eighteen months in prison.

The character of Mr Hyde first makes an appearance in the opening episode of Season 2 of *Scooby-Doo Where Are You!* as a ghost – the great grandson of Dr Jekyll. The story, 'Nowhere to Hyde', which Joe Ruby and Ken Spears revealed was amongst their favourites, sees the gang investigating the ghost of Hyde as a jewel thief. He is seen entering a creepy house that belongs to Dr Jekyll who is worried that he might be transforming into the ghost of Mr Hyde without knowing it and undertaking the robberies. It turns out that he is, but that he very much knows about it!

The ghost of Mr Hyde, who made it into the revised title sequence for this season, glows green, as do many of the early ghosts. The colour is often seen as unlucky in folklore. The mechanic for this, which provides a clue to the gang on more than one occasion, is the use of phosphorescent paint. In the previous season, a sheet is painted with the substance in 'Which Witch is Which' to resemble the witch. In the following episode, 'Go Away Ghost Ship', the ghost of Redbeard the Pirate has phosphorus on his face. There are glow-in-the-dark footprints left behind in the wake of Spooky Space Kook, a grinning skull looking out from inside a white space suit; that looks as if it should have been (and maybe was) the inspiration for Steven Moffat's visual embodiment of the Vashta Narada (once the humans had been attacked) in the 2008 *Doctor Who* episode 'Silence in the Library'.

This idea of painting yourself with phosphorescent paint comes directly from the Victorian practice of ghost hoaxing, an undertaking that led to a number of famous cases being recorded in chapbooks and pamphlets in the nineteenth century. Springheeled Jack was probably the most famous of these, but there were numerous examples both in the United Kingdom and abroad, where the practice could also be found. One man dressed in a white sheet and wore a sugar-loaf hat soaked in phosphorus. Another wore black robes decorated with glow-in-the-dark paint. The same techniques were in use, of course, on the stage at the time. The ghost of Hamlet's father was invariably portrayed glowing in this way, probably leading to the establishing of the colour green for spectres.

What the ghost hoaxers were unfortunately not aware of at the time that they were operating was the carcinogenic nature of phosphorescent paint, meaning that some of them may very well have returned soon after and haunted the streets for real.

We know that there is a complex interplay between folklore and the old stories of smugglers. Needing to keep people away from the areas in which they were operating, much like the majority of the villains in Scooby-Doo, smugglers would employ tales of ghosts, demons or other such strange events. This accounts for a number of stories of coastal hauntings around the United

Kingdom, for example, where there is evidence that wreckers and smugglers used practical demonstrations that would be at home in an episode of the cartoon. Phantom coaches, for example, could be mocked up by the use of phosphorescent paint. By binding the horse's hooves and padding the wheels, they could be made to move silently. Leave the paint off the horse's head and a viewer at a distance would see a ghostly carriage being pulled by a headless horse.

What is not always clear in such examples is where the smugglers used a pre-existing legend and recreated it, and where they essentially formed a legend through their actions. In both cases, what they did would inform and drive the narrative, embedding it in the area for the future. We see this whole idea play out in the very first season of the original *Scooby-Doo Where Are You!* with Captain Cutler and his scheme to steal yachts.

The moon is an important part of the traditional cycle of death and rebirth; a cycle which horror arguably went through itself. By the 1940s, the traditionally frightening 'Universal monsters' were being reduced to comedic forays with Abbot and Costello in much the same way that *Scooby-Doo and Guess Who?* features Ricky Gervais battling the mummy of the Egyptian goddess Bastet or the ghost of Bigfoot crosses swords with Laurel and Hardy in the episode of the same name in Season 1 of *The New Scooby-Doo Movies*. In the case of mainstream cinema, the 1950 release of *The Curse of Frankenstein* saw a return to the Gothic roots of horror. Scooby-Doo has begun to see a restoration of its original design and use of folklore in recent years but it hasn't quite got there yet.

The visual path of horror cinema that was to come over the decades following the release of *The Curse of Frankenstein* was effectively mirrored from the inception of Scooby-Doo in the late 1960s onwards. It would be reflected both in the visual imagery used in the landscape, and then later also in a wide-reaching use of cinematic parody which we will touch upon later.

In the classic early designs of Scooby-Doo, death is always on the periphery. Sometimes, that is in an obvious way with an animated corpse or a haunting, but it might also be in more subtle ways too. Buildings are usually run-down, even in towns. Woodwork is rotting. And as with the Gothic generally, and a lot of folklore in particular, the haunted landscape has the feel of death about it too. Trees are often twisted and bare. Dead leaves blow along the ground. Even in episodes that are set outside of the usual American backdrop you get the same feel, such as the remoteness of the mountains in episodes that feature the Abominable Snowman.

All of these stereotypical Gothic elements serve to codify for the viewer the evil villain or the supernatural event that we come to expect. The make-up of the show arguably uses two key theories within the Gothic as part of this: Edmund Burke's theory of the sublime and Tsetvan Todorov's theory of the fantastic.

Edmund Burke (1729-97) is probably known mostly for his political career and the foundation of modern conservatism. But in 1757 he published a tract on aesthetics titled *A Philosophical Enquiry into the Origin of our Ideas of the Sublime and Beautiful*. In this, Burke posited that the beautiful was well-formed and aesthetically pleasing to a person, whereas the sublime had power within it to compel one, or even to bring about destruction. At this time, the qualities of the sublime were taking the place of those of the beautiful in terms of literary preference. This marked a change to the Romantic from the previous era of Neoclassical works and with this came the growth of the Gothic.

As an empiricist, Burke thought that our understanding of and interaction with the landscape came from our senses and emotions. This led to a mix of fear, excitement, terror and awe when faced with the natural world, whether it be mountains and canyons, forests or lakes. He wrote that "the passion caused by the great and sublime in nature is astonishment, and astonishment is that state of the soul in which all its motions are suspended, with some degree of horror." Burke goes on to add that this is heightened when it is also accompanied by an awareness of the unknown; it increases the sense of terror. Where we cannot see an object clearly, says Burke, then it gives rise to a "terrible uncertainty".

All of this can be found in the environments where the gang find themselves solving a mystery. There is terror to be found in nature which, in Burke's words, "comes upon us in the gloomy forest, and in the howling wilderness".

Forests are represented as dangerous or enchanted way back into the earliest folk tales. It is in the forest that Hansel and Gretel are captured by a witch, and where Baba Yaga might be found residing in her enchanted hut on giant chicken legs (although as we shall see in another chapter she makes forays elsewhere in the Scooby-Doo universe too). Many stories use the forest as a mechanism for evil. There is danger to be found in the forests of Oz if Dorothy and her companions stray from the yellow brick road. The forest around Harry Potter's Hogwarts is literally named 'Forbidden'.

There is an understanding that if one ventures among the trees at night, then something frightening will happen. An unnamed murderer who was on the run from the police was said to have tried to conceal himself in Collingbourne Woods in Wiltshire. He did not stay long and when he emerged and was arrested by the police, it was said that "he had dark hair when he went in, and when he came out he was white". He had been scared by the apparition of a black dog, with blazing eyes[4]. This is a common trope found in many folk tales, and also in historical legend. Marie Antoinette's hair was said to have turned white overnight through stress on the eve of her beheading. The hair of third class *Titanic* passenger Edvard Bengtsson Lindell reportedly turned white in

---

[4]. Sometimes there are people, not one. And sometimes they are robbers. Or robbers and murderers. Sometimes it takes place in the 17th century and sometimes it doesn't. Because, folklore. But the location is always the same.

an hour due to stress before he perished when the liner went down. Medically, it is impossible for hair to lose its pigment so quickly, since the hair that isn't at the root is dead and does not change colour at all.

Many of the trees in Scooby-Doo look like contorted human figures. They appear to be able to come to life and pose a threat at any time. In some cases, they do. Season 2, Episode 4 of *Scooby-Doo and Guess Who?*, 'The Hot Dog Dog!', sees the gang investigating a hot dog factory that appears to be being haunted by a tree monster. It has all the hallmarks of the trees in the Gothic landscape of the show – its bark is dead and jagged, its anthropomorphic face is set in a perpetual scream and its eyes glow with the green of so many of the show's luminous villains.

The trees of the Scooby-Doo forest are generally devoid of leaves. They represent death in the natural cycle of death and rebirth touched upon earlier. In fact, they represent the death that we know will not be found elsewhere in a children's show. This is the very thing that makes frightening experiences sublime: they become so when we know that there is no danger of death or injury.

In the Commedia dell'arte roll-call of character tropes that we examined in the first chapter, Shaggy and Scooby's roles as clowns exist to dilute the terror that would otherwise be found in this landscape that the characters inhabit. They admit this themselves in 'How to Train Your Coward', the fourth episode in Season 2 of *Be Cool, Scooby-Doo!*. The two have decided to quit Mystery Incorporated when the gang end up investigating a vampire that has been terrorising a village, because they don't feel that they have any skills that are worthy of giving them a place in the team. They set about training a replacement man and dog pair who end up being far more fearless, which results in the derailing of the investigation for a while. Through this problem, they learn that their fear is actually beneficial to the gang. Shaggy points out that by not wanting to go into scary places they remind the others that this should provoke fear, and thus their roles are justified and fulfilled.

In the psychogeographical landscape of the show's urban environments, decay is still often represented. Buildings are run down, wood rotting and festooned with cobwebs. Even the most modern of skylines is portrayed as having something unusual about it. For example, in the first season of *Scooby-Doo and Scrappy-Doo*, the episode 'I Left My Neck in San Francisco' pushes the modern skyline to the back, and foregrounds Alcatraz Island with its foreboding lookout tower dead centre. Everything is shrouded in mist and tones are muted. A year or so earlier in 'The Diabolical Disc Demon', the home of Decade Records looks more like a prison than a musical establishment. Out front, an ornate metal lamppost casts a shadow right across the front of frame – presumably from a full moon just out of shot.

Even the more modern approach of the artwork in *Scooby-Doo Mystery Incorporated* does not fully escape this treatment. In an episode towards the end of the second season story arc, Fred is pulled through a mirror into a dystopian future of Crystal Cove where everyone appears to have died. Of course, it turns out to be a ruse, but the concept plays with various ideas in folklore relating to the mirror either as a gateway to another realm, or a repository in which the soul may become trapped if precautions are not taken.

In medieval times, the mirror was thought of as a way to allow the lower mortal beings to be able to communicate with higher forms such as angels. The mirror acted as an interface to blur the divide between the physical and the spiritual – a boundary over which humans could not communicate otherwise, being unworthy of direct dealings with the higher plane.

Superstition tells us that we should cover a house's mirrors with cloth or other material if a person dies within. This simple protection would prevent the soul from becoming trapped in the mirror when it left the body, leaving the deceased in a sense of limbo and unable to pass to the other side. The earliest example of this appears to come from the Orkney Islands in the late eighteenth century. The concern was very real for our more superstitious ancestors and many extended the practice as far as covering the mirrors in rooms where sick people lay recovering.

Where the landscape in Scooby-Doo may be seen to be reflective of Burke's ideas of the sublime, the supernatural itself arguably utilises the concept of Todorov's theory of the fantastic in its representation.

Tzvetan Todorov (1939-2017) was a Bulgarian-born philosopher and literary theorist. He emigrated to France in 1963 and from there went on to teach in many prestigious establishments including both Yale and Harvard. The author of a large number of books, the two areas for which he is probably most remembered are his work on concentration camps and the Holocaust and, in one of his earliest titles, his analysis of storytelling in fiction.

It is in Todorov's 1970 work *Introduction à la littérature fantastique* that we see the development of the theory of the fantastic. The book was translated into English three years later with the title *The Fantastic: A Structural Approach to a Literary Genre*. In the book, Todorov argues that the fantastic is a term that can be situated between the uncanny and the marvellous. It is, to look at it in terms of folkloric definitions, a liminal state – a border between two other things. The fantastic reflects that brief moment of uncertainty that a person might have between believing that what they are experiencing is supernatural, or disbelieving it and finding a more rational explanation. In Todorov's own words:

> "The fantastic occupies the duration of this uncertainty. Once we choose one answer or the other, we leave the fantastic for a neighbouring genre, the uncanny or the marvellous. The fantastic is that hesitation experienced by a person who knows only the laws of nature, confronting an apparently supernatural event".

So what is the difference between the uncanny and the marvellous? In terms of Todorov's thinking, the uncanny is characterised by the way that a character responds to something that is unexplained. Often, that response is fear. The thing being responded to might be impossible, or might defy normal explanation, but it has something strange and familiar about it.[5] The marvellous, on the other hand, needs no character response at all. It is an amazing event that just occurs.

In short, the uncanny is the supernatural explained[6] and the marvellous is the supernatural as supernatural. Scooby-Doo traverses the path from one to the other and passes that tipping point between belief and disbelief. There are episodes and iterations of the franchise that represent the marvellous, as we have seen, but they are the minority and outside of the original construction of the series. It is probably no surprise that the versions where the supernatural is portrayed as real rarely feature Fred or Velma as characters. This removes both the person generally responsible for trapping and unmasking the real-life villain behind the supernatural, and the voice of rationality when looking for plausible explanations. In the case of *The 13 Ghosts of Scooby-Doo*, when the series was completed with a one-off telefilm years later, Fred and Velma were reintroduced and the whole concept of the marvellous supernatural ended up being brought into question.

A similar thing happens with one of the classic feature-length films where the supernatural is probably real, *Scooby-Doo on Zombie Island*. The film ends with the gang leaving the island having witnessed what are undoubtedly real zombies and werecats, but with no evidence to demonstrate this to anyone else. When they return in a later film, *Scooby-Doo! Return to Zombie Island*, enough time has passed that Velma is able to supply a possible rational explanation, because she cannot change her views to see the supernatural as real rather than explainable. She suggests that the previous events were hallucinations brought on by swamp gas. In doing this, the show is playing on an idea in real-world folklore where swamp or marsh gas has been used often as an explanation for sightings of UFOs or other mysterious lights.

Executive producer at the TV channel Nickelodeon, Mitch Watson, was one of the key people responsible for the two seasons of *Scooby-Doo: Mystery Incorporated*. He believes that one of the reasons for the longevity of the show is:

---

[5]. This differentiates it slightly from Freud's definition of the uncanny which explains it as the sense of dread that ones feels in a situation where the fears or fantasies that we experienced as children feel more real than the views that we hold as adults.

[6]. Ann Radcliffe, one of the earliest authors working in the Gothic mode, frequently did this in her novels. Velma would have been a fangirl, no doubt.

> "…because at the end of each episode the supernatural villain turns out to be fake. That is very reassuring to kids, and their parents. In my opinion the versions of the show that hold to this work the best."

Watson also has a fondness for the supernatural elements, however, and believes that they still have a place in the show.

> "In SDMI (*Scooby-Doo: Mystery Incorporated*) we held off on introducing the supernatural until the back half of Season 2. A lot of purists were not happy with it, but it was the only logical place we could go, and it allowed us to tell a much bigger story."

This is alluding to the story arc that develops during Season 2 surrounding the Nibiru Cataclysm, a collision or near-miss between the Earth and 'Planet X' which has been predicted by some groups as taking place early in the twenty-first century. This is explored in detail in the chapter on modern folklore.

Watching Scooby-Doo develop over the years from the initial shows in the 1960s onwards, you can see how the more heavily Gothic interpretation in the landscape gradually became lost over time. The elements were still present – the moon was still full and castles still had the expected architecture – but the colour palette became more vibrant and the whole mood was generally lighter. Mitch Watson also notes how, with the development of *Mystery Incorporated*, there was a conscious effort to reintroduce the feel of the original. What better way to do this than to draw on a cinema style that is often acknowledged as rebooting the Gothic itself? As Watson notes in private correspondence:

> "We wanted to give the whole series a 'Hammer Horror' vibe. That is to say a more 'Gothic' vibe than maybe the show has had before. We took our cues from old Hammer Horror movies of the 60s, wood cuts from storybooks, and the thicker lined graphic style you'd see in old horror comics like 'Eerie Tales'. Up until then most children's cartoons were well lit and not so moody. We wanted it to be scary and so did Warner Brothers."

Interestingly, Hammer did not produce any horror content until after 1955, when they adapted Nigel Kneale's work *The Quatermass Experiment* for the big screen. Kneale was very interested in folklore, as can be seen from the titles of some of his other shows such as *The Abominable Snowman*, *The Witches* and *The Stone Tape*.

Watson's views almost bring the show full circle back to its origin point, where the creators were originally told to draw inspiration from the Universal Horror franchise monsters. This turned out, of course, to be poor advice, leading to the need to play down the horror and play up the comedy although the monsters themselves would appear on numerous occasions, as we will see when we move on to look at monster stereotypes.

When the two-season run of *Be Cool, Scooby-Doo!* emerged from the Warner Brothers Animation stable in 2015, it offered audiences a quite different look and feel for the show. The standard plot line and its elements were all present: the supernatural was just a ruse by someone with criminal tendencies, the chase scene fell in the middle of the episode, the criminal "would have gotten away with it if it hadn't have been for you meddling kids". The visual feel was far more modern and caricatured, however, with ridiculous Mystery Machine modifications and impossible happenings now the norm. Each story was still an investigation, but the scripts were very much produced for comedic value. It is arguably the funniest of all the iterations both for younger audiences and for their parents.

Some episodes of *Be Cool, Scooby-Doo!* bring the Gothic more to the foreground than the modern because their plots demand it. In Episode 13, 'Where There's a Will, There's a Wraith', a member of a family dies and leaves a bequest to everyone who has saved their life in the past, which includes Scooby. In order to get the inheritance, Scooby has to spend the night in the Gothic mansion belonging to the family, along with various other relatives. These include the deceased man's twin nieces, Ruby and Trudy, who are obviously based on Alexie and Alexa Grady, the two girls dressed in blue dresses who are seen in the west wing of the Overlook hotel in Stanley Kubrick's *The Shining*.

Whilst Ruby and Trudy are obviously twins, even going so far as to finish each other's sentences, the girls in *The Shining* are sisters but not twins, despite being played by real-life twins Lisa and Louise Burns. Alexie and Alexa Grady are different heights and their dresses actually vary slightly although they are designed to reflect the common practice that parents used to follow of dressing twin children in the same clothes. Overlook manager Stuart Ullman describes the two girls as being aged 8 and 10 at the beginning of the film.

Although not confirmed, it is probable that the family name of Lutz in this episode of Scooby is a reference to the couple who bought the Dutch Colonial house in Ocean Drive, Amityville, which was alleged to have been the scene of various paranormal events and which sparked a series of books, films and other media appearances over the following years.

Gothic styling appears for the house portrayed in the episode 'Party Like It's 1899', a little earlier in the same season. The location for this story is Wuthering Manor, obviously drawing inspiration from the novel *Wuthering Heights*, where Mystery Inc are taking part in the Annual Monster Mystery Party – a whodunnit mystery-solving evening where everyone plays a different character as part of the mystery. Lady Pipi Wuthering and her husband, Lord Randolph, have based the story on events that happened in Wuthering Manor's past. The participants have to solve the mystery of the Headless Count, a ghost who wanders the manor house looking for a new head.

The Headless Count in the mystery is portrayed by the Wuthering's butler, Colander, but before too long the 'real' Headless Count appears and begins to abduct members of the party. The gang eventually unmask the Count as Bradwick Haverall, a childhood friend of Daphne's who has also been champion of the mystery-solving party for the last few years, achieved through cheating. He disguised himself as the Count and controlled the game in order to systematically rob the wealthy guests, having squandered his own fortune.

There are many headless ghosts in our folklore and myth. Probably the one conjured up first by many when asked to name one would be the Headless Horseman from Washington Irving's *The Legend of Sleepy Hollow*. Written in 1819, the story tells of a small town, Sleepy Hollow, which lives in fear of the restless spirit of a man on a horse, whose head had been blown off by a cannonball during the Revolutionary War.

We can't be certain where Irving drew his inspiration for *Sleepy Hollow* but it was possibly from various sources. Certainly, there are a number of tales of headless horsemen found in Germanic folklore, many of which were told through the work of the Grimm brothers. Some of these feed from the legends of the Wild Hunt, the ghostly procession of demonic hunters and dogs said to ride abroad on wild nights searching for souls. Stories of the Wild Hunt spread out from Germany in our past and are found in many other areas, with the leader of the Hunt drawing on more geographically local cultural sources. In the South West of England for example, we find leaders as diverse as Sir Francis Drake and the devil; in Wales meanwhile, the god Gwyn ap Nudd performs a similar role alongside his supernatural white hunting dogs, the Cwn Annwn.

Washington Irving wrote *The Legend of Sleepy Hollow* while living in the British town of Birmingham, so it is also probable that he found inspiration from other UK sources. His parents were from opposite ends of the United Kingdom. His father William Senior was born in Orkney, Scotland, and his mother Sarah was from Falmouth in Cornwall, England. They may have related stories as the author grew up that stuck with him. Also well-known would have been the Arthurian story of the Green Knight, who arrived in Camelot from nowhere and challenged any member of the King's court to strike him a blow, with the condition that, one year later, the Green Knight would strike the same blow. We have already discussed the importance of the colour green both in folklore and in the supernatural aspects of Scooby-Doo.

Sir Gawain takes up the challenge and decapitates the Green Knight, but the mysterious figure picks up his own head and rides off with it. A year later, Sir Gawain fulfils the bargain and meets with the Knight again, but survives as the Knight only touches his neck with his sword. The story is essentially a parable on the value of truth and honour.

There are countless examples of stories relating to saints who were beheaded, but who were able to pick up their head and walk off with it. In many of these, the blood dripping from the head falls to the ground and, where it hits the earth, particular types of flowers spring up – such as foxgloves, in the case of Saint Nectan. Many of these stories become associated with holy wells and the flora which surrounds them.

As we are discussing ghosts, this seems like an excellent time to start a new chapter on that very subject...

# CHAPTER THREE

## GH-GH-GH-GH-GH-GHOSTS

The appearance of ghosts is part of the bread and butter of classic Scooby-Doo episodes and so in this chapter, named after Shaggy's usual way of announcing their presence, we will take a look at many of the traditional features of hauntings and apparitions, both in the real world and in Scooby-Doo.

At the end of the previous chapter we touched on the subject of the headless ghost. This motif was one of the earliest variations of the ghost portrayed in Scooby-Doo, first making an appearance in the second season of *Scooby Doo Where Are You!* in the episode 'Haunted House Hang-Up'. Eagle-eyed readers may recall that this was the episode that was later reimagined in *Be Cool, Scooby Doo!* as 'Party Like It's 1899'.

The Mystery Machine is driving through the suitably spooky rural landscape with the gang on their way to a 'groovy' rock festival (because we are back in the 1960s now and everything is groovy). With his usual impressive navigation skills, Fred is lost and they pull over to look for a road sign. While inspecting a fallen and illegible sign, a figure looms out of the mist. It is a local farmer, Asa Shanks, who points the gang in the right direction towards an upcoming fork in the road. They can take either path, but he advises taking the longer left-hand route rather than the shorter road to the right, because this passes an old mansion that is reputed to be haunted by a headless spectre.

The left-hand path seems sensible, but of course the fates have other ideas and Fred notices that the van is low on gas and so elects to take the short route. But, quelle surprise, the normally reliable Mystery Machine overheats, coming to a stop right outside the eponymous mansion. Shaggy and Scooby go to fetch water from an old well, but are scared by a white-sheet ghost that rises from the depths.

The white-sheeted ghost is memorable from Scooby-Doo, appearing in the original opening titles, and frequently appears in modern times in GIF form on social media whenever anyone wants to tweet about hauntings. It is also one of the more stereotypical forms of apparition, particularly amongst children.

This might be because it is both easy to draw and also makes for a cheap fancy-dress costume for exhausted parents to throw together at Halloween.

In terms of folklore, the white-sheeted ghost finds its origins in the Early Modern Period – that is from the mid-fifteenth to the mid-eighteenth century. It was usual in this period for any deceased person to be wrapped in a winding cloth, or a shroud, before they were interred. Those who could afford it had their bodies placed in a coffin as well, but for the poorer majority the body would be placed into the ground in its shroud.

It should be no surprise, therefore, that people believing that they are witnessing a ghost will see a shape which appears to be in a shroud or sheet. In the same way that smugglers drew upon folklore as previously discussed, the criminal classes took advantage of this. The white-sheet was an easy way to hoax a ghost and scare someone for nefarious purposes. We can find reference to this in Chapter Fifteen of Reginald Scot's classic book *The Discoverie of Witchcraft*:

> "But certeinlie, some one knave in a white sheete hath cousened and abused manie thousands that waie… But you shall understand, that these bugs speciallie are spied and feared of sicke folke, children, women, and cowards, which through weaknesse of mind and bodie, are shaken with vaine dreames and continuall feare."

In other words, naughty people have fooled and attacked loads of folk using this disguise, but you'll only fall for it if you're a child, or a woman, or a coward and not if you're a manly man (presumably in tights).

It should be noted that although the white-sheet was a common idea and an easy disguise at this time, it wasn't the most common method of portraying a ghost, especially not in the 'media' of the time such as the stage play. Here, ghosts were normally portrayed using a suit of armour. This was possibly an influence of Horace Walpole's eighteenth century novel *The Castle of Otranto*, and the image is found in the first ever episode of *Scooby Doo Where Are You!*, 'What A Night For A Knight'. Haunted armour was to return in the first season of *Scooby-Doo and Guess Who?* where, in the episode 'Hollywood Knights!', a gardener forges the deeds to the mansion of a film director in order to try to make money.

The image of the white-sheeted ghost probably became culturally embedded in the early nineteenth century with the London case of the 'Hammersmith Ghost'. In the winter of 1803, reports began to come from the Hammersmith district of London that people were being attacked by a ghostly figure. The man was said to have been very tall and dressed in a white shroud. It was believed that he was the spirit of a suicide victim who had been buried in the area the year before.

Robert Peel's Parliamentary Bill which led to the formation of the Greater London Police was still more than twenty years away at this time, so vigilantes would often take the law into their own hands. This is what happened in Hammersmith, with tragic consequences. Excise officer Francis Smith, aged 29, was out hunting for the ghost one night when he spotted a figure dressed all in white. He fired his gun at it, shooting and killing the innocent bricklayer Thomas Millwood.

The trial that followed this incident drew massive publicity and did much to solidify the image of the ghost in a white-sheet in the public imagination. The whole affair turned out to be a hoax, with the Hammersmith Ghost having been a creation of a man named John Graham, a local shoemaker who concocted the story just to scare people. From this point on, in various English-speaking countries, the white-sheeted ghost image spread, taking over in theatre from the supernatural suit of armour and leading to many a Halloween costume, all of which cemented its stereotypical nature still further.

Back to the haunted mansion... The headless ghost here ultimately proves to be Penrod Stillwall, the owner of the building and a descendent of Jefferson Stillwall whose treasure is said to still be in the house somewhere. This is the first time that the main villain is not up to something criminal, as Stillwall is simply trying to keep people away while he searches for what is rightly his. The gang assure Penrod that they don't want his treasure, and will help him to search for it. In doing so, they all find yet another white-sheeted figure in the attic. Whilst the one at the well had turned out to be a helium balloon covered with a cloth, this one is actually a disguised Asa Shanks who is himself searching for the Stillwall fortune. At least, until he is stopped by the meddling kids.

The headless motif shows up in other episodes and doesn't always relate to ghosts. In the 2002 'A Scooby-Doo! Christmas', part of the first season of *What's New, Scooby-Doo?*, a New England town does not celebrate Christmas because of their fear of a headless snowman. The town, Winter Hollow, makes a cultural reference to the location of a more well-known literary headless figure, and the owner of the local inn, whose name is Asa Buckwald, may well reference 'Haunted House Hang-Up'. In turns out again, in fact, that the motive for the creation of the monster is a hunt for treasure.

In the first season of *Scooby-Doo! Mystery Incorporated* we find another variation of the headless creature. This time we travel as far as the Amazon to come across it, but it does draw from well-established legend in its design. The story centres around an explorer, Dr Rick Sparton, who is something of an Indiana Jones character. He becomes cursed by a headless creature and Mystery Inc. try to help him to break the curse. The story behind the mystery is rather sad. The creature turns out to be Rick's wife Marion[7] who is fed up with exploring

---

[7]. A coincidence, or might this be a reference to Karen Allen's character Marion Ravenwood in the 1981 Spielberg movie *Raiders of the Lost Ark*?

and just wants to settle at home. She thinks that if the curse is discovered to be fake, her husband will just go back to exploring the jungles again.

The monster here is humanoid in appearance. It wears only a loincloth and has no head, but instead sports facial features on its chest. It is in essence a rendering of the mythical headless species known as the Blemmyes, described in antiquity in a roundabout way by Herodotus who names them akephaloi in the Greek, and then later by Roman geographer Pomponius Mela and philosopher Pliny the Elder who both placed the creatures in African regions.

Headless men appeared in a number of places around the world, with similar descriptions to the Blemmyes. They often appeared on old maps; the version in *Scooby-Doo! Mystery Incorporated* is a more ferocious-looking rendering of one drawn by French explorer Guillaume Le Testu in the sixteenth century.

Later explanations for the stories of Blemmyes suggested that they were a misinterpretation of peoples who happened to have their heads much more deep-set in the shoulders than the Western travellers who observed them, or even that they were a description of animals such as Bonobo apes for whom this is a common trait.

Aside from the ghost in a white sheet and the one that has carelessly misplaced its head, there are a number of traditional ghost stereotypes represented within the spirits of Scooby-Doo.

We often see the trait of walking through walls and doors exhibited by ghostly villains in the show. An early example is the Creeper from 'Jeepers, it's the Creeper' in Season 2 of *Scooby Doo Where Are You!*. The episode title is, of course, a play on words of the classic song which we discussed in the opening chapter, along with Daphne's use of both 'Jeepers' and 'Creepers' as expressions of surprise.

The Creeper as a ghost perhaps looks more like a zombie, but fits into the ghostly category. He ends up being unmasked (unusually by Scooby himself) and revealed as the bank manager, Mr Carswell, who is trying to steal money from his own bank. It seems highly likely that Carswell's name references the alchemist and occultist Karswell who is central to the plot of the M.R. James story 'Casting the Runes', and who in turn influenced the mad scientist Dr Julian Karswell in the 1957 film *Night of the Demon*.

A key difference, in terms of folklore, between the wall-traversing ghosts of Scooby-Doo and those in real world stories lies in their sense of purpose and interaction with other people. The ghosts of Scooby are frequently chasing the gang when they pass through solid objects, or spying on other events that are going on around them. This means that they have intent (of course they do, apart from the rare cases where the supernatural is real, they are criminals trying to cover their tracks).

Whilst we cannot, of course, say for certain that ghosts exist, and when we look at them in terms of folklore that point is moot anyway, there are

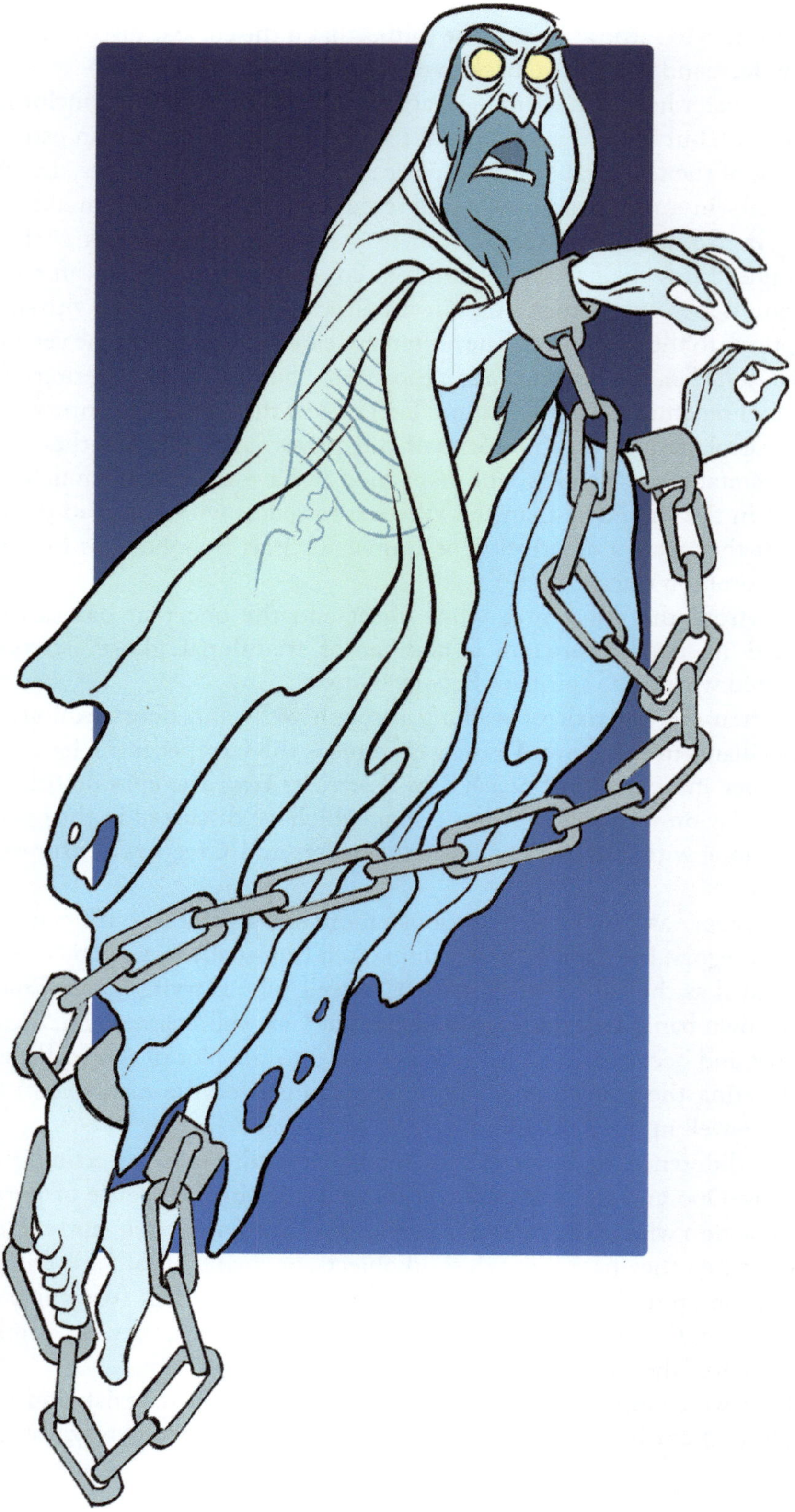

plenty of theories put forward by those who investigate the subject as to what particular types of spirit are and how they manifest. In the case of ghosts walking through walls, the most common theoretical explanation pertains to the ghost being a 'residual haunting'.

Put simply, in a residual haunting the ghost would be following a pre-defined pattern without variation. It might always appear at two in the morning. It might always perform a particular function. And it might always follow the same route between appearing and disappearing. It is this latter point that would account for the ability to walk through walls and doors.

If the ghost is connected with a location in a particular time period, there would be a high chance that the layout of that location will have altered over time. If it is the interior of a property, new walls or doors may have been put in during renovation work. Where a person once moved between rooms using a particular set of doors and stairs, these may have now gone and so their ghost might appear to walk through a wall where there was once a door.

One of the most famous examples of the idea occurred in 1953. At the Grade I listed National Trust property Treasurer's House, in the UK city of York, an eighteen-year-old plumber's apprentice named Harry Martindale was undertaking pipe repairs in a cellar. While up a ladder, he was startled by something that sounded like trumpets. Looking down, he was shocked to see what appeared to be Roman soldiers emerge from a wall and walk across the cellar, along with a cart horse. They were remarkable as being visible only from the knees upwards. Martindale was so unnerved that he fell from the ladder and would not return to the cellar for a number of weeks. The reason for the lower part of the legs not being visible is the change in floor levels at the location over the centuries.

Whilst this apparition can never be evidenced more than anecdotally and the original observer has now passed away, there are certain things that hint at it being particularly remarkable. One of these is the unusual description of the soldiers, which at first appeared anachronous to York but was later shown to precisely fit a particular reserve force who held the garrison when the regular army returned to Rome. It is interesting to note that Harry Martindale never once changed his story in the decades after the sighting took place, and never sought any reward for sharing it. Whilst none of this is proof, it all adds veracity to the tale.

The third obviously stereotyped ghostly trait that we can find in the show is the idea of the ghost being in chains. In the episode 'A Night of Fright is No Delight', towards the end of the original first season, Scooby finds that he has been included in the will of the late Colonel Beauregard Sanders; this is apparently not the creator of any kind of fried chicken, but rather someone who Scooby saved from drowning some years before.

In order to share in the inheritance, Scooby and the other characters who are also potential heirs must spend the night in the Colonel's haunted manor house. Anyone leaving during the night will forfeit their share of the money, which will be divided between those who remain. The gang, of course, decide to stay with Scoob.

Two menacing green (of course) phantoms, with glowing orange eyes and horrific looking pumpkin-carved faces, appear at various times to try and scare people away. Both phantoms have black chains secured to their wrists with manacles.

The phantoms turn out to be the two lawyers, Cosgood Creeps and Cuthbert Crawls, who want to keep the fortune for themselves.

The image of a ghost in chains has a very old origin, but is not as common throughout history as one might imagine. I discuss the story in my book *Dark Folklore*, which has a chapter looking at folk ghosts in history. As far as can be ascertained, the first appearance of a chained spirit relates to an event recorded by Pliny the Younger in a letter to Sura. It is, in fact, one of the earliest ghost stories to be written down at all. Pliny writes in the letter:

> "There was at Athens a large and roomy house, which had a bad name, so that no one could live there. In the dead of the night a noise, resembling the clashing of iron, was frequently heard, which, if you listened more attentively, sounded like the rattling of chains, distant at first, but approaching nearer by degrees: immediately afterwards a spectre appeared in the form of an old man, of extremely emaciated and squalid appearance, with a long beard and dishevelled hair, rattling the chains on his feet and hands. The distressed occupants meanwhile passed their wakeful nights under the most dreadful terrors imaginable."

The story is essentially one of those types where an unquiet spirit cannot find rest until some unfinished business has been dealt with. The house is eventually purchased by a philosopher called Athenodorus, who is not worried about the stories but does want to take advantage of the much reduced price for the property.

Athenodorus sees the ghost for himself and follows it. The spirit leads him out to the courtyard, where it disappears in a particular spot. Being a clever, scholarly sort of person, Athenodorus marks the spot and then goes back to bed. The following morning, he has his servants dig up the spot that he marked, where they discover a skeleton with chains attached to it. Once the bones have been properly buried, the ghost does not appear again. It is the beginning of what will become a common folklore trope.

It would probably be the case that stories of figures with chains would be consigned to the more legendary appearances associated with the Wild Hunt if it wasn't for a couple of notable literary appearances of shackled figures. The first of these is published in 1843, and describes the appearance of the ghost as

> "…in his pigtail, usual waistcoat, tights and boots; the tassels on the latter bristling, like his pigtail, and his coat-skirts, and the hair upon his head. The chain he drew was clasped about his middle. It was long, and wound about him like a tail…"

The ghost here is that of Marley (or the Marley brothers if you prefer your spirits more Muppety) from Charles Dickens's classic *A Christmas Carol*. In this particular instance, Dickens ascribes a meaning to the chains that isn't found in general folklore. He describes, through the education being given to Scrooge in the story, how the chains are formed by the sins or bad deeds of the person in life. The more the sins, the longer the chains will be.

The second instance is rather more comedic, referring to the ghostly figure of Sir Simon de Canterville in Oscar Wilde's 1887 short story *The Canterville Ghost*, originally published in two parts in 'The Court and Society Review', a British literary magazine. In Wilde's tale, Sir Simon appears in a variety of different guises in his efforts to haunt the American family who purchase his old family seat, many of which use common ghostly tropes such as carrying your own head or wearing a white sheet. When he tries appearing shackled in chains, it results only in Sir Simon being offered some oil to stop the squeaking.

Between them, these two mentions in popular literature probably did more than anything else to embed the motif of the spirit in chains into the world of supernatural folklore.

There are many other examples of different aspects of ghosts represented in episodes, from the way that they appear to the function that they perform and typical locations associated with them.

## Mirrors

There are many superstitious beliefs attached to mirrors, aside from the well-known one that breaking a mirror will bring seven years of bad luck. We have already touched upon this idea slightly in the previous chapter. Mirrors are considered by some to be a form of portal to the spirit realm. Arranging two mirrors to face each other, for example, is said by some to be able to create a gateway that will allow spirits to pass through to our world.

Ideas of the mirror as a spirit portal such as these undoubtedly led to the development of urban horror legends such as Bloody Mary and Candyman, and another similar one known as Blue Baby. The first and last of these are genuine urban legends, whilst *Candyman* features the folkloresque story based around the premise of summoning the hook-handed killer of the title by chanting his name five times into a mirror. Based on a short story, *The Forbidden*, written by horror author Clive Barker in 1985, it spawned four movies between 1992 and 2021.

In the lesser-known version Blue Baby, the participant must stand in front of a mirror in a dark room and repeat the phrase 'blue baby' thirteen times. There are connections here with thirteen being an unlucky number and of the power of repetition in magical use. After doing this, a baby is said to appear in your arms and scratch you. If you don't drop the child and run, then the image of the mother will appear in the mirror, demanding her baby back, screaming loudly enough to shatter the glass. Staying put through all of this will lead to her killing you.

The number thirteen appears in an episode of the (not terribly good) *13 Ghosts of Scooby-Doo* which features a mirror, or more precisely a demon. In the episode 'Reflections in a Ghoulish Eye' (a parody on the 1941 novel *Reflections in a Golden Eye* by Carson McCullers) Scoob and his friends are attending a paranormal convention at a hotel in Marrakesh, where they are booked into room 1313. They end up encountering a mirror demon, who captures a maid at the hotel and some others and drags them through into a mirror dimension. Fortunately, a mysterious merchant who later turns out to be Vincent van Ghoul (an invited and seemingly immortal magician, based on – and voiced by – the horror legend, Vincet Price), gives Daphne a magical amulet that is inscribed with mirror writing. When she and the others are finally captured, remembering that the supernatural is real in this iteration of the show, the amulet allows them to return to their own dimension and capture the demon.

The making and wearing of amulets as a form of protection is particularly ancient, and has been subsumed into many ongoing cultural beliefs. Morocco, where this story is set, enjoys a mixture of Islamic beliefs and older practices which means that symbols occur frequently, although the wearing of any amulet or talisman other than one bearing Islamic verses is strictly forbidden.

The more modern urban legend ideas surrounding mirrors are riffed on in the episode 'The Legend of Alice May' in the first season of *Scooby-Doo: Mystery Incorporated*. The storyline follows the idea of an online urban myth; that of a Ghost Girl who lures boys to her with her attractive appearance, before revealing herself to be a crone and asking them if they want to be her boyfriend forever. The girl turns out to be a new student called Alice May who has transferred to the school at Crystal Cove. In the episode we see her looking into a mirror, with the reflection looking back being the hideous image rather than the attractive one. Looking into a mirror and seeing something unexpected looking back is a staple of many a creepy movie sequence.

Alice May turns out to be the daughter of another character, Deacon Carlswell, who was the bank manager previously unmasked by the gang as 'The Creeper' in the episode of *Scooby-Doo Where Are You!* 'Jeepers, it's the

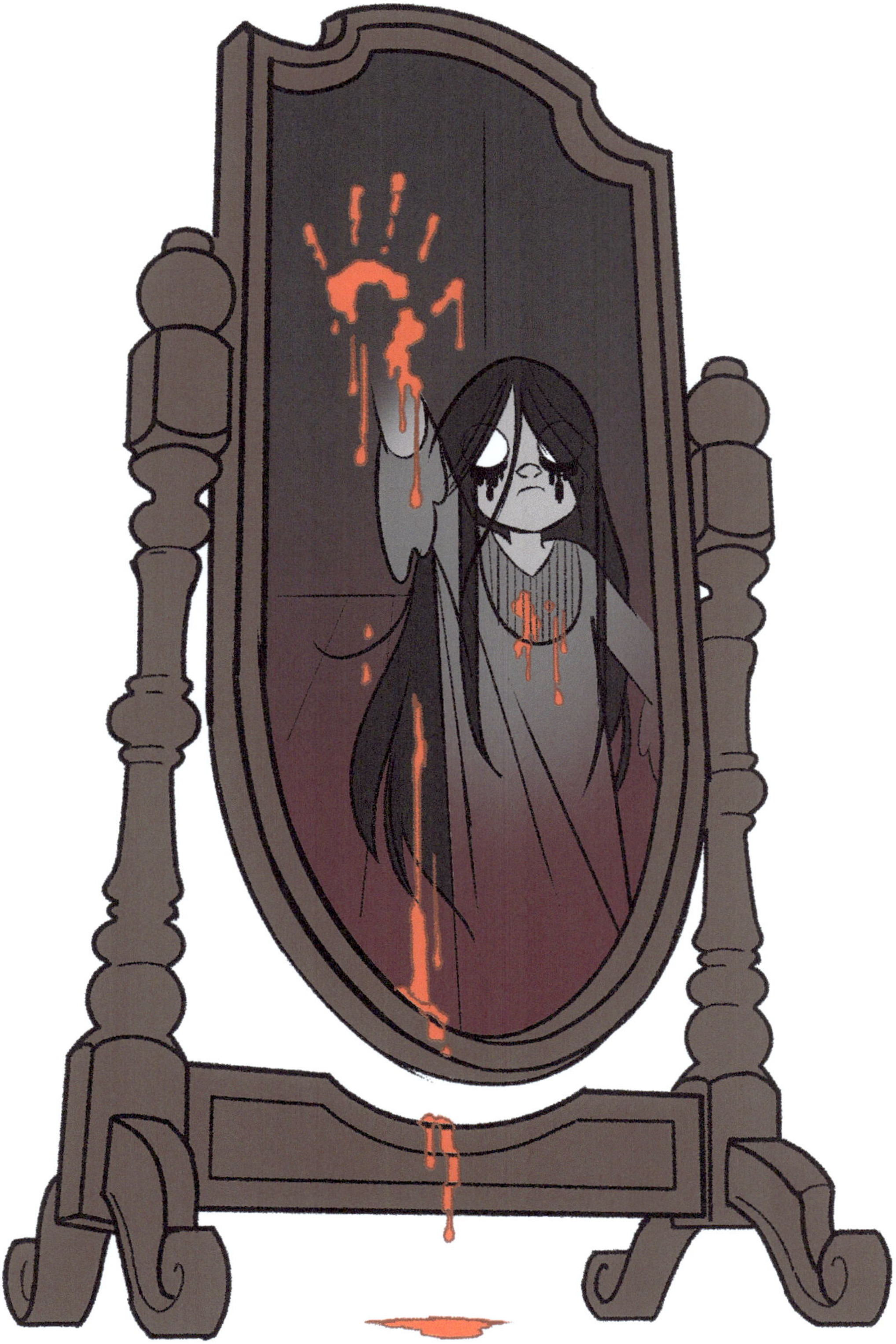

Creeper'.[8] Alice wants to exact revenge on the gang for the previous capture and incarceration of her father and so she uses her father's costume as inspiration for her own and draws on an old internet legend, kidnapping another student at the top of the episode as a way of getting the old Ghost Girl legend back into the public consciousness again. It's a modern twist on the old idea of smugglers adopting folkloric stories for their own ends.

## Curses

When we think of mirror ghosts such as Bloody Mary or Candyman, we naturally think of their evil aspects, and there have been a few occasions in the show where these aspects have been shown specifically in relation to ghosts rather than any other form of more demonic entity.

The idea of family ghosts is used many times, but in Episode 6 of the first season of *Scooby-Doo Where Are You!*, 'What the Hex Going on?', we find one enacting a particular curse. The gang are travelling to see a friend, Sharon Wetherby. At the start of the episode, we see Sharon's Uncle Stuart being lured into the house by the voice of an old family ghost, Elias Kingston. He subsequently goes missing in the house, and when the gang find him, he has been affected by the family curse, which ages people, and is significantly older.

As the story develops, Sharon goes missing and the gang find a set of mummified bones. It appears that Uncle Stuart had another run-in with the ghost and the aging curse took its toll. The gang are threatened by Elias Kingston and follow him into an old family mausoleum. He disappears, but they do find some clues – including a book that, from the cover, is described (in the episode) as being about 'crystalomacy'. They head into town to visit the local swami and find out more.

We need to pause here and unpick some of the folklore before we unmask the villain.

Let's start with the curse. There is certainly plenty of folklore connected with curses to be found. Curse tablets, cursed objects, witches cursing animals or people are all well known. Family curses are a little more complex. We find in the Bible the idea of a generational curse within a family; that is, where the sins of one generation are atoned for by future generations. This idea is more prevalent in Greek religions and those from around the area of the Mediterranean, both historically and contemporaneously.

Western family curses are often connected with something more portentous. Many generations of the Oxenham family in Devon, in the South West of England, were said to have seen a white bird appear just prior to the death of

---

[8]. In the original episode, which we discussed earlier, the character was named Carswell and there is no explanation offered for the slight variation in the *Mystery Incorporated* reference to the back story.

the head of the household. Lord Byron, who inherited Newstead Abbey from his uncle, also inherited a death omen in the form of a spectral Augustinian friar in a black robe, who would appear at the deathbed of family members, as well as at weddings and christenings. At these last two he reportedly looked angry at the celebrations, whereas he was joyful at the deathbed.

It is perhaps within literature that we find one of the most famous of all family curses, in the form of the spectral animal that haunts the Baskerville family in Sir Arthur Conan Doyle's famous Sherlock Holmes novel. This, itself, draws on many aspects of folklore in its construction. A number of these were related to Conan Doyle by his friend, journalist Bertram Fletcher Robinson, whose family home was on the edge of Dartmoor, where the story is based.

Both the Sherlock Holmes story and the concept of Black Dog ghosts more generally have been taken into the show and parodied. In the *New Scooby and Scrappy Doo Show* episode 'Hound of the Scoobyvilles', first broadcast in 1983, Scoob, Shaggy, Scrappy and Daphne visit the Scottish estate of the Barkervilles, where sheep have been going missing. This is said to be due to the curse of the Barkerville Hound, who was banished before and whose return is said to signify the falling of the estate. There is some confusion as Scooby is accused of being the Hound, but it turns out that he has been put into a trance by the caretaker Bentley using an ultra-sonic ring. This is all part of Bentley's scheme to secure the estate for himself.

A giant black hound appears in the first season of *Scooby-Doo: Mystery Incorporated* in the guise of the Fright Hound. Although this turns out to be a robotic dog, and that fact is used to good effect in some *Terminator* parody set-pieces, the image of the dog is very much based on that of a demonic hound. Its fierce-looking glowing red eyes are a common motif in terms of this symbol.

To return to the book that the gang uncover, whether by error or design the invented term 'crystalomacy' undoubtedly refers to the practice of crystallomancy. Also known more simply as crystal gazing, this is a method of divination that in its most stereotypical form would see the practitioner gazing into a crystal ball. In fact, any transparent surface could be used. The term is sometimes conflated with scrying, where one would look into an obsidian mirror and hope to see shapes and visions within, that could then be interpreted.

The gang head into town to see if there is a connection with a 'Swami' who has a shop there. The term swami here refers to a fortune teller, operating in the manner of a fairground sideshow practitioner. The 'swami' would wear a cloak and a turban, usually containing some kind of jewel, making them look like an oriental mystic.

The true use of the term swami, however, comes from the Hindu religion. To be a swami, in the original Sanskrit use of the term, is to be 'at one with the self'. A Hindu swami is one who has chosen a path of abstinence. The title is bestowed as one of honour and precedes the person's name, which is usually adopted from the religious faith.

Cultural appropriation then took this image and ascribed it both to the fairground fortune teller and to the penny arcade and boardwalk automatons such as the Zoltar machines, where a fortune on a printed card would be dispensed by a bearded mystic figure with a crystal ball. These machines are still manufactured and distributed today, with possibly the most popular reference being within the Tom Hanks film *Big*, in 1988. The Zoltar trademark is owned by the Nevada-based company Characters Unlimited.

A fraudulent swami also showed up in the feature length *Scooby-Doo on Zombie Island* where she conjured up a skeletal ghost that turned out to be a projection.

Back to the plot – in case you didn't see it coming, the ghost was Uncle Stuart, who also used the swami as an alias and aged himself using make-up before hiding out in the mausoleum, which had a secret passage to the Weatherby mansion. Unusually, he does not explain his motive, stating instead that he will explain it to the sheriff rather than telling his own daughter, who he had captured when she had seen his wig blown off.

Curses appear in a number of other episodes in relation to Egyptian mummies for example, or to the ill-effects of removing ancient items from caves or tombs. But from the crystal ball gazing of the swami, we move to another aspect of dealing with the spirit realm that has come up in a few of the later iterations of the show and that, if they were still monitoring it today, would have had members of 'Action for Children's Television' running for their complaining trousers.

## Séances

The act of attempting to commune with the spirits of the deceased is an important part of many cultures, but the séance as an organised event for doing so found its foothold as a more public event with the rise of spiritualism in the mid-nineteenth century. The legitimacy of many séance rooms has been called into question over the years due to the uncovering of 'parlour tricks' and other fakery, but this is not the forum to discuss the authenticity or otherwise of the practice. In Scooby-Doo, at least, we know for certain that things are rarely what they first appear to be.

A very simplistic séance scene is included in the *New Scooby-Doo Mysteries* episode 'Doom Service', which we have already discussed regarding its parody of *The Shining*. The participants try to contact the spirit of Ebenezer Overview, whose voice is heard thanks to a remote-controlled tape machine in the air vents. We see the characters sitting around a circular table with their hands on it and one calls out to the ghost, but there are no physical effects and the character's hands are not joined in the traditional séance fashion. It is, at best, a rough approximation to give the idea in what is a very short scene within a fifteen-minute episode.

A more standard-looking séance scene opens up the episode of *Scooby-Doo and Guess Who?* that features Whoopi Goldberg as special guest. In 'The Nightmare Ghost of Psychic U!', Goldberg is studying to graduate as an animal psychic having enjoyed some success finding lost pets[9]. She leads a séance to try to find a lost puppy called Snuggly Puggly (parodying Scooby himself from *A Pup Named Scooby-Doo*), but appears to inadvertently open a doorway and call through The Nightmare Ghost which proceeds to haunt the school.

The Nightmare Ghost is extremely tall and thin, looking in some respects a little like a tentacle-free version of Slenderman – only bright blue. At the end of the episode, it is revealed that the shape of the ghost is due to its being the lady who runs the school cafeteria, in disguise and wearing stilts. She is trying to scare everyone away so that she can cause the psychic school to close down and leave the way clear for her to open a stilt-walking ski school. Yes, really… it's complicated.

One interesting aspect of the design of The Nightmare Ghost has a direct relation to real world lore, though is never explained, or even commented upon, in the episode: the ghost has coins in place of its eyes. Released in 2020, it seems probable that this element draws from the demonic entity known as The Ferryman in the previous year's film *Annabelle Comes Home*, a part of *The Conjuring* franchise.

In the film, The Ferryman was a supernatural collector of souls, and the coins over the eyes are in direct reference to the Greek mythological character of Charon, who conveyed the dead across the river Styx. It was traditional for people to place coins over the eyes of the deceased before burial; these coins were the toll with which to pay the ferryman Charon in the afterlife.

These are not the only filmic references to this to be found, interestingly. In the 2004 Canadian werewolf horror sequel *Ginger Snaps 2: Unleashed,* coins are placed over the eyes of the mutilated body of Beth Ann. Recently, in the 2022 animated film *Puss in Boots: The Last Wish*, Death (in the form of an anthropomorphic wolf) places two coins over his eyes as Puss and the other hero characters escape from Big Jack Horner's guards.

'The Nightmare Ghost of Psychic U!' is also significant because Velma acknowledges that she has at least some time for psychic work. She notes that, whether you believe in its veracity or not, the police and the FBI use psychics to track down criminals, and "that's good enough for me".

---

[9]. Goldberg had previously played charlatan psychic Oda Mae Brown in the earlier movie *Ghost,* starring Patrick Swayze.

According to the American journal *Law and Order* in September 1993, whilst approximately twenty of the large police agencies in the country had used psychics at the time of publication, the FBI did not hire psychics and had no plans to do so. Maybe even Velma makes a mistake occasionally? Or maybe not... in fact checking this, a colleague in the United States spoke to an ex-federal agent friend of theirs to enquire about this. She said that, although it was not the official line, it was an open secret amongst agents that psychics have sometimes been used in investigations involving the Bureau, generally in missing persons cases when all other avenues have been exhausted.

One such case was the high-profile crash landing of an aircraft carrying the Uruguayan rugby team on which the 1993 film (and 1974 book) *Alive* was based. A psychic was brought in to try to locate the missing team in the mountains.

Using perceived psychic ability to try and help solve crime was not just confined to the United States either. In 1966, a British psychiatrist named John Barker tried the same thing with the establishing of the 'Premonitions Bureau'. He figured that if he could find enough people who were sensitive to such things, he could build a network which would act as an early-warning system to help to combat terrorist incidents, avert natural disasters and prevent shootings and other serious crime. The story is told in the book *The Premonitions Bureau*, by Sam Knight.

Of course, Velma does not (to the best of our knowledge, unless she is an undercover clandestine agent) work for the FBI, so how would she have known this? Maybe she has someone on the inside...

If all these séances were not enough to shock the 1960s sensibilities of the Action for Children's Television parents, then the final one we will look at would certainly do the job. This takes place towards the end of the first season of *Scooby-Doo: Mystery Incorporated* in the episode 'A Haunting in Crystal Cove', which sees Fred's father Mayor Jones being troubled at home by a poltergeist.

Velma thinks that one of her mother's herbal sleep remedies will help Mayor Jones to sleep. Whilst at the Spook Museum arranging this, the new barista Lady Marmalade learns of the case and suggests that an exorcism may be required. She arranges to perform a séance, during which she uses a spirit board to contact the other side.

A spirit board, also sometimes known as a talking board and more commonly as a Ouija board from its brand name, is a flat board generally made of wood, bearing the letters of the alphabet, numbers 0-9 and words 'yes' and 'no' as standard. Some boards also have the additional greetings of 'hello' and 'goodbye' on them. A moveable indicator called a planchette will point to any of these markings in turn to spell out words and phrases in answer to questions when those using the board place their fingers on it. Believers in the spirit world and the effectiveness of the board see this as communication from the deceased. The scientific explanation for the movement is the amplification of small involuntary muscular movements from the participants, known as the ideomotor effect. And sometimes, fakery. A 2004 television special in the United Kingdom, created by psychological illusionist Derren Brown and named *Séance*, explored the idea. Twelve students were gathered in a room where it was explained to them that the location was chosen because twelve other students had previously met there and all died as the result of a suicide pact. A séance was then undertaken to try and contact the spirits of the deceased twelve.

A number of seemingly supernatural events took place, including a Ouija board spelling out messages, but at the end of the programme it was revealed that the participants, who had been carefully selected for their susceptibility to suggestion, had taken part in a hoax.

The Ouija board is notable for being the only patented board game that includes an occult method of communication in its make-up. There has obviously been supposed communication with the spirits for many centuries across the world's cultures and this has taken many different formats. In America, following the popularity of the Fox sisters[10] and their public displays of 'mediumship' and the terrible losses of the Civil War, there was an appetite amongst the public to try to communicate with deceased relatives.

Around the year 1886, use of talking boards to attempt this was growing in the Ohio area and it caught the attention of a businessman named Charles Kennard and his office neighbour E.C. Reiche. Kennard was something of an entrepreneur. Reiche was a coffin maker so he had some practical skills and, presumably, plenty of wood. Together, they developed something that we would now recognise as a Ouija board.

Four years later, in 1890, Kennard moved to Baltimore where he set up a real estate business. He took the talking board with him and began to try to sell the idea to local investors, now speaking of it purely as his invention and cutting Reiche out of the picture. There was little interest shown until an attorney called Elijah Bond came across the board. His sister-in-law, Helen Peters, was, he claimed, a competent medium. He financed the idea and the Kennard Novelty Company began producing Ouija boards. Peters is not only responsible for convincing the government to grant a patent, but also for the name.

---

[10]. Recognised as being responsible for the birth and spread of spiritualism, the Fox sisters had alleged that they were conversing with spirits through a series of rapping sounds. Despite the fact that they confessed to staging the whole thing, producing the noises by cracking the bones in their feet, spiritualism continued to take hold after their performances.

It is believed by many people that the popular name 'Ouija' for the spirit board is an amalgamation of the French and German words for 'yes'. This is not true, but is a story that was spread by one-time investor and employee of the Kennard Novelty Company, William Fuld, when he managed to buy out control of the Ouija business. Ouija was originally a name spelled out on a spirit board during a session by Helen Peters in response to a question as to what the board should be called. The 'spirit' explained to Peters that the word meant 'good luck'.

In fact, Ouija was engraved on the locket on a necklace that Helen Peters was wearing at the time.

Lady Marmalade's board in the episode spells out "I am an old friend and I want what you took from me" when she asks who the spirit is, before it then catches fire in what may be a reference to the 2007 low-budget horror movie *Paranormal Activity*. The 'spirit' turns out to be Professor Pericles, an anthropomorphic parrot who was the mascot of Crystal Cove's original 'Mystery Incorporated' gang many years before Fred et al. Pericles went rogue and is the villainous mastermind behind the sophisticated story arc that runs beneath all episodes of *Scooby-Doo: Mystery Incorporated*. We will return to this arc in a later chapter. Suffice to say, for now, Professor Pericles fakes the shadowy poltergeist and rigs the house to appear to be haunted by poltergeist manifestations so that he can, indeed, steal back an important artefact which Mayor Jones once took from him.

## Reasons for hauntings

In folklore, many ghosts have an identifiable purpose behind their appearance. Sometimes, this is because there was some kind of unfinished business left over when they died. An important document might have been left undiscovered, or a hidden cache of money intended for a relative never had its location disclosed. Sometimes, a wrong needed to be righted. Consider the earlier story of the haunting of Athenodorus in the discussion of chained ghosts by way of example. These ideas carry forward into some of the ghostly episodes of Scooby-Doo as well.

The character of the ghostly Miner Forty-Niner is introduced in the first season of the original *Scooby Doo Where Are You!* in Episode 4, 'Mine Your Own Business'. The gang end up in an old western town called Gold City; as usual, they were not intending to be there but are lost, this time not due to Fred and his appalling sense of direction but rather because Shaggy was holding their map upside down.

The Miner is the ghost of an old prospector who, it is said, cannot rest until he has mined the last vein of gold from the shaft he worked in life. The ghost has scared away all the customers from the guest ranch where the gang stay, according to the ranch owner's assistant Hank. The mine is said to be heard moaning for the ghost.

In terms of actual cultural references, the ghost takes his name from the slang term 'Forty-Niner', which was used to refer to gold miners who were a part of the Californian gold rush of 1849. It was later immortalised in the famous song 'Oh, My Darling Clementine' written in 1884, most probably by Percy Montross although some attribute it to Barker Bradford:

"In a cavern, in a canyon
Excavating for a mine
Dwelt a miner forty-niner
And his daughter, Clementine"

The song has reached such cultural significance as to be considered a Western folk ballad and has been used (or the well-known tune has at least) around the world with different lyrics. The origin of the tune itself is uncertain but has been cited as a traditional Spanish melody by author Gerald Brenan. In parody of folk ballad, it is possibly equally as well known, again around the world, as the traditional children's parody song 'Found a Peanut'. This version's origins are less clear, although a Florida newspaper covering events at the Florida State University does note in an article in 1945 that the parody is an "old song".

'Clementine' can be heard a number of times in the soundtrack for the episode 'Mine Your Own Business'.

Moaning, along with banging, creaking and other auditory phenomena, is a very common part of mining lore. In July 1902, at the Cwmcos Glyncorrwg Colliery in West Glamorgan, Wales, workers ceased mining after they said that they heard the wailing of women and children coming from an adjacent disused mine. They believed this to be a sign of some impending disaster.

In this episode, the explanation for the moaning is said to be the mine itself calling for the ghost. In terms of folklore, mine spirits are often responsible for making noises. In some areas of the UK, particularly in the South West of England, these spirits were known as Knockers, and in Wales, they were named Coblynau. The knocking noises that they made served a particular purpose, and interestingly, over time as mining practices changed, so did the reason for the noise.

Originally, the knocking sounds made by these gnome-like creatures were said to be made to guide the miners to the places in the mine where the richest seams could be found. At this time, most mines were small concerns and tended to be owned and operated by one family. Over time, as industrialisation caused mines to grow larger and become more business and profit-focussed, miners became increasingly concerned about safety practices within the mines, or the lack of them. It is at this time that the purpose behind the Knockers changes, and the sounds are said to be reflective of a warning against impending collapse. In this way, miners were able to use superstition to avoid working in areas that they felt were not safe. In the 1902 example above, in fact, newspaper articles from the period show that there was already a concern that sealed-off adjacent workings to the mine were unsafe, and that there was a real threat of flooding from water incursion to the tunnels.

In the early 1800s many skilled miners went from the mines of Wales and Cornwall to America, where their expertise was employed to set up mine workings in Pennsylvania, Colorado and a number of other areas. As if often the case in folklore, as the people migrate they take their stories with them, and in America the folklore of the Knockers became established with the slightly altered name of Tommyknockers. It is possible that the prefix Tommy was added later in response to British soldiers becoming known as 'Tommies' in the war.

The moaning in the mine in the case of 'Mine Your Own Business' comes not from the mine itself, but rather from a tape recorder concealed in the mine. Because, unsurprisingly, the ghost turns out to be Hank. He has discovered that, although the gold veins in the mine are depleted, there is a large quantity of oil underneath, which he wants to exploit himself.

As well as dealing with their own unfinished business, ghosts might sometimes act as a portent of disaster to come, or sometimes they may be associated with particular families as a death omen that appears before an important member of the family is scheduled to depart from spiritual pastures new. The premise is included in the episode 'Haunted House Hang Up', which we have already discussed for a number of other reasons – nobody was said to have met that particular phantom and lived to tell the tale.

Many of the ghosts in Scooby-Doo, and in folklore more generally, are rooted firmly in history, and we will finish this look at some of the phantoms of the Scoobyverse with one particular type.

## Civil War Ghosts

Taking place between 1861 and 1865, the American Civil War was a pivotal point in US history. The northern Union's victory over the Southern Confederacy was to lead to the abolition of slavery in the country and heralded the start of a period of reconstruction for a land devastated by widespread bloodshed, not only over the four years of the war itself but during more than a century of torture and killing of enslaved Black Africans and other racial groups before that. It is no wonder that there should be a great number of paranormal events and haunted locations connected to such a period of trauma and loss, and therefore only natural that the subject come up multiple times in Scooby-Doo.

The episode 'A Mystery Solving Gang Divided!' in the first season of *Scooby-Doo and Guess Who?* is unusual because, in universe at least, it contains both fake ghosts and real ghosts. Iterations of the show normally treat the paranormal as either one or the other, as we saw earlier, but this is something of a diversion.

The show is also something of a dichotomy of serious and silly as it provides an important commentary on the war while at the same time is a vehicle for Hanna-Barbera to parody its own property.

A sign in the ground tells us that this episode takes place at 'Pennsylvania Historic Battlefield'. In actuality there is no battlefield with this generic name, but Pennsylvania is home to many historic battlefield sites such as Gettysburg and Pickett's Charge. A family is posing for a photograph at dusk when behind them, soldiers from the monument appear to come to life. They take on the green glow of a Scooby ghost, which by now should be very familiar, and are described as 'zombie ghosts'. Shaggy explains that these are "like regular ghosts only more zombie-er".

Whilst investigating the mystery, the gang lock horns with another gang of mystery-solving teens called the Funky Phantom Crew. Canonically, they had never previously met although in fact both groups did appear in the same story in issue 50 of DC Comics' *Scooby-Doo*. The Funky Phantoms are unusual for having a real ghost as part of their team, Jonathan Wellington Muddlemore, who died in the 1776 Revolutionary War and appears as a soldier, although all in white. The character had originally appeared in his own short-lived show produced by Hanna-Barbera in 1971, where he was voiced by Daws Butler using the voice he had originally developed for the character of Snagglepuss.

Although he is a real ghost, Mystery Incorporated of course do not believe this, and spend the whole episode disputing it. Velma at one point wonders whether he is created using Pepper's Ghost, the classic stage technique of reflecting an actor playing a ghost onto the stage in translucent form using an angled mirror. It was named for scientist John Henry Pepper, who first demonstrated it in 1862.

The plot of this episode centres around the lost payroll of 1863, a shipment of gold that is said to have gone missing and led to those who fought and died on the battlefield not being paid.

The real-life cold case surrounding the legend of the lost Civil War gold is a mystery in itself. It is far too involved to go into in any detail here, but in essence, the legend tells that a caravan of Union soldiers were transporting a shipment of gold bars to the US Mint in June of 1863. At some stage the caravan went missing and a search took place, resulting in the discovery of the wagons but no gold. Detectives from the Pinkerton agency worked the area disguised as lumberjacks and similar local traders but came up with nothing.

Two years later, two and a half ingots were thought to be dug up, along with some skeletons.

The rest of the gold remains missing, although there is an ongoing legal battle between treasure hunters and the FBI; the former believe that they discovered the site and alerted the latter to it who, they allege, excavated it and took the gold, declaring afterwards that the site was empty.

In the show, the two mystery-solving gangs are constantly squabbling and therefore failing to make progress in solving the mystery, before the ghost of Abraham Lincoln appears to set them straight. Abe explains how the soldiers remained unpaid because of the loss of the gold, which is why they are still haunting the area. Reflecting themes discussed in the previous section, Lincoln asks the teens to "help them (the soldiers) for they clearly have unfinished business". By doing this, he says that they will be able to rest in peace.

After the advice, the two groups do pull together, resulting in the solving of the mystery. One of two brothers from a local antique store, Jebb, has found a map that showed the location of the gold. The map had been concealed by the other brother, who knew that Jebb wanted the gold for himself but personally believed that it should be put into a museum and be kept safe, in true Indiana Jones style.

In a strange plot twist, the ghost of Abraham Lincoln turns out to be the ghost of Jonathan Muddlemore in disguise, with the same motive of encouragement. At the end of the episode, Fred and the gang remain ignorant of the ghost being real.

Abraham Lincoln's ghost has reportedly been seen in the White House a number of times, with the earliest being in the 1920s, when he was seen by the First Lady at the time, Grace Coolidge, in the Oval Office. A number of witnesses of reported seeing the ghost in a bedroom in the guest suite known as the Lincoln Bedroom because it served as his office during the Civil War. The most high profile of these, Queen Wilhelmina of the Netherlands, is said to have admitted that she fainted at the vision. Of course, like all good celebrity ghosts he has been seen in various other locations outside of the White House, including his grave site at Oak Ridge Cemetery in Illinois.

There can be no doubt that, in its various forms, the ghost has been a staple of Scooby-Doo stories over the fifty-plus years of the show, in the same way as it has been the driving factor behind the continued interest in the paranormal, especially through the mediums (no pun intended) of television and the internet. Spirits are found in cultures around the world, but then again, so are many other creatures of folklore… and the gang have had their run-ins with many of these in the past, too.

# CHAPTER FOUR

## SNIPS AND SNAILS
### Witches in Scooby-Doo

We have looked at the development of Scooby-Doo as a concept and we've examined the settings in which many of the stories take place, along with the look and feel of the Scoobyverse itself. It's about time, therefore, that we actually moved on to meet the monsters!

The way that characters from folklore and horror settings are represented in Scooby-Doo can be something of a mixed bag. Sometimes, things are done purely for plot advancement or entertainment and bear no resemblance to real-world folklore. Sometimes, supernatural creatures or tropes are entirely stereotypical. On occasion, representation of actual folklore goes very well… and then once you are lulled into a false sense of security it derails at the last moment. And sometimes, things can be spot on.

The figure of the witch is one which spans the whole gamut of these scenarios and so makes a good starting point to dive into our investigation of Scooby and real-world folklore.

We only have to wait until Episode 2 of the first season of the original iteration, *Scooby Doo Where Are You!*, to find our first witch in the franchise. The episode in question is 'A Clue for Scooby-Doo' and, technically, the witch is not the villain of the piece, although we could consider her as 'aiding and abetting'.

Boats have been disappearing off the coast near Rocky Point Beach, where the gang see the ghost of a man in an old diving suit. This is said to be the spirit of Captain Cutler, who died at sea when his boat was wrecked, and is out for revenge.

Up at the lighthouse, bizarre witchcraft practices are taking place. Mrs Cutler says that she is responsible for having raised the ghost of her late husband. Of course, nothing of the kind has happened – in fact, Captain Cutler has faked his own death so that he can merrily get on with his new hobby of stealing yachts around Rocky Point. And he would have gotten away with it too if it wasn't for… Shaggy, in this case. This is the only time that Shaggy discovers the identity of a villain before Velma.

Mrs Cutler is a stereotypical looking and sounding witch in every sense; in fact, the original storyboards for this episode portray her as even more unsightly than she finally appeared on screen. No doubt, the depiction was toned down for air by concerned producers who were acting on the guidance discussed in Chapter One of this book for a more wholesome Saturday morning cartoon. Whilst she has normal looking human skin colouration, she has the hook nose and the cackling laugh that is so stereotypical of witches in media.

In terms of folklore, we might think of the widow Cutler as a 'crone' or 'hag'. The word hag entered the English language around the thirteenth century, although it was rarely used for the next three hundred years or so. Its original use at this time described an old and ugly woman more akin to the Mrs Cutler of the original storyboard than the final one on screen, but its root is most likely from the Middle English word 'hægtesse', meaning 'witch'. Similar words can be found in other languages, such as the German 'Hexe', from where we find both the word for a particular type of magic spell and also the inspiration for the Gothic girl rock band in Scooby-Doo who we will meet shortly.

The stereotype of the hag as the symbol of a witch probably emerged in Renaissance art, which in itself gained popularity at around the time that the word hag itself began to become more widely established in common linguistic use. German artist Albrecht Dürer (1471-1528) produced a print around the year 1500, 'Witch Riding Backwards on a Goat', which was one of the earliest portrayals of the old and ugly witch. The woman sits on a horned goat; she is naked with wild hair and holds a form of broomstick, the preferred mode of air travel for the cartoon witch as we shall see later.

Witchcraft expert Marion Gibson points out that at this time, however, there is a dual representation of the witch who may often be particularly beautiful if not shown in this way. Dürer himself paints both types, with his work of three years earlier, 'The Four Witches', showing young women with the body type favoured by artists of the time.

As a sidebar, the character of Captain Cutler is notable in a few ways. He is unique as a villain as he is the only character who is disguised as a ghost of himself. He can also be found in other places within the Scooby-Doo universe, probably because of his role as one of the iconic early spooks from the original title sequence. Captain Cutler can be found as a statue who comes to life in the live action sequel *Scooby-Doo 2: Monsters Unleashed,* and his costume is also a part of the Crystal Cove Spook Museum which is owned by Velma's parents in the *Scooby-Doo Mystery Incorporated* iteration of the show.

The Spook Museum is a great concept. If you have ever visited or seen online the Museum of Witchcraft and Magic in Boscastle, Cornwall in the UK, you can imagine that as a resource for investigating mysteries and you end up with the Spook Museum. Velma's mum Angie Dinkley has a very useful occult library, which is consulted from time to time, as well as a large collection of past disguises used by villains who have been unmasked by the gang. There is also a great set piece acted out in this location where the gang walk past a statue of Scrappy-Doo. Daphne tries to mention the subject, but Fred cuts her off, reminding her that they all vowed that they would never talk about that again.

Technically, the next appearance of a witch in Scooby-Doo is in the original 1969 Season 1 of *Scooby-Doo Where Are You!* – Episode 9, 'Puppet Master'. The plot centres around a counterfeiting operation running out of a theatre, with a puppet master theatre ghost accounting for the haunting. As well as a creepy clown and a jack-in-the-box, there is a scary witch puppet too. But for the next proper appearance of a witch character we need to move on four more episodes to Season 1 Episode 13, 'Which Witch is Which?'.

When the gang get lost in a swamp, they stop and ask a bystander for directions. In a bizarre mix of folkloric themes, the man turns out to be a zombie who has been brought to life by a witch. Fleeing and ending up in a local shop, they meet Zeke who explains that the witch lives in the swamp and has voodoo powers. He had spotted her months ago creating the zombie when out in the swamp with his business partner Zeb. The two naturally turn out to be behind the characters. Years before, they had stolen an armoured truck and sunk it in the swamp. Returning for the contents, they realised that they had forgotten where they secreted the vehicle, and so created the witch and zombie disguises to scare people away while they searched.

In folklore, of course, there is a good track record of supernatural events coming about as such a diversion around bodies of water. Smugglers would both create and draw upon and use folkloric creatures or ghosts to keep people away while they landed and hid contraband goods, as we have already seen. Many of the spectral black dog stories concerning fearsome creatures such as the Shuck, found on coasts and in fenland areas for example, have such a root.

In terms of the folklore record, these smuggler stories can sometimes create a headache for researchers because they both used existing stories and developed their own (which then became embedded in the landscape where they were operating). When we look back from an historical perspective, we are left with something of a 'chicken and egg' situation where we cannot easily tell which stories fall into which category.

The witch in the swamp in this episode is a classic European stereotype in terms of appearance, but uses voodoo magic and thus seems to demonstrate the ability to make or control zombies. We will examine zombie lore in more detail when we turn our attention to non-Western cultures. Suffice to say, whilst it makes perfect sense to have voodoo magic and zombies together, and for them to be located in swampland, the European witch playing a large part in this is somewhat anachronistic in terms of folklore.

Chronologically, the next time that a witch appears in the show is a few years down the line, in the 1977 second season of *The Scooby-Doo Show* where Episode 6 is entitled 'The Ozark Witch Switch'. It seems almost as if the writers of this episode enjoyed 'Which Witch is Which?' so much that they decided to do it again! Once more, the action takes place in a swamp. And again, the witch's accomplice is a zombie. A strange combination the first time around, and equally strange again this time.

The Mystery Machine is transporting the gang to the Ozark river, a water course that rises in the south east of the Ozark mountains in Missouri and flows into Arkansas where it joins the Black River before finally ending up as part of the Mississippi. En route, the van is unfortunate enough to pick up four flat tyres. and so the planned rafting trip is curtailed. Seeking shelter, our heroes find an old cabin in the woods that used to belong to the McCoy family but is now home to the Hatfields. They have been terrorised by the ghost of Witch McCoy who was, they say, "a wicked old crone hung for witchcraft a hundred years ago". The witch has been trying to drive away the Hatfields because of a long-running feud between the two families. She appears to everyone and proclaims that they will all be doomed if they do not leave, before seemingly turning the family into frogs.

The gang, of course, is compelled to investigate the mystery. Much like the previous witch-themed encounter, they again find a zombie who is digging for something. Scooby and Shaggy go for help to nearby Spooky Hollow, no doubt named after the village of Sleepy Hollow found on the bank of the Hudson River and made forever famous by Washington Irving's 1820 novel. The owner of the local store, Aggie Wilkins, warns them about the witch and tells of her cave on Spider Mountain before the witch, who has transformed into a cat, appears and scares the duo off.

Investigation of the cave reveals the staples of any witch: spell books and a cauldron. Eventually, after more clue-hunting, the gang naturally succeed in trapping the witch and the zombie. They discover that the witch is none other than Aggie, the store owner, and the zombie is her ex-boyfriend Zeke Harkins, who was a bank robber and had hidden a large sum of money in a pit in the area. The two were independently trying to find it. Part of the directions needed were hidden in the cabin and so Aggie had needed to create the witch to scare away the Hatfields, who were not frogs after all but had been tied up and hidden at the local sawmill.

Transformation into animals is a common part of folklore surrounding witches, both from the perspective of the witch themselves transforming and also cursing others to become animals. Way back in Greek mythology, Circe changed someone into a pig. Being turned into a frog or toad has become a common threat in terms of folk and fairy tales featuring witches. We cannot say for certain why this idea became so popular. It may in part draw from

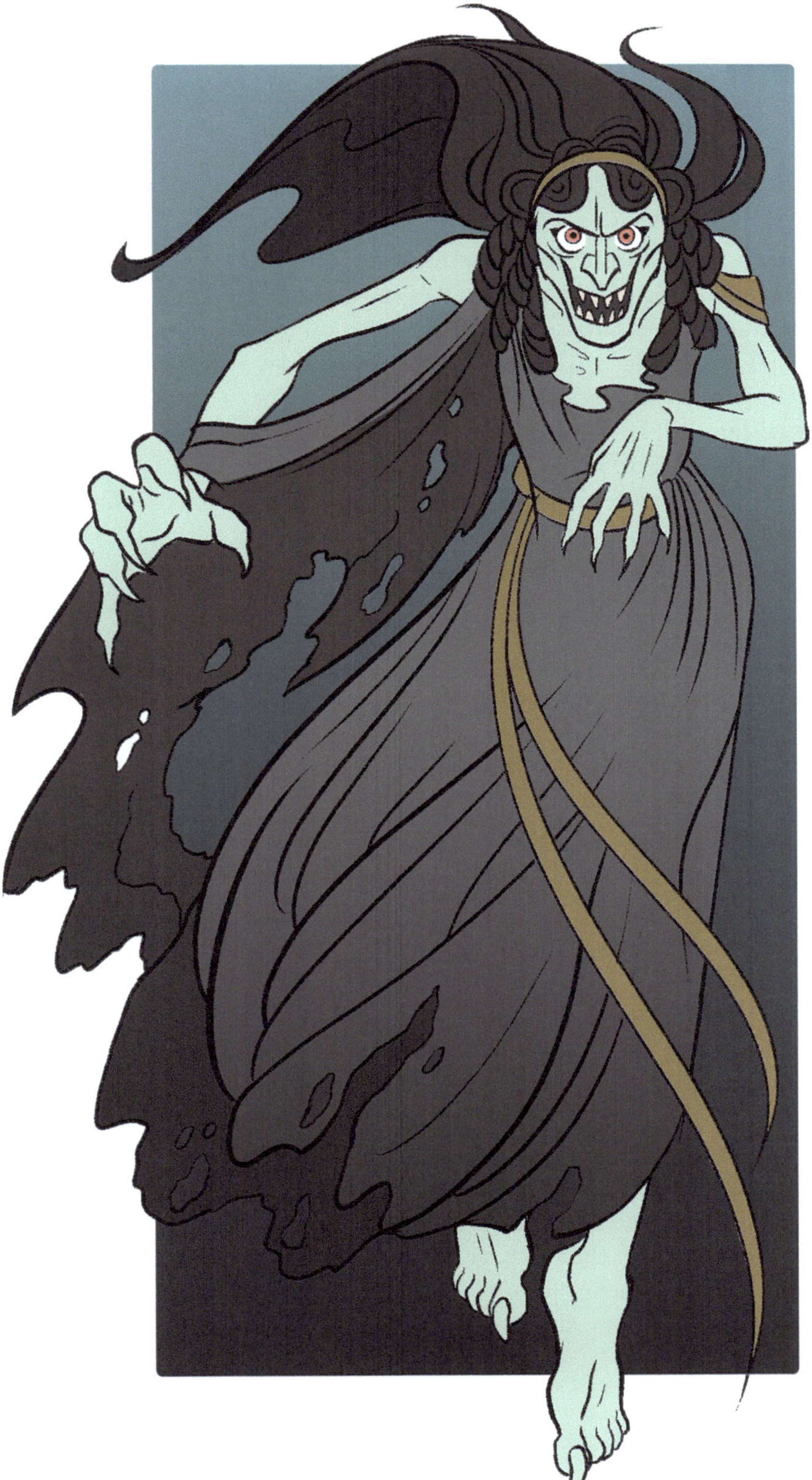

other amphibious transformation stories such as 'The Frog Prince' but might equally evoke the importance of frogs and toads for certain charms and folk magic. Cats also have ancient magical roots. Whilst some were seen as deities in ancient Egypt, the Catholic Church made links between black cats and the Devil as early as the thirteenth century, and this depiction was probably influenced by the way in which they were viewed culturally in previous periods. From here, the link with witches became quite a natural one, with the symbol of the cat as a witch's familiar becoming embedded through both story and art.

Also of cultural significance with this episode is the fact that the two feuding families, the Hatfields and McCoys are based on real-world clans, with a real-world feud behind them. The actual Hatfield-McCoy feud was relocated to the Ozark area from its original location of West Virginia and Kentucky, where the actual families fought between 1863 and 1891. This came off the back of the American Civil War and a number of reasons seem to have been involved, including land disputes, animal theft, revenge killings and many more. The feud entered into American folklore, where it became a reference point for any parties involved in a bitter battle, and it has featured in countless examples in the media, also including appearances or references in *The Flintstones*, *Merrie Melodies* cartoons, *Warehouse 13*, *My Little Pony* and many more.

More anachronism along the lines of the previous witch-zombie-voodoo hybrids comes with the next episode to feature the image of the witch, where we find a real mix of stereotypes, real-world folklore and standard Scooby-Doo artistic licence. This comes in the third and final season of *Scooby Doo Where Are You!*, which was originally broadcast as part of *Scooby's All Stars*. This is a more obscure season of the show for many. For example, it was rarely broadcast and has never been officially released on DVD in the United Kingdom. For the purposes of research for this book, I had to enlist the help of an overseas friend to buy an American region DVD for me and ship it to the UK. But it was worth the trouble: Episode 4 of this season, 'To Switch A Witch', is an interesting one in terms of folklore.[11]

The 'monster' of the piece this time around is the 'Ghost Witch of Old Salem'. So, we have a witch. But she appears as a ghost. The episode features a number of solid folklore tropes, but they are mixed together in something of an odd way. The artistic licence comes into play when we look at the actual historical facts behind the character of the witch. Milissa Wilcox was said (in the show) to have been a witch at Salem who was burned at the stake 200 years ago in order to protect the town, and who then cursed the town by saying that she would rise from her grave on Halloween night to avenge herself. The plot centres around Milissa's descendent Arlene, who bears more than a passing

---

[11]. For fans of trivia, the cackling laugh of the Witch McCoy in 'The Ozark Witch Switch' was reused for the witch in 'To Switch A Witch'. This seems natural considered they almost reused the title as well!

resemblance to the historical witch. Arlene's twin sister frames Arlene, making it seem that the ghost has returned and is manifesting through her, in the hope that the townsfolk will drive Arlene out, leaving her sister free to receive the entirety of the family inheritance. We might compare the glowing witch ghost scaring Arlene away with the family legend in Conan Doyle's *The Hound of the Baskervilles*, another glowing 'entity' trying to remove the head of a household.

There are two main problems with the story of 'Ghost Witch of Old Salem'. Firstly, nobody who was executed as part of the Salem witch trials was burned. The idea of those accused of witchcraft being killed in this way is often applied wholesale to the history of the witch trials and, while it is true that this method was employed in many places, Salem was not one of them. Like those accused in England (who were also not burned despite the method being in common use over the border in Scotland) the Salem accused died in other ways. Fourteen women and five men were executed by hanging, one was pressed[12] for refusing to plead (Giles Corey, for fans of *The Crucible*) and a number died in jail.

Secondly, the Salem trials took place between 1692 and 1693 and so the maths that would place Milissa Wilcox amongst them is around a century out.

In both this and the previous swamp-based foray we start to see the image of the witch becoming very much the expected stereotype that is seen so often around Halloween. In both cases, the skin is green and the witch wears a pointed hat. Along with the broomstick, these are all iconic ideas surrounding the witch of literature and media.

We can look to cinema to find the origins of the common physical features of the witch in terms of biology. In particular, the image of Mrs Cutler in the very first season of *Where Are You!* is perhaps more accurate. Prior to 1939, representations of witches generally had normally-coloured skin for the most part. Where this did deviate in some Halloween pictures, tones of orange were used. But, with the release of *The Wizard of Oz* (a film that historian Carol Karlsen notes did "more than any single witch to shape the popular stereotype"), Margaret Hamilton's character of the Wicked Witch of the West cemented the green-skinned witch firmly in place for the future.

Author L. Frank Baum drew inspiration from fairy tales, as did the two illustrators that he used for the *Oz* series of books, but despite using some other examples found in folklore, such as being afraid of water, the witch in the books does not have inhuman skin colouring. The decision to use green in the film version came down purely to a desire to make Hamilton look frightening and, more importantly, because the use of colour in the film was so important.

---

[12]. Trying to extract a confession through pressing involved laying a person underneath a board and then adding more and more heavy stones on top. The hope was that the person would confess before being crushed to death. Giles Corey, however, just kept calling for 'more weight' until he was crushed to death.

The famous transition from a monochrome Kansas to fully coloured land of Oz is one of the first mainstream uses of the Technicolor film process.

Disney's animated feature film telling of the story of *Snow White and the Seven Dwarves* came out two years earlier and also made use of the emerging three-colour Technicolor system. It was from this film that we find the beginnings of other common physical attributes of the witch – the hooked nose and the wart.

For the origins of the other two staples of the stereotypical witch outfit, the hat and the broomstick, we need to look further back in our historical sources.

The first appearance of a witch wearing a black pointed hat in print is probably one in a woodcut made as an illustration for Cotton Mather's account of the 1691 Salem case. Entitled 'Wonders of the Invisible World', this was published in England in 1693. At this time in history, however, this could be rather ambiguous and might be viewed in terms of Quaker dress, to which we will return shortly.

More obvious is a woodcut from 1720 depicting Mother Shipton and two other women, all of whom wear black pointed hats. This was a period in which cheaper methods of printing were starting to become more established, and relatively inexpensive publications such as pamphlets and chapbooks were widely purchased. Although typesetting was a fairly quick process, which helped to meet the demand for more new materials, the woodcuts used for illustration took a lot longer to produce. This led to pictures often being reused in many pamphlets, and this process certainly helped to embed images into popular culture and allowed them to carry forward to the present day. The witch's hat is definitely one of these.

There is a popular misconception that the pointed hat worn by witches comes from the much earlier wide-brimmed and cone-shaped Judenhat – headgear that was compulsory for Jews across Europe in the Middle Ages. Antisemitism became rife, and both Jews and witches were accused of similar crimes and victimised in the same way, leading to parallels being drawn between the two. This was particularly the case in Germanic parts of Europe, which also saw the emergence of larger parts of the witch-hysteria.

Whilst Judaism is a real faith, most of those who were accused of witchcraft were not actually involved in anything that might be described as an occult practice. What is exhibited here are two very distinct forms of oppression.

Although similar in some respects to the hat more commonly seen in depictions of wizards or sorcerers, the most obvious clue that leads to this theory being disputed is found in the way that Jews were treated in England. Here, the Judenhat was not a requirement, with Jews instead being told that they must wear a star on their garments to signify their race. As the image of the hat for witches comes from this country, the link does not stand up.

This is not to say that the now popular image of the black pointed hat for witches is not based on historical prejudice. But that prejudice is not from antisemitic roots; it comes from the rise in England of the Religious Society of Friends, more commonly known as the Quakers.

The Quakers were formed as many dissenting Christian groups started to make their presence felt after the conclusion of the English Civil War. Instrumental in their formation was George Fox, a man who believed that anyone could have direct experience of Jesus without the intervention of the clergy. Following a religious vision, he travelled extensively, converting people to his faith, wherein the Gospel was taught by Christ himself rather than through representatives of the Church. Interestingly his vision, which took place in 1652, occurred on Pendle Hill in Lancashire, a site notoriously connected only forty years earlier with the series of witch trials that resulted in the execution of two percent of the entirety of those accused of the crime in England.

The progressive views of the movement, which placed women in equal positions to men such that they led many of the religious meetings and preached the idea that people were not automatically sinful, alongside the concept of direct experience of God, led to a backlash from the established Church. Quakers were painted as blasphemous and wicked. Essentially, they were imbued with the traits also associated with witches, and we might speculate that this link with Pendle Hill might have fed into this comparison also.

The form of dress chosen by Quakers gave them a distinct look, and part of this was the wearing of tall black hats, cone-shaped and wide-brimmed. Aside from the fact that the very top of the hat terminated in a flat section, looking like the tip had been cut off, they are identical to the modern witch's headgear. As fashions subsequently changed and the Quaker hat stopped being worn, it remained firmly connected with the image of the witch, who was so closely connected with Quaker women and perpetuated in Western culture.

The image of a witch riding a broomstick is even older than the pointed hat. We first find it in a marginal illustration in the 1451 illuminated manuscript *The Defender of Ladies*, written by poet Martin Le Franc. Two women are depicted – one on a stick and the other on a besom.

Although created some 200 years earlier than the formation of the Quakers, there are interesting links that should be drawn. The dress of the women pictured suggest that they are Waldensians. This was a religious movement that shared certain ideas with the later Society of Friends, notably that women could preach as well as men, and a refusal to recognise the role of the ordained clergy. This led to their being viewed by the established Catholic Church as heretical – very much an early mirror of the Quakers' position in society.

Traditionally linked with domestic life for women, the broom was probably adopted in this case because of its phallic shape, being used to link these deviant women with earlier pagan fertility rituals that employed similar symbols. The suggestion being made was that the women were corrupt, and therefore evil in nature. It is easy to see how this link with the symbol of the witch would also carry forward.

Back to Salem, and the Ghost Witch. As part of their investigations, the gang visits Salem's Witchcraft Museum, of which there is a real-world version. Here they see on display a set of stocks and what Fred refers to as a 'dunking stool'. He here misnames the ducking stool which is usually associated with witchcraft accusations in the Early Modern period, particularly to test whether the accused was a witch.

In fact, the ducking stool was not used for this purpose as often as people think. The more common method of trial by water was floating – that is, throwing a person into water with a rope attached. The guilty floated and the innocent sank. The confusion arises with the 'cucking stool' which was a chair to which both men and women were bound and put on display in a form of public humiliation for various transgressions. There was no water associated with this (apart from any that might have been thrown at the prisoner by passers-by).

Whilst investigating Milissa's grave, the gang find an apotropaic mark, which they refer to as a witch's mark. Coming from the Greek word Apotropaios, divinities who could ward off evil, these protective marks are often found incised into old buildings and may take the form of daisy wheel patterns, known as hexafoils, Marion marks (capital M symbols referencing Mary) and other shapes. This moves us into an area of the story where the folklore has been covered really well.

We know that apotropaic marks were put on many buildings and other places to give magical protection from witches and other supernatural threats. In the episode, we learn that the mark on the gravestone is the 'sign of Mormo', which was placed there to stop the witch rising from her grave. The writers could easily have gotten away with telling the meddling kids anything in this case. But they didn't.

Mormo was a female spirit in Greek folklore who acted as a bit of a bogey. Mothers and nurses would use Mormo as a threat to stop children from being naughty. The name can be found with this connotation as early as the First Crusade. The etymology borrows from Greek, and has a rough translation of 'fright'. In modern times, it frequently refers to a female ghost or phantom of some kind. Although the origin is unknown for certain, it is interesting to speculate as to whether the name of the creature from the 'Momo Challenge' internet panic was a contraction of the Greek. The original Mormo ate her children and then flew off.

In terms of modern entertainment, Mormo crops up in other places as well as this quite relevant inclusion in Scooby-Doo. H.P. Lovecraft's *The Horror at Red Hook* has an inscription to Hecate, Gorgo and Mormo. She is depicted as an evil witch in the movie version of Neil Gaiman's *Stardust* (though the character is not in the book) and also a flying cat in the videogame *Tales of the World: Radiant Mythology*.

We should note at this stage that not all witches were, or are, women. Whilst the majority of those who were persecuted and executed as such were women in most countries, in Russia, Iceland, some areas of Eastern Europe and France, the statistics are reversed. In 1453, just two years after the marginal illustrations in Le Franc's manuscript, the first person to confess flying on a broom was a man – Guillaume Edelin.

The next depiction in Scooby is also male, coming up in a story set in England that appears towards the end of Season 3 of *Where Are You!*. The protagonist is the warlock Anthos and the episode, 'The Warlock of Wimbledon', centres around tennis star Jimmy Pelton, who is cursed by Anthos and told to forfeit the Wimbledon championship or be forever doomed.

Much like the plot of 'To Switch A Witch', the story uses ideas of magical ancestry in its narrative. The villain, Jimmy's trainer Nick Thomas, and his brother John are both revealed to be descendants of Anthos, and use the story of his curse on the Pelton family in order to try to lay claim to Jimmy's mansion, which he would not be able to afford to keep up mortgage payments on if he lost the tournament.

The story is set up at the beginning of the episode when Jimmy and Nick are out jogging and pass by what is described as an ancient Druidic ruin, called Rothmore. They conveniently find a magical staff that summons Anthos, who appears with his demon hound to pronounce the curse. There are some interesting folklore elements here that we can unpick.

The warlock's name, Anthos, matches the Ancient Greek term for flower. This may be connected, in terms of Greek mythology, with a couple of characters named Anthus: one of these was attacked and killed by horses who he had driven aware from pasture, and the Gods – in sympathy for the family – turned them all into birds. The other was lost as a child, and subsequently rediscovered as a cupbearer by his visiting sister. Neither of these stories have any bearing on the plot of the episode and so it is likely that the name was just chosen at random – maybe from a book of mythology.

The ruined stone monument named in the episode looks very much like it has been based on Stonehenge in terms of its design, albeit relocated from the rolling fields of Salisbury to Wimbledon Common. Although there are stone monuments in Britain that probably are druidic in origin, the description also draws heavily on the misconception that most stone circles or menhirs were used for Druidic rituals. This idea comes from a desire exhibited by many that humans need – as a species – to find longevity in traditional practices. This particularly applies to many 'new age' or recent religious magical paths that seek to evidence a long-standing unbroken traceability to historic rituals. The feeling is that this creates some sort of extra legitimacy, whereas in fact such traceability is often speculative or without strong grounds for accuracy. The idea is far from new. Sir James Frazer did exactly the same thing when writing *The Golden Bough*, as many of his ideas were deemed to be clutching at straws and have been robustly rebuked by modern researchers.

The idea that Iron Age druids constructed and used megaliths became prevalent in the eighteenth century, particularly at the hands of the antiquarian William Stukeley. In fact, all that was happening was that the druidic hypothesis was being used to replace older ideas for the origin of structures whose original intention is shrouded way back in the mists of time. One hundred years later, the Victorian commentators and curators, who became so smitten with the concept of folklore and the superstitions of the 'common people', totally missed the fact that these beliefs and stories are fluid and change all the time based on their cultural standing. They accepted the druidic hypothesis without investigation and the idea has been with us ever since.

One other minor character in *The Warlock of Wimbledon* seems to profess some magical ability, or at least is particularly superstitious. Ms Warren, John Thomas's housekeeper, warns Jimmy that she sees danger in his future by reading tea leaves. This method of divination, known as tasseomancy, probably has its roots somewhere in the Middle East but gained in popularity in the seventeenth century when tea found its way along trade routes from China into Europe. It has connections more with the figure of the village wise woman than with the Western stereotype of the witch, who is generally portrayed as maleficent rather than employing methods to provide people with help.

The term tasseomancy draws from its probable origins in the Middle East. The suffix 'mancy' is common in many compound words for methods of divination as it comes from the Greek for that very term. 'Tassa' is an Arabic word that translates as 'cup'. Prior to the increase in the tea trade, fortune tellers in medieval Europe tended to use patterns found in molten wax or lead to make their readings. The same method is applied with tasseomancy, but the patterns used for divination are those formed by tea leaves left in the cup, or sometimes saucer.

There are two ways of interpreting the patterns left behind in the tea leaves when the liquid has been removed. Firstly, well-established interpretations of symbols can be consulted to give an indication of a possible future. A line, for example, is taken to indicate a journey and in conjunction with other symbols nearby it might be possible to suggest what the journey is heading towards. Some symbol meanings come from ideas about objects that have been around for some time: a clover indicates good luck and prosperity, whereas a fox indicates that danger of being crossed or stabbed in the back by a close friend, indicative of the trickster archetype associated with this animal. Other symbols are more unusual in their meaning: a kettle symbolises death, and a pig symbolises a lover who will remain faithful (but cause jealousy amongst one's friends).

The second method of interpretation is to look at the symbols intuitively and consider what they make you feel[13], or what ideas they conjure up in your head. This could bring about a completely different reading, so whereas an apple is generally thought to symbolise knowledge it might conjure up ideas of bitterness (if you thought of a cooking apple rather than a dessert one) or it might bring about ideas of red and green being important colours in the reading.

All in all, *The Warlock of Wimbledon* is the typical mish-mash of stereotypes and folkloric snippets that is a common feature of early iterations of the franchise.

Witches, and swamps, make a return at the start of the 1980s when Scooby-Doo starts to appear with his rather troubling (for many) nephew Scrappy in the ABC Saturday morning Hanna-Barbera produced package *The Richie Rich/Scooby-Doo Show*. The stories in these shows were to have little substance to them, due mainly to their approximately seven-minute run-time. This iteration of the show built on a previous Scooby and Scrappy vehicle, with Shaggy being the only other member of Mystery Incorporated present – the others having been sidelined.[14] It also forms one of the versions of the franchise where the supernatural is treated as being real rather than a mechanism for crime to be committed. It an approach that, arguably, simply does not work most of the time… with one or two exceptions. It is also generally written mostly for the 'comedy'.

Season 1, Episode 6B's 'Swamp Witch' sees the titular character having run out of frogs' legs for her stew. She despatches her goblin familiar, Globby, to find someone to turn into a frog to complete the recipe. Who gets chosen probably does not need explaining!

This is another crone or hag-styled witch, who, with the exception of normal rather than green skin, is essentially a double for the witch in the previous 'Ozark Witch Switch'. The witch's robes again appear as purple, a representation used on a few occasions. Purple as a clothing colour tends to

---

[13]. This could be considered in terms of how Freud's theories surrounding dream interpretation, which postulated that dreams act as a way of fulfilling repressed wishes, differed from previous code-based methods of interpretation or more modern ideas suggesting that dreams are a way for the brain to self-organise disconnected ideas into a meaningful narrative.

[14]. Maybe it is this that leads to Fred making the comment that he does when they find the statue of Scrappy in the Dinkley's Spook Museum.

be associated more with royalty. Queen Elizabeth I's Sumptuary Laws banned anyone outside the monarchy from wearing purple garments. The original dye that would have been used by Byzantine or Roman rulers was extremely expensive, being made from the mucus of a certain type of sea snail, so the suggestion here is probably one of power. This is partially backed up by more recent surveys that show that people associate the colour with magic, although there is no firm folkloric reason for this.

Ironically, when there was an outcry in Romania in 2011 when self-identifying witches were forced to pay taxes for this first time, it was noted that the then-president Traian Basescu and some of this staff would wear purple on particular days in order to protect against evil forces. Witches threw mandrake into the Danube River in protest, and cast spells on members of the government… who presumably quickly donned their purple garments.

Globby is a strange creature. He appears as semi-transparent, suggesting that he is a ghost of a goblin. His name will probably have a certain familiarity to it, not being a million miles away from the later Dobby who is found in the Harry Potter universe (and is possibly at least as annoying as Scrappy-Doo). This is because both the writer of this episode and J.K. Rowling have taken their inspiration from the late 19$^{th}$ century word Dobbie, or Dobby, deriving in turn from the earlier English 'Dob', meaning a benevolent elf or house spirit who worked secretly on domestic tasks.

In Episode 11C later in the season, 'Scooby's Trip to Ahz', Scoob goes to fetch sandwiches for himself, Shaggy and Scrappy to eat while they watch the movie *The Wizard of Oz*. Whilst returning with the food, he accidentally knocks himself out and the episode becomes a dream-state parody of the dream-state trip of the original film. The episode is incredibly similar to 'Scooby in Wonderland' (just slightly earlier in the same season at Episode 7B) where Shaggy is reading Scoob and Shaggy *Alice in Wonderland* as a bedtime story and Scooby dreams the story. The writers were obviously short on plots for this season.

There is no good witch in this story, and Margaret Hamilton's original character is renamed as the 'Wicked Witch of the North by South-East', which is in itself a cultural draw on the 1959 Alfred Hitchcock film *North by Northwest*. Otherwise, in terms of design, she is essentially another carbon copy of the 'Ozark Witch Switch' and 'Swamp Witch' characters.

Another missing ingredient storyline turns up in the next season of the *Richie Rich/Scooby-Doo Show* vehicle. This time, in Season 2 Episode 4B 'Scooby's House of Mystery' the witch, Madame Olga, is concocting a beauty spell. The recipe requires 'snips and snails, and puppy dog tails', but she has run out of the latter. Scooby and Scrappy, who have entered Olga's House of Mystery with Shaggy, look set to provide the perfect solution to the problem.

The rhyme, of course, is familiar but it has been misappropriated here. 'Snips and snails, and puppy dog tails' are what little boys are made of, rather than the more pleasant 'sugar and spice, and everything nice' for the girls. The rhyme, catalogued with a Roud Folk Song Index entry of 821, comes from the early part of the nineteenth century and is generally attributed to the poet Robert Southey.

There is some debate about the etymology of the word 'snips' in this rhyme. Some versions substitute the words frogs or snakes, or most commonly slugs. In very early versions of the rhyme, we sometimes find the line recorded as 'snigs and snails', with a 'snig' being a dialect word for a small eel in the North-East of England. Another theory points to the word 'snip' as a noun, being an off-cut of something. The suggestion might be that the component is something discarded, picked up from the floor or bin, or that maybe it is an alteration of 'snips of snails', as in snail parts. Whichever is the correct version, for a misappropriated rhyme for a beauty spell, you would have thought that the sugar and spice would be the more logical ingredients.

The year 1983 saw a single season of *The New Scooby and Scrappy Doo Show* broadcast. In an effort to add back into the show a part of the original premise, the two dogs and Shaggy are joined by Daphne Blake again. Each of the thirteen episodes was made up of two separate eleven-minute stories, meaning that once again, little in the way of plot development was possible. Investigation in the season comes in the form not of Mystery Incorporated, but rather through the auspices of the Scooby-Doo Detective Agency.

In the first part of Episode 7, 'Wizards and Warlocks', the gang are visiting a gaming convention when they find that everyone there has been trapped by the Tower Wizard. For most of *The New Scooby and Scrappy Doo Show*, the emphasis shifts back onto the villain being a normal human in disguise rather than something supernatural, but in this episode, the wizard does have genuine magical ability. However, there is no real crime here, and the wizard has the look of a kindly mage such as you might find in a traditional Disney cartoon. In fact, the Tower Wizard is conjuring monsters as part of a live-action role play version of 'Wizards and Warlocks'; the Hanna-Barbera team playing with the concept of the popular 'Dungeons and Dragons' role-playing game that had first come out in 1974.

In terms of its first broadcast date, this episode is somewhat ironically juxtaposed alongside the rapidly snowballing moral panic regarding the playing of Dungeons and Dragons, led by fundamentalist religious groups and then subsequently by the moral watchdog group Bothered About Dungeons and Dragons (BADD), formed by mother Patricia Pulling in the same year that *Wizards and Warlocks* was broadcast. The group seems strangely reminiscent of the original action group whose campaigning had effectively led to the creation of Scooby-Doo back in the 1960s.

In 1982, Pulling's son Irving Lee had tragically died after shooting himself. The boy had had difficulty fitting in at high school and apparently suffered from other psychological issues. Amongst other actions, the mother had attempted to sue the principal of her son's school, who had run a game in which Irving Lee had taken part, stating that the curse put upon his character was real, and had also brought a lawsuit against Tactical Studies Rules (TSR) Inc. who were the original publishers of Dungeons and Dragons.

These actions followed in the wake of a case in 1979, when 16-year-old James Dallas Egbert vanished from his accommodation at Michigan State University. Egbert, a child prodigy, suffered from mental health issues, including depression, and also had a drug misuse problem. He had hidden in the university utility tunnels when self-harming. The boy's parents hired a private investigator, William Dear, to try to locate the child and Dear had drawn a link between the boy playing Dungeons and Dragons and going missing. No evidence, or indeed particular knowledge of roleplaying games, was offered up by Dear, but this episode was undoubtedly the start of the panic that would follow.

Like his successor, Irving Lee Pulling, Egbert also ended his life using a firearm. His mental health was overlooked by many in favour of the scapegoat of Dungeons and Dragons.

The broadcast date for 'Wizards and Warlocks' was, by pure chance, an unfortunate one, but the show does not seem to have been seen to be making light of the moral panic or the tragic deaths and fortunately seems to have come out unscathed.

Daphne remains with the other characters for the 1985 one-off season of 13 episodes, *The 13 Ghosts of Scooby-Doo*, which also sees a return to the misguided idea, in terms of plot mechanics, of the supernatural being real. The title itself turned out to be something of a misnomer as the series was cancelled and cut short due to budget problems, finally being completed years later in 2018 in the direct-to-video *Scooby-Doo! And the Curse of the 13th Ghost*.

This series is unusual for having an overall arc tying all of the episodes together, an idea which was later used to greater effect by the creators of *Scooby-Doo: Mystery Incorporated*. Shaggy, Daphne, Scoob and Scrappy are travelling to Honolulu when unforeseen problems cause them to have to ditch their plane in Tibet, where they are tricked into opening the powerful Chest of Demons, a receptacle keeping thirteen of the most powerful ghosts and demons imprisoned. Legend (and script) tell that only those who open the chest are able to return the ghosts to it again, and so the gang must travel the world to track down and trap the escaped creatures. They are aided in their quest by the warlock Vincent Van Ghoul, who – as mentioned before – was a clear caricature of horror actor Vincent Price (who also provided his voice).

Witches and warlocks appear twice in the season. In Episode 2, the gang have to capture a ghost of a warlock, Maldor the Malevolent, who resides in a haunted forest for added spookiness. This episode is essentially a retelling of the Sleeping Beauty fairy tale. Maldor is trying to capture a wizard's wand to destroy the world. He captures Daphne and puts her under a 'sleep of the centuries' spell that stops her from being able to stand in his way. Scooby finds the wand in Maldor's castle where it has been hidden by another wizard who is being held captive there, along with Princess Esmeralda, the actual owner of the castle, who is also under a sleep spell. He tries to use the wand, but he is not magically trained and so turns himself into a fly. This ends up working in Scooby's favour, as when Maldor turns himself into a frog in order to eat Scooby, he is easily trapped in the chest.

The idea of being turned into a fly is used to parody the classic 1958 film *The Fly*, with Scooby asking for help with his trademark 'rhotic replacement'… "Relp me, relp me!" Vincent Price, who voices Van Ghoul throughout the season, is paid homage here as the star of that movie.

Like most classic fairy tales, the story of Sleeping Beauty that we know now has very old origins, well before the traditional examples that we might naturally turn to (published by Charles Perrault in 1697 or Jacob and Wilhelm Grimm; whose later version was soundly based on the orally disseminated Perrault tale). The earliest variant that we can identify comes from the French prose romance *Perceforest*, written sometime around the year 1340.

The episode plays with one of the most well-known elements of the Sleeping Beauty story – that the maiden can only be roused from her long-running slumber by a kiss from a prince of some kind. Usually, the prince is stated as being 'charming' or 'handsome'. In *13 Ghosts*, the 'sleep of the centuries' spell can only be broken by a kiss from a Great Danish Prince. Scooby, as we have already learned, is a Great Dane, and so he licks Daphne's face, causing her to wake up. He rouses Princess Esmeralda in the same way. She turns out not to be human, but to be another Great Dane, albeit a rather formidable one. The episode closes with the Princess chasing Scooby into the distance, to the backdrop of a rising sun.

The episode title for this story, *Scoobra Kadoobra* is an obvious play on the well-known magical term 'Abracadabra'. These days, we recognise this word mostly from its use by some stage conjurers, along with others such as 'Hocus Pocus', but the historical use of the word Abracadabra can be traced back to an early medical book from somewhere between the second and fourth centuries AD. The word is used as a charm for curing malaria, and later also other diseases. The Roman physician Serenus Sammonicus is often credited as being the author of this work and hence one of the first to use the term Abracadabra, although evidence that he was the writer of the work appears to be scant and unreliable.

As a folk magic cure, the word was inscribed on an amulet in a triangular form, with the full word across the top leading down to just the letter A at the point at the bottom – one letter being removed from the end of the word in each row. The use of amulets as charms in this way is very common in history across the world. Other words are similarly found in written charms, or inscribed upon objects, such as the 'Sator Square'. This is a five-by-five grid of characters that can be read in different horizontal and vertical directions, generally beginning with the letters SATOR (meaning one who plants or seeds) on row one. The earliest probable example of this is found at the archaeological site of Pompeii.

Theories have been put forward suggesting that the word Abracadabra derives from Greek or Aramaic phrases describing creation through the power of speech, but there is no supporting evidence to either back up or refute this claim.

A later episode of the *13 Ghosts* vehicle, 'When You Witch Upon A Star' sees a trio of witches in the form of Brewski Sisters, who are given a book of spells by escaped demon Marcella. She instructs them to recite spell number thirteen at Stonehenge at midnight in order to become all-powerful.

We might think of the Three Witches from Shakespeare's *Macbeth* here, but there are of course many other places in folklore, myth and legend where the image of three powerful women crop up: the Fates symbolising destiny in classical myth; the Norns from the North pantheon who weave the fate of humans in the same way; the Greek Moirai or the image of the triple goddess image of the maiden, mother and crone. Any of these could have offered up a good connection between the episode and the folklore. But instead, the Brewski sisters are essentially a witchy rendering of the Three Stooges, an American comic vaudeville act who performed regularly between the early 1920s and 1970, known in particular for their film and television work.

As far as the spellcasting here is concerned, we can see that midnight is used as the stereotypical liminal time, and that Stonehenge is a prime example of an unusual British ancient site in the landscape that would be recognisable to an American audience. The number thirteen is perceived in many cultures as both a magical and an unlucky number, leading to a fear of its use because it will tempt bad fate. In its worst form, this is given the medical term triskaidekaphobia.

Many point to the Biblical story of the Last Supper as the reason for the number thirteen to be considered unlucky, as this was the number of people who were said to have sat at the table. Some take this idea even further, saying that Judas Iscariot, the disciple who betrayed Jesus to the authorities, was the thirteenth person to take a seat at the table. The Bible makes no mention of the order at which people sat at the table, so there is no evidence to support this idea.

Any kind of Biblical connection is unlikely, in fact. Many aspects of the fear of the number that have a religious association come from the medieval period, and there is nothing in the writings of the Bible to suggest anything directly. Even the Last Supper has a much earlier mythological version, in the story of the trickster god Loki being the thirteenth person to arrive at a dinner of the gods, having not been invited; an appearance that ultimately led to the death of the god Baldur.

In some countries, the number thirteen is said to bring good fortune rather than bad, but these are certainly in the minority and the fact that the number is considered unlucky across Western countries has led to its representation as mysterious or maleficent in magical terms.

Salem is a location once again for a witch story when we fast forward to 2017 and the second season of *Be Cool, Scooby-Doo!*. In the episode 'World of Witchcraft', a parody of the popular *World of Warcraft* videogame, the gang arrive in Salem and, coincidentally, the town is suddenly troubled by its first witch in 400 years.[15] She proceeds to summon a demon, who then terrorises the entire town. The whole story is naturally a ruse, concocted by the innocent-looking Mrs Baker, owner of 'Ye Old Pie Tent', and her son, so that they can rob the local bank.

This episode is important as it is one of the few (outside of the feature length *Scooby Doo and the Witch's Ghost*, which we will turn to shortly) to offer a social commentary on the persecution and oppression of people for witchcraft in the past. The view is put forward by Daphne and her defence of witches leads to her ironically being accused by the town mayor of being one[16]. He cites as evidence for this, aside from her sarcastic 'confession' that she is one, the fact that the trouble started when Mystery Inc arrived in Salem (in a paralleling of the real-world scapegoating of women in particular as witches).

Shaggy sums it up in his own inimitable style. As they are turned upon by a pitchfork-wielding crowd and Shaggy and Scooby are tied to stakes next to Daphne, Shaggy says

"Like, I can't believe these people. They pounce on the free-spirited woman, but they have no problem with the guy who can eat 20 pies at once and his talking dog! I mean, if anyone here was using magic, it would be us."

One very well-done folklore reference comes up during the usual set piece where Shaggy and Scooby don disguises in order to hide from the monster. In this case, they take refuge in a blacksmith's shop, disguising themselves as

---

[15]. Not only have the writers seemingly forgotten about the previous Salem ghost witch incidents with Milissa Wilcox, but they have also not improved their maths skills, being now 100 years out from the Salem trials in the other direction.

[16]. This is the second time in this season of the show where Daphne suffers this problem. The same thing happened to her in the third episode, *Renn Scare* at a renaissance fair that was attacked by a monster in the form of a jester.

smiths. What follows is a skit that references the folk tale of 'The Blacksmith and the Devil', which was shown through work undertaken by researchers at Durham and Lisbon universities in 2016 to be probably the oldest known folk tale across the world. There are many versions of the tale in existence and a few stories of smiths who spot the cloven hooves of the Devil and fit him with ill-fitting shoes or similar. Here, Shaggy and Scooby as smiths measure up the devilish-looking Demon of Salem for shoes before attaching him to a donkey wheel (a wooden wheel that was driven by a donkey or horse before the introduction of water or steam power) and making their escape.

An earlier episode in this season, 'Halloween', finds the character of the Slavic witch Baba Yaga making an appearance. We learn that Fred will not go out with the others at Halloween because he has traditionally always failed to solve mysteries on this date. The problem, it is revealed, stretches back to when he was a child and went out trick or treating with his friends Rose and Scott. They came across an old house in the woods but got scared away from it by a witch. When they returned with the police, the house had mysteriously gone.

Eventually, the gang goes out trick or treating. Velma has been moaning constantly about the crass commercialisation of the traditional Gaelic Halloween, so to visualise her having fun, Daphne dresses as a zombie version of Velma. Fred becomes very nervous because some of the children trick or treating seem to resemble some of the villains from the gang's previous investigations. Suddenly, the witch's house from Fred's childhood appears. Shaggy and Scooby go to knock on the door for trick or treat, but a witch scares them all off. Much hilarity ensues, as you would expect.

The witch turns out to be a woman called Mrs Clune who is working alongside her husband to try to end Halloween as a celebration. They have fitted hydraulic chicken legs to their house (to resemble the house in the Baba Yaga tradition) and every year they go to another town, make themselves popular and become a part of the neighbourhood watch, and then come Halloween frighten everyone with their house and flying broomstick – the latter being powered by mercury and copper.

The gang cannot understand why the couple would want to end Halloween until Velma points out that it is obvious that they, like her, cannot stand the commercialism. Her evidence for this can be found in Mrs Clune's cauldron room, which is full of the hallmarks of ancient religion and ritual – apples, nuts and books on ancient Gaelic traditions. This is a nice mention of our older ways, and the episode could be seen as a social commentary on both the cultural appropriation debate over traditions being integrated into foreign cultures and tensions between new alternative pathways and older beliefs. This was also the topic of the movie *Halloween III: Season of the Witch*, for which Nigel Kneale wrote the first draft. He was later to request that his name was removed from the credits after producers added more horror and gore than Kneale believed necessary.

The most recent TV appearance of a witch in the show (at the time of writing) is the first of two more examples of the witch appearing in the form of a ghost, in the manner of the 'Ghost Witch of Old Salem' examined earlier. This comes up in Episode 22 of the first season of *Scooby-Doo and Guess Who?* in 2020; this iteration of the show being a vehicle for the regular characters to appear alongside guest stars who voice their animated likenesses.

'The Wedding Witch of Wainsly Hall!'[17] sees comedian Jeff Foxworthy join the gang to solve a mystery surrounding the appearance of the ghost of a bride named Lenore who was going to marry a famous chef back in the 1880s but who was jilted at the altar. The episode title is, in fact, a bit of a misnomer because there is no other mention of witchcraft in the entire episode and the title 'witch' relates more to the fact that the legend tells that Lenore cursed everything after her groom left, including the house, the guests and herself – finally turning into the Wedding Witch, who has an horrific green skull-shaped face and is dressed in her wedding dress. Lenore's name is probably a nod to the poem of the same name by Edgar Allen Poe.

The plot here is about as convoluted as the trap that Fred inevitably constructs in order to trap the villain. Essentially, mansion house Wainsly Hall has to be moved in order to allow a six-lane freeway to be built. The Hall is known for the fact that it still has the mouldy remains of the wedding feast laid out on the table from the failed ceremony, not unlike Miss Havisham's meal in Charles Dickens's *Great Expectations*. The Wedding Witch turns out to be the unnamed lady who owned the food truck that Jeff Foxworthy, who is transporting the mansion on the back of a flatbed truck, hired to feed the crew needed for the operation. (Are you keeping up?)

Food truck lady is, as Velma explains, a "culinary archaeologist" who specialises in recovering old and decayed food, which she uses to reverse engineer the original recipes and create new cuisine that nobody else makes. She uses the legend of the Wedding Witch to keep people away from the house so that she can obtain the preserved wedding feast before the property is moved.

The story, as well as the food, is based on that of Miss Havisham, but also puts one in mind of the backstory behind the 'Haunted Mansion' and 'Phantom Manor' dark rides at Disney theme parks.

Also of folkloric interest is the fact that the archaeologist uses her knowledge of Incan recipes to create a pie that, using a particular combination of spices,

---

[17]. The episode titles in this season hark back to the original version of the show by inserting an errant exclamation mark at the end of each title. In fact, this season returns to the original format in many ways, to its credit, with even the opening titles and theme tune being a reflection of the 1960s show.

creates a dream state that allows Shaggy, Scooby and Jeff to visualise that they are actually part of the wedding ceremony, with Shaggy marrying Lenore. This references shamanic practices from cultures around the world who used different ingredients in order to alter consciousness and commune with the spirits and ancestors or achieve some form of purification. There is no obvious Incan connection with spices (the show obviously having to make sure that it specified that it was using legal ingredients in the recipe) but substances such as vilca snuff and a derivative obtained from the San Pedro cactus, which contains mescaline, were certainly recorded as being used in Peruvian areas for similar purposes, for example.

Witches turn up in a few of the direct-to-video and telefilm features. There is one in the very Gothic *Scooby-Doo and the Reluctant Werewolf* and another in *Scooby-Doo and the Ghoul School*, both of which feature renderings of the famous Universal Monsters. Another, the Crimson Witch, appears in the frankly bizarre crossover movie *Scooby-Doo! And KISS: Rock and Roll Mystery* – most notable for its specially composed doo-wop/barbershop song by the band, 'Don't Touch My Ascot'.

The key direct-to-video feature to examine in terms of the representation of the witch, is *Scooby-Doo and the Witch's Ghost*, released in 1999. Like most of the direct-to-video stories, the plot of this sits in the realm of the marvellous, according to the literary theories which we explored in the chapter on Landscape and the Gothic. There are no villains to unmask. The supernatural is real, but justice still needs to be meted out.

This story is set in the fictional New England town of Oakhaven, in the suburbs of Salem, which was said to have been founded by Puritans in the 1600s. If the name Oakhaven seems familiar to folk horror fans, then it could be that this is a probable reference to the 1970s American very-folk-horror supernatural TV movie *Crowhaven Farm*. In this, Maggie and her husband Ben move from the city to the rural Crowhaven when Maggie inherits a farm there. Maggie ends up having strange visions, the neighbours seem overly friendly and just a little odd, the couple adopt the inevitable creepy child and Maggie (who couldn't have children) falls pregnant after meeting the village doctor who has a whole different skillset in terms of medical knowledge. There's a lot of witchcraft, devilishness and talk of the Salem Witch trials.

One of the early residents of the Scooby-Doo based town of Oakhaven was Sarah Ravencroft, who was executed as a witch and whose spirit was trapped in a spellbook to prevent her from returning and exacting revenge on the town. In modern Oakhaven, townspeople decide to create a fake version of Sarah's ghost to act as a tourist attraction.

Mystery Inc. are invited to Oakhaven by the famous horror author Ben Ravencroft, who is a modern ancestor of Sarah as well as being a parody of both Stephen King and HP Lovecraft. The gang solve the mystery of Sarah's fake ghost but unfortunately, along with Ben, they inadvertently raise her real spirit from the spellbook.

This film actually does a lot for the plight of women who were persecuted as witches and it tries really hard to put across that point. But unfortunately, it then also includes some horrendous errors that would make any witchcraft historian shudder. The plot takes pains to point out that many of Sarah's neighbours said that she was a healer and was wrongly accused.

Sarah is described as having treated people under an oak tree that was known for its healing powers. Certainly, the oak is very important in terms of mythology and folklore and there are various healing properties associated with it. Oak bark was used, and is still used, in medicine because of its antiseptic properties. It can be given instead of quinine for fevers, for example, when powdered and mixed with water. Bruised oak leaves can relieve inflammation. Botanist Sir William Turner Thistleton-Dyer's *The Folklore of Plants*, published in 1889, contains a Germanic cure for gout involving the oak, and it is one of many trees that were used in charms for the transference of pain.

Ben Ravencroft also says the same thing about his ancestor:

> "…unjustly persecuted, Sarah Ravenscroft was a medicine woman who practiced natural healing, and was unfairly accused because of her eccentric ways."

Unfortunately, Ben also suggests that Sarah was a Wiccan who used her natural herbs to heal people. The message here alludes to the fact that practitioners of Wicca tend to follow a strong ethical code and believe in the power of doing good over ill. But it is the morality and not the religion itself that can be placed in the seventeenth century, as Wicca as a modern nature-based religion was first named in 1954 by Gerald Gardner.

Daphne compounds the confusion here by stating that Wiccans were "in tune with the forces of nature and used them for healing purposes". Velma, at least, explains the origin of the word 'witch' pretty accurately. It is a shame that this conflation of modern Wicca is made with ancient healing, because the message which the show was actually trying to put across in this case was a good one.

There is one other notable set of residents of Oakhaven worthy of mention, because they went on to become very important for a lot of people in a totally unconnected way. Those people are Dusk, Thorn and Luna, or if you don't recognise those names, The Hex Girls. Described by the writers at this time both as 'eco-goths', a term which all the voice artists for the girls laughed about at the time, and Wiccan pop goth, the Hex Girls certainly made their mark. Interestingly, although the episode pre-dates it, 'eco-Gothic' is now an accepted concept within theoretical Gothic studies.

Much was made of the fact that they were Wiccan and used that particular religious persuasion as a force for good. Sally, the real name of the lead singer of the group, is seen using peppermint and cloves to soothe her vocal chords. These were certainly part of an old herbal remedy for toothache and score another mark for good research.

The Hex Girls took the show full circle to the initial problem that led to its creation in 1969, as conservative parent groups complained that the film was 'promoting Wiccan practices'.

But the decade in which the film was released was one in which it was easier to weather the storm than back in the 1960s. Such was the popularity of the Hex Girls that the studio even began talks, which ultimately didn't come to fruition, of spinning them off into their own show. Their image was toned down a little over the years, but they returned a few times to the Scoobyverse.

# CHAPTER FIVE

## INDIGENOUS, ANCIENT AND NON-WESTERN CULTURES

Acting as a social commentary on the political unrest of America at the time, highlighting hope through the well-intentioned youth of the country and coming directly from concerns over the state of children's media of the period, it is no surprise that Mystery Incorporated concentrated their investigation on home ground for the first two seasons of the show. Even in episodes that dealt with the lore of more distant cultures, such as 'Scooby Doo and a Mummy, Too' where the gang lock horns with the Mummy of Ankha[18], the story takes place in an American Department of Archaeology.

The show begins to become more adventurous in terms of its locations with what we might think of as Season 3 of *Scooby Doo Where Are You!* (Certainly, as far as DVD releases go, it is packaged as that but the episodes in question came from various programmes and were originally put together under the umbrella of *The Scooby-Doo Show*.)

The first episode, geographically, takes place on the US-Canadian border, but it deals with First Nations American culture, and so it is important to make the correct distinctions with the way that this material is treated, certainly as far as this book is concerned. Firstly, we use the term First Nations American here, rather than 'native American', which is the term used within the show itself. This is done after taking advice from people closely connected with tribes in this area. Whilst the term native American is still found in use now (in America rather than Canada specifically), most tribes prefer the term First Nations. Whilst America and Canada are generally considered Western cultures now, tribal philosophy often describes their culture as non-Western as there is more at play than simple geography. After taking advice from a

---

[18]. The show described Ankha as a feared ruler of ancient Egypt. The name is purely fictional, possibly being drawn from the middle part of Tutankhamun or alternatively from the ankh, meaning life. In either case, it sounds plausibly Egyptian. Interestingly, the name Ankha would later become far more significant in pop culture in reference to a cat villager in the game 'Animal Crossing', who also resembles as ancient Egyptian pharaoh.

cross-section of First Nations representatives, and with the best of intentions to get this as correct as can be possible for a British author, these storylines are included in this chapter, along with a request for forgiveness from anyone who thinks that I may have this wrong.

The episode 'Watch Out! The Willawaw!' (yes, they still love an exclamation mark) sees the gang travelling to a First Nations reservation on the border to meet up with Velma's uncle Dave. While there, they suffer from a lot of owl-based trouble. Having spotted what they think is a large owl whilst sailing in, Scooby later believes that he sees two more large owls while they are all puzzling over the fact that Uncle Dave seems to be missing. At this point, some members of the local tribe arrive on the scene.

The tribal visitors are Chippewa, an indigenous group more commonly known as the Ojibwe, of which there are some 300,000 or more members spread across the Northern Plains and southern Canada today. The tribal chief, in the show, bears the appropriate name Red Herron (because it turns out that he isn't the villain). He explains that Dave has been taken by a legendary creature called a Willawaw – a monster that comes down from the sky and captures anyone whose name has been given to it by an owl.

There is no actual cryptid or spiritual creature fitting the description of the Willawaw in real-world lore. The name might well be taken from the word williwaw, which describes a gust of cold wind that suddenly blows offshore from a mountainous coastal region. The term, originally spelled williwau, was first noted as being used by British sailors in the nineteenth century.

Owls are certainly important in the lore of many First Nations tribes, including the Ojibwe or Chippewa. For most, the owl is seen as symbolic of death, and for some, there is also a connection with the afterlife. In the mythology of the Choctaw, the owl deity Ishkitini hunted for human and other souls by night. Other tribes such as the Seminole and some near-Mexican cultures believed that the owl could shapeshift into human form.

For some cultures, owls were also seen as messengers, and it may be this aspect that the writers adopted in the plotline for this episode, with the Willawaw taking those who had been named. Of course, this being a standard episode of Scooby-Doo, there must be a rather more human villain behind the escapade, and in this case, it is another member of the reservation, Grey Fox, working with a couple of cronies to steal valuable items. In line with typical First Nations practices, Red Herron takes them to the village elders to sit in judgment for their crimes.

Maybe surprisingly, this episode is one of the very few that feature any prominent storyline involving First Nations Americans. This may possibly be because, as the franchise developed over the years towards more inclusive times, it was considered too dangerous to use the normal comedic approach that the show takes and remain respectful to these cultures.

That being said, just a couple of episodes later, in *A Scary Night with a Snow Beast Fright,* some more indigenous symbolism does crop up, albeit slightly out of place.

Professor Kreuger is a friend of the gang. He has been working at the North Pole, based at an Eskimo village nearby. We should note that the term 'Eskimo' was in common usage at the time to describe the indigenous peoples of the Arctic and Alaskan regions; it is disappearing from use now, with Inuit being used across the Arctic and Alaska, but we use it here purely because it was current at the time and is still adopted by some agencies today.

When Scooby and the others arrive, the Professor has gone missing. Scoob discovers a giant paw print in the snow, which the village elder Chief Manook tells them belongs to a snow monster, who turns out to look rather like a giant anaemic Godzilla. Tribal legends say that the monster arrived because the village was built on sacred lands.

The idea of a curse being centred around lands that were sacred to the previous occupants is a well-used one. We find it at the heart of many a horror story, such as Stephen King's *Pet Sematary* (1983) where trouble begins when a family cat is interred in a burial ground once used by the Mi'kmaq people. The house at the centre of the alleged true-life paranormal events portrayed in *The Amityville Horror* (1977 – book, 1979 – movie) was declared somewhat controversially by a visiting medium to have been built on an Indian burial ground. There seems little evidence for this, with the local Montauket tribe having no records of burial land in Amityville, and further stating that even if one did turn out to be there, that did not automatically mean that the spirits of their ancestors would just start possessing people.

Such stories often come up in real-world locations that seem beset with problems, and usually without any real evidence to back up the claims. Take the example of the golf course built by one of the sport's most famous players, Jack Nicklaus – Muirfield. The annual tournament held here is well-known for being washed out and flooded by torrential downpours. It used to happen with such frequency that the timing of the tournament was moved, but this made no difference. And so, the fact that the course was built over an 'ancient Indian burial ground' was blamed, the curse having apparently been put on the tournament by Chief Leatherlips.

It is worth noting here that the phrase 'ancient Indian burial ground' persists in American folklore to this day, but it is not used by First Nations peoples themselves.

In the case of Muirfield, it is true that the course is built on the ground which was used by the Wyandot tribe for burials.[19] The tribe were the last

---

[19]. Although the Wyandot do not refer to themselves as Indians, this term was used historically by others, such as in the wording of the 1760 Huron-British 'Treaty of Peace and Friendship' for example.

Native Americans to leave the Ohio area, being sent to a reservation in Kansas in the 1840s. Thirty years before this, in 1810, they had executed their own tribesman, Leatherlips. His crime was being too friendly with the white settlers. His name, 'Leatherlips', had been coined by them because he never went back on his word.

Of course, none of these historical facts account for why he should have a dislike of golf.

Whilst investigating the disappearance of their friend, Velma discovers a drawing in the Professor's hut that seems to show three totem poles. In time, the gang find the actual poles themselves, which seem to be surrounded by black snow.

Totem poles, which can vary in height from a mere three metres to over twenty, are usually carved out of red cedar and are probably one of the most common symbols associated with First Nations people. The images represented on the poles can symbolise many things, from family ancestry to particular events or periods of history. They are not, however, found at the North Pole, being created by tribes from the Pacific Northwest rather than the Arctic. This should have been the most obvious clue for Mystery Incorporated, who failed to pick up on it at all.

The oil around the poles was black because the totems had been created to mask a secret drilling operation. Each one contained an oil derrick, which accounted for the strange unearthly thumping noises that were heard in their vicinity. The snow beast was, unsurprisingly, not from local legend, but was rather (perhaps more surprisingly) a giant robot.

Tangentially, if you really want to find a link between the North Pole and Alaska, then you should pay a visit to the village of 'North Pole', near Fairbanks, Alaska. First populated in 1944, it gained its name from a development company who tried to encourage toy manufacturers to set up base there, so that they could advertise their products as being 'made in North Pole'. The village has year-round Christmas decorations and road names including Santa Claus Lane, St Nicholas Drive and Snowman Lane. In all the fifty-plus years of Scooby-Doo, the gang have never encountered a scenario as horrific as this.

We will stick with the idea of snow beasts to continue with a look at some different cultures from around the world and the ways in which they are represented in the Scooby-Doo franchise.

## The 'Abominable Snowman'

Scooby-Doo has had a bit of an odd take on this famous cryptid over the years, as it seems to use terms like 'abominable snowman', 'yeti' and 'bigfoot' somewhat interchangeably. Let's be sure to make sure we have our hairy cryptids defined correctly from the start. Bigfoot is the popular colloquial term for Sasquatch.

This is purported to be a large ape-like creature that lives in areas across North America, with a main concentration in the Pacific Northwest region. As such, this is outside of our focus on traditions that come from outside of western regions.

'Abominable Snowman' is a term coined in 1921 in the west to describe the Yeti, an alleged cryptid again resembling a large ape, which is said to inhabit areas along the Himalayan mountain range. Yeti itself is a generic term, as Tibetan folklore describes three different creatures that range from three to fifteen feet in height.

Of the various appearances in different iterations of the show, the only story that is actually stated as taking place in the Himalayas is the 2007 direct-to-video feature *Chill Out, Scooby-Doo!* The movie was dedicated to character designer Iwao Takamoto, who passed away just a few months before its release.

The story opens with Professor Jefferies on an expedition to find the city of Shangri-La. He is accompanied by a Sherpa named Pemba who has navigated the couple by means of an old tablet to a point high up the mountain, but who refuses to go any further as it would mean entering territory that belonged to the Yeti. (The characters use the term Abominable Snowman generally throughout the film, even those who were Tibetan in origin, but we will use the indigenous term here.) Jefferies cuts himself free from the Sherpa's rope and continues alone.

Scooby and Shaggy are flying to Paris to join the rest of the gang on holiday, but strangely the plane they are on belongs to a French hunter, Alphonse LaFleur and he is taking them to the Himalayas to use them as bait in his quest to trap the Yeti. (Are you with me so far?) Shaggy manages to place a quick mobile phone call to Fred who tracks them using his GPS and the rest of the gang set off to rescue them. LaFleur throws Shaggy and Scooby off the plane, along with his equipment, and they end up in the local village where Jefferies and Pemba are based, along with the Sherpa's sister, Minga. She has a crush on the man working at the weather station in the village, which has the only local telephone and radio equipment.

A convoluted plot then ensues that sees Professor Jefferies become a main suspect when he is found to be mining crystals in the area. Shaggy and Scooby have previously seen a statue of the yeti, which was holding a similar crystal. The High Lama had explained to them that the crystal was a form of protection against the Yeti.

What can we make of all this so far? In our world, Shangri-La has become representative of the search for something that will always be just out of reach. The place itself was a fictional utopia created by James Hilton in his 1933 book *Lost Horizon*. There has been much speculation over the sources that Hilton might have used, or where else he might have taken inspiration for the valley. He certainly stated that he found information at the British Museum, and from records of the exploration of Tibet by two French priests, Huc and Gabet. He is also known to have visited the Hunza Valley in Kashmir.

There are several ancient folk tales and writings in old Buddhist texts about a Tibetan utopia, but nothing that provides anything remotely like solid evidence that such a place exists or existed. Consequently, most of the searches that have taken place over the years have been for areas that might have been a source of inspiration, rather than for Shangri-La itself. Various places stake a claim on the name themselves, not least of which is Zhongdian County in Yunnan province which changed its name to Shangri-La in 2001 in an effort to increase tourism to the area.

There is no parallel in real-world folklore or mythology to the idea of crystals offering a form of protection from Yeti. The Lepcha people saw the Yeti as a deity and believed that it should therefore be appeased, but this was done with offerings of fish, dried bird and ginger.

Crystals are, of course, seen by many people to offer protection in a metaphysical way against all sorts of things. In the Himalayan area naturally occurring quartz crystals are quite rare, but those that are found are said to protect the owner from negativity. But not Yeti.

In *Chill Out, Scooby-Doo!*, the usual ending is subverted a little. Professor Jefferies goes to jail because he has been mining the crystals without a permit, but he was not responsible for the Yeti attacks. That turned out to be Minga in disguise, her motive being that she wanted to prevent the weatherman, Del, from leaving because she liked him. In the end, Del and Minga live happily ever after, and justice is served elsewhere.

Ironically, the one episode that actually called the Yeti by its proper name, and refers to its Tibetan roots, locates it in an American downtown cheese restaurant! The 2015 *Be Cool, Scooby-Doo!* episode 'Kitchen Frightmare' sees the restaurant Cheese Volcano troubled by a Yeti. Its appearance is heralded by the air turning cold enough to freeze all the mirrors, reflecting its mountainous homeland. The gang, who are visiting the restaurant because chef Chazz Larkin was mentor to Shaggy when they worked in a food truck, naturally decide to investigate. Notably, this episode covers the ascribing of the term 'abominable snowman' to the Yeti by westerners very well. Velma describes how early 20th century British explorers encountered stories of the creature, but can find no explanation as to why one would have turned up in an American restaurant.

The answer is more straightforward than she could have imagined. The Yeti is a costume created by Jack Howard, the man who lives in the apartment over the top of the restaurant. He objects to there being a restaurant below where he lives, as the noise keeps him up all night. And so, he has scared away a string of restaurant businesses, with Cheese Volcano being the latest. He uses the Yeti disguise because the first restaurant to open served Tibetan food, but he has never bothered to change the costume.

The 1969 episode 'That's Snow Ghost', which closes the first season of *Scooby-Doo Where Are You!*, forms a strange bridge between the Tibetan cultural references of the Yeti and the location of sasquatch stories as it is set on the US-Canadian border.

The gang are on a winter holiday near the border and get a less than happy welcome from Mr Greenway, the owner of Wolf's End Lodge, where they have chosen to stay. He suggests that they should keep their windows and doors locked at night – to stop the Snow Ghost from capturing them and turning them into spirits.

After the Snow Ghost inevitably turns up, the gang follow it to a cave that contains various objects of Tibetan origin and is home to a man named Fu Lan Chi. He tells the gang the story of how he came across a Yeti once in Asia and how the creature fell to its death while chasing the man. He says that he thinks that the ghost of the Yeti has followed him to Wolf's End.

After eagle-eyed Velma spots some sawdust in the tracks left by the Snow Ghost, the trail leads Mystery Inc to a sawmill where various dangers befall them. After dealing with these, Shaggy (who has become separated) appears, completely white. The others fear that the Snow Ghost has turned him into a ghost, but Shaggy falls into the water which causes the white powder that was coating him to wash off. It appears that the Snow Ghost is not turning people into ghosts after all. Daphne finds another clue as to what might actually be going on when she discovers jewels in a hollow log in the mill.

There is an inevitable chase scene that ends when Scooby and the Snow Ghost become encased in a giant snowball as they roll down the hill. This allows the Snow Ghost to be unmasked, revealing it to be none other than Mr Greenway. In cahoots with a partner, he has been floating stolen jewellery down the river, using the story of Fu Lan Chi as inspiration for his disguise.

Other Asian cultural references have recurred within Scooby-Doo over the years, particularly Chinese and Japanese references, although these non-Western cultures are still sometimes placed in an American setting.

## Japanese Supernatural

It is not surprising to find Japanese ghosts and monsters in Scooby-Doo as the country is so rich in spirits and superstition. What is more surprising is really that there aren't more examples than can be found, especially when you consider that there are many hundreds of examples of Japanese demons, or Yokai, that can be explored.

Probably the first time that the Scooby gang deal with Japanese influences is in the episode 'Now Museum, Now You Don't'. This is because it comes from the 1988 vehicle, *A Pup Named Scooby-Doo* which is set in Coolsville and has the characters at a pre-teen age, running the Scooby-Doo detective agency

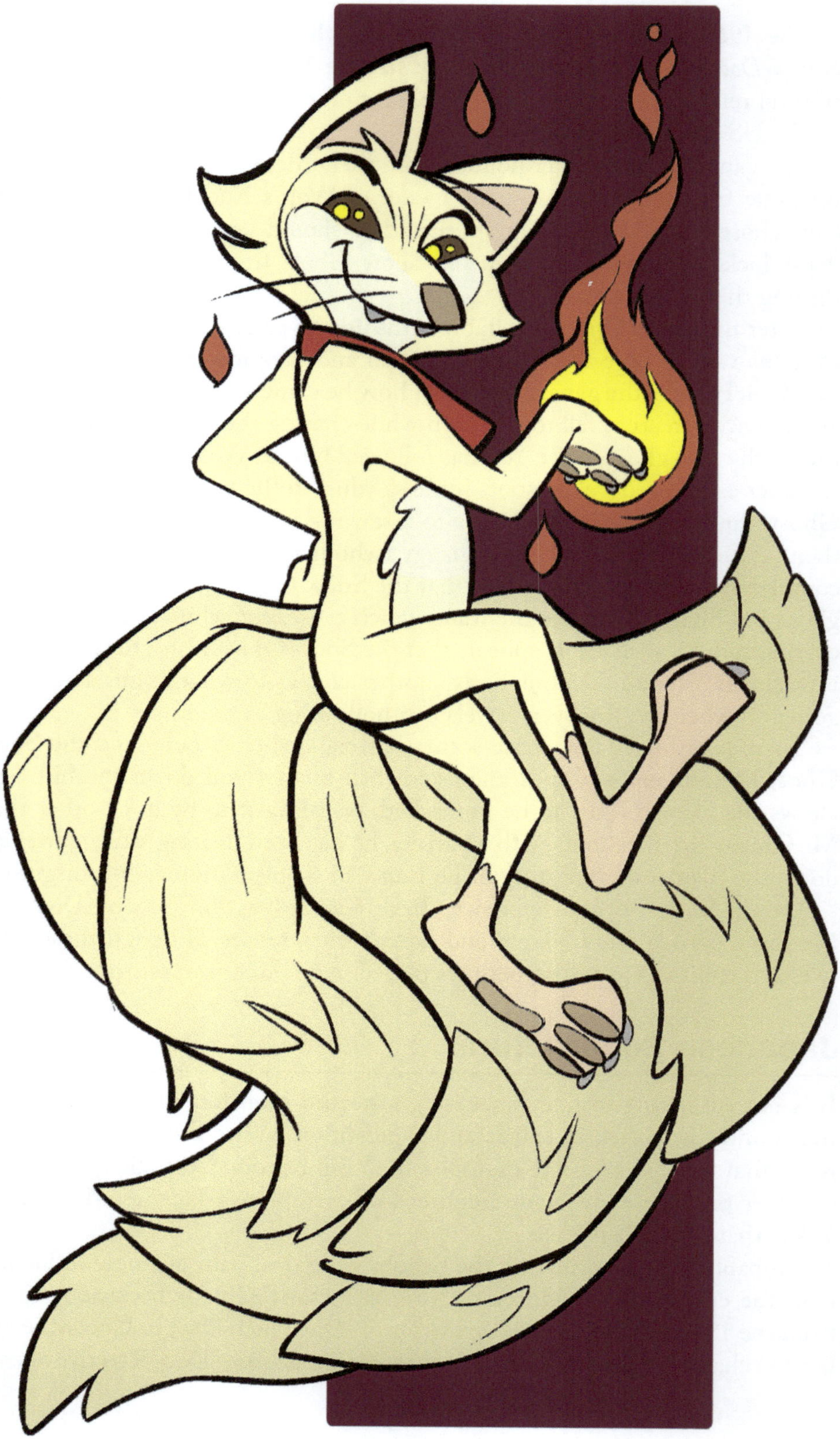

in a Hardy Boys and Nancy Drew style. Although the overall construction of the show remains the same, *Pup* is far more fantastical in that it employs every trick in the cartoon book in a similar way to classics such as *Tom and Jerry* (eyes out on stalks, characters morphing into odd shapes or doing impossible things, for example).

The kids are on a visit to the Coolsonian Museum where they are shown a pair of Japanese swords, which are said to curse anyone who touches them. The swords subsequently go missing and Scooby and Shaggy initially get the blame, although they were witness to the actual thief in the form of the ghost of a Samurai warrior. They spend the rest of the episode trying to convince the authorities of their innocence, which they eventually do when the villain turns out to be the museum owner trying to cash in on a million-dollar insurance policy against the loss of the swords.

Aside from the Samurai ghost, the episode is really quite light on Japanese cultural references, although at one point Shaggy and Scooby don a Japanese dragon disguise to chase the ghost. The dragon is an element of Japanese folklore often seen depicted artistically. Also known as ryu, or tatsu, the first mention in the mythology of the country is around the year 680AD. As they are seen as ancestors of the first Japanese Emperor, dragons are an important symbol in Japan.

In terms of art, the Japanese and Chinese dragons (the latter of which we will meet shortly) appear on the surface to be quite similar, which is unsurprising considering the closeness of their heritage. The main physical difference can be found in the feet, where Chinese dragons are five-clawed and Japanese generally three. Otherwise, the main difference in terms of the animal itself can be found in its demeanour. Japanese dragons are considered more aggressive, which might be seen as referencing their origin as an ancestor of the powerful Emperors, whereas Chinese dragons are generally thought of as more benevolent.

The villain of the *Scooby-Doo and Scrappy-Doo* story 'The Demon of the Dugout' is named as a Dragon Beast but has no similarity to Japanese dragons other than nomenclature. The gang are visiting Japan to watch the final of a baseball competition between the US and Japan; the trophy for this is the Baseball Diamond. But the match is thwarted by the arrival of the demonic Dragon Beast. The stadium owner Mr Husai, who suspiciously has many other business interests across Tokyo, decides that he will just sell the stadium if the demon sticks around.

Quelle surprise – it turns out that Husai is indeed the Dragon Beast. Years ago, he switched the real diamond in the famous baseball trophy for a forgery and he is worried that if the American team win and take it back to US soil, his crime will be uncovered.

Baseball is a hugely popular sport in Japan, so the plot of this episode is not as odd as it might first appear. There is, however, no particular connection to the traditional dragons. The demon looks more like a man wearing a *Kabuki* mask. This classical Japanese theatre style features heavily costumed performers who often wear one, or a number, of masks. Its origins probably lie in the early Edo period (between 1603 and 1868). Kabuki began in Kyoto with a female dance troupe but, after laws were passed in the seventeenth century banning women from performing, it developed into the all-male format that survives to the modern day.

The episode 'The Curse of Kaniaku' takes place in Japan itself, with the gang travelling to Tokyo, and also features a curse. In this case, a 700-year-old golden scroll is said to contain a recipe that curses the person using it if it is not followed exactly. Bandits steal the scroll before the cook has finished preparing the recipe, which leads to the appearance of a crab demon. This monster comes from an ancient Japanese legend about the recipe, which was said to have originally been given to someone by a sea serpent to make their prospective lover fall in love with them.

The whole construction of this legend is very much in the style of Japanese folk tales, although Kaniaku is a fictional construct for the show. Author and broadcaster Thersa Matsuura, creator of the podcast *Uncanny Japan*, says that the character and story are based on Japanese Yokai and legends generally, but not on one specific one.

The crab demon, of course, is not a demon at all, but the owner of the local kimono shop, whose family have been forced to sell their seafood business.

The closest we might find within the Japanese yokai is the Kani oni, a crab demon which is blue-green, vaguely resembling a crab but with six limbs instead of eight. The Kani oni has blue lips and sharp, black teeth, which may hark back to the old Japanese fashion of blackening the teeth with iron filings and vinegar known as *ohaguro*.

In turn, this Yokai may have been informed by a real-life species of Japanese crab known as Heikegani. Sometimes called the samurai crab, the carapace sports of a series of indentations that resemble the face of a Samurai warrior. The crab takes its name from the Heike, a medieval Japanese clan whose soldiers were said to have been reincarnated in the crab form. It has been suggested, by scientist Carl Sagan most famously, that these crabs thrived because Japanese fisherman would throw them back as a mark of respect for the warrior ancestors. Whilst this is quite plausible, it is also unlikely as, although the crabs are edible, they are not a common Japanese seafood.

'The Sword, the Fox and the Scooby Doo!' in the 2020 *Scooby-Doo and Guess Who?* vehicle has much basis in both real-world folklore and in the history of its guest, actor Mark Hamill. The story begins as Mark Hamill is appearing as guest of honour at a reunion of his class at Yo-Hi high school. Proceedings are interrupted when a giant fox monster appears and kidnaps his old drama teacher Mr Berle. As it runs off, the fox monster causes the Mystery Machine to crash into the barriers of a bridge, where Hamill appears and saves the gang, who then help him to solve the mystery. The fox monster, it turns out, is Hamill's old physical education teacher, Coach Roachner. He has discovered an ancient Japanese sword, which he hopes to sell for millions. Mr Berle discovered this and so the Coach kidnapped him to stop him from revealing the plan.

Yo-Hi is a real school. Established in 1946 in occupied Yokohama, from where it got its nickname, and relocating to the Yokosuka naval base in 1959, the school was renamed Nile C. Kinnick High School in 1990 after a previous scholar and athlete who was killed during a training mission in the Second World War. Mark Hamill's father William served in the US Navy and was stationed in Japan during Mark's high school years, leading to his real-life graduation from Yo-Hi in 1969.

Although the design of the fox monster seems to draw a little on the fictional animal spirit Totoro from the 1988 Studio Ghibli animated movie *My Neighbor Totoro*, written and directed by Hayao Miyazaki, in terms of folklore, the character definitely takes influence from the fox yokai *kitsune*, and is referred to as such by Hamill in the episode.

Foxes are seen as trickster characters in the folklore of many cultures. The European 'Reynard the Fox', whose origins most likely lie in medieval writings from the Lorraine region of France, has many parallels with Aesop's fox, who is the subject of a number of fables. West African Dogon beliefs have a similar fox spirit, and indigenous Siberian Chukchi myths may feature a similarly cunning animal. The nineteenth century folk tales of the fictional Uncle Remus, compiled by journalist Joel Chandler Harris in 1881, pit the wily but ultimately hapless Br'er Fox against the similarly tricksy Br'er Rabbit. It is a common mechanism which works equally well with wily but hapless coyotes and tricksy roadrunners. Beep beep!

The kitsune of Japanese folklore are highly intelligent supernatural beings who, like all foxes in yokai descriptions, can shapeshift and take on a human form. Kitsune are closely linked to the Inari spirits of the Shinto religion. These are messengers for the gods and act as protectors for some Shinto shrines.

The supernatural magic manifested by kitsune takes on a fiery-look and can often cause strange floating lights to appear, which led to the effect being called kitsunebi, or 'fox fire'. There are obviously links here with the ghost light phenomenon often known as will-o-the-wisps. There has also been speculation that the use of the term fox-fire to describe the fungal bioluminescence that is often responsible for this effect, and that has the usual greenish tinge of supernatural magic that we have already discussed, comes from this root. However, a contradictory argument for this suggests that this biological glow is named from the French root 'faux', translating therefore as false fire.

A Samurai sword is also central to the plot of the 2009 direct-to-DVD feature *Scooby-Doo! and the Samurai Sword* – I guess the clue is in the title. Another of the more unusual versions of the show featuring the supernatural as real, a dragon also crops up in this one, although it has no legs and so technically, in terms of the lore of such creatures, should be classed as a wyrm.

In some respects, the plot of this feature is not dissimilar to *Scooby-Doo! and the Witch's Ghost*, which we examined in the last chapter. Both centre around a fake ghost that ends up releasing a real one. The Mystery Inc. crew have travelled to Japan because Daphne has been invited to take part in a martial arts tournament at Miss Mirimoto's academy, where she proves her worth by defeating Mirimoto's bodyguard Sojo.

At the Tokyo museum, the curator Mr Takagawa has seen a set of newly exhibited armour transform into the resurrected Black Samurai. The legend of this warrior tells that he asked a swordsmith named Masamune to make a powerful sword. Masamune accepts the task, but his evil apprentice, Muramasa tells the Samurai that he can do the same work in six months, and so the warrior agrees. This leads to the sword being imbued with the evil of the apprentice, which in turn passes into the Samurai. This sword then became known as the Sword of Doom.

Masamune's sword, which he made anyway, became the Sword of Fate. The swordsmith gave this weapon to the Green Dragon, who used it to defeat the Samurai in battle, forcing the Samurai's soul into the Sword of Doom, which the dragon concealed. Its location could only be revealed by solving a riddle recorded on a scroll.

Back in modern times, the scroll, which was at the academy, leads the gang to recover the Sword of Doom and to unmask the Black Samurai, which was the bodyguard Sojo in disguise. This appears to be an end to the mystery – but is far from it. Miss Mirimoto, it turns out, has staged the whole tournament just to lure the gang to Japan, where she created the fake Samurai ruse in order to use their skills in mystery solving to find the sword for her. Her evil plan sees her attempting to enact her wish to return the country to its feudal past.

Miss Mirimoto succeeds in resurrecting the actual spirit of the Samurai – but fails to get him to bend to her will. Shaggy and Scooby, who through a convoluted plot mechanism earlier in the feature have been trained as Samurai, are able to summon the Green Dragon. Scooby destroys the Sword of Doom using the Sword of Fate, which breaks the curse for the Black Samurai, leaving him able to finally rest in peace in the afterlife.

Aside from the aspects of Japanese history and culture that we have already covered, the central plot theme of the swords merits some attention.

Whilst the Sword of Doom and the Sword of Fate are fictional, the legend of the swordmakers is based in some fact. Sengo Muramasa was a Japanese swordsmith working in the sixteenth century. He founded his own school, which has become famous in Japanese culture. Contemporary texts on Muramasa also state that he was a student of Masamune, as represented in the show, but this has been widely dismissed now as all the swords made by Muramasa that still exist to be examined date from a period far too late for this to be the case.

Muramasa does, however, have a reputation for producing cursed weapons. Some are said to be unable to be sheathed unless they have drawn blood; others to drive their owners to kill regardless, even if it is their own life that they are taking.

This was not the view at the time that they were made, but rather was a later invention. This came about because the swords were popular with the samurai of the Tokugawa shogunate, and so most warriors carried one. Over time, this meant that whenever an incident happened due to internal political fighting or family feuds, any crime would have been committed with a Muramasa sword. Later, as the shogunate was replaced, the idea that the swords used by its warriors carried a curse that led to such events taking place was naturally formed. The fact that they are still viewed in this way now, in terms of lore at least, is a result of their depiction in this way in the kabuki plays of the eighteenth century. The popularity of the plays with the general public caused the legend to take shape and stick.

The way that legend narratives change in this way over time is actually neatly summed up by Daphne in *Samurai Sword*. Whilst she is sitting in a sushi bar, Daphne makes the prophetic comment,

> "you know what I like about legends? New chapters are being written all the time. You never know what is going to happen next."

Joe Sichta, the writer of this feature, had it right.

## The Middle East

Arabic folklore is, on the whole, quite under-represented across Scooby-Doo and most of it centres around magic, and in particular the jinn.

Jinn, commonly anglicised as genies, in which form they are stereotypically associated with confinement in a bottle, come from the early religions of Arabia and later become a part of Islamic folklore and culture in which many people still believe in their power today. Jinn live within their own tribes and are not as prone to interfering with the lives of humans as our stories about them might suggest. If they are caused harm, however, they are said to possess a person's body in the same way that a demon of western religion might, having to be forcefully removed by exorcism in a similar way. Unsurprisingly, in Scooby-Doo, things are rarely this dark.

The franchise's first foray into Middle Eastern culture comes in the episode 'Mystery in Persia', part of Season 2 of *The New Scooby-Doo Movies* and first broadcast in 1973. The episode is notable for three particular reasons. Firstly, it is a crossover episode with another Hanna-Barbera product, *Jeannie*, which ran for sixteen episodes in the same year. Secondly, it marks the first time that the gang venture outside of the US. Thirdly, 'Mystery in Persia' is the first occasion in which the supernatural is portrayed as real – albeit via another cartoon character.

After Jeannie rescues the gang following a not-uncommon Mystery Machine crash, she and her bungling apprentice Babu are summoned to ancient Persia where the uncle of a Persian prince named Abin believes that he should be the sultan and is plotting to displace the Great Hajji with the help of an evil jinn, Jadal.

Arriving at Prince Abin's palace, everyone divides up to stay overnight in different rooms. Shaggy sees a ghost in a veil, who Jeannie drives away. One of her friends, Henry, witnesses his reflection in the mirror behaving differently to himself. After a vulture appears overhead, everyone is suddenly transported to a room with many locked doors, from which they are again rescued by Jeannie. Abin reveals that there have been many such events. The reason, it transpires, it that Abin will only become Sultan if he resides in the palace for a year. Someone (his uncle Abdullah) is trying to drive him away.

Jadal, who is working for Abdullah, imprisons Jeannie in a bottle and places it in a hole in a wall. He himself was imprisoned in a bottle for 10,000 years before Abdullah released him and we all know that this is where he will invariably end up when retribution is served. Velma finds an old bottle in Jadal's cave and, after some of the others have found Jeannie and set her free, she manages to force Jadal into it. After it is revealed that it is Abdullah who freed Jadal to help him in his quest for the sultanate, Jeannie magics him into the bottle as well until the current sultan can decide what to do with him.

Culturally, being set in Persia rather than being Arabic, the term sultan is not accurately used, as the Persian ruler would have been named Shah. There are a couple of well-worn Middle Eastern stereotypes represented in this episode, not least in the style of clothing and general décor. The most obvious trope in 'Mystery in Persia' surrounds the jinn being trapped in a bottle. The commonly thought of 'genie in a bottle', which is freed and serves a master, probably finds at its heart the story of 'The Fisherman and the Genie' from *The Arabian Nights*. In this tale, a poor fisherman brings up a brass vessel in his nets that, when the lead seal is removed, releases a 'genii'. After being threatened, the man tricks the spirit back into the vessel by telling it that he does not believe that it ever fitted in it.

This story then becomes conflated with the idea of the three wishes and the magic lamp to form the popular Aladdin tale and other similar derivations. The story, as it is known now from 'Aladdin and his Magic Lamp', was never a part of the original Arabic *Thousand and One Nights*. Along with other modern classics, such as 'Ali Baba and the Forty Thieves', the stories were added by the French translator Antoine Galland in 1704.

The *Scooby-Doo and Scrappy-Doo* story 'Scooby-Doo and Genie-Poo' brings these elements together, while simultaneously parodying *Jeannie* and the show on which that cartoon was based, *I Dream of Jeannie*. Once again, the entrapment in a bottle theme is key to the motif of the genie.

Scooby, Shaggy and Scrappy are having a picnic on a beach, when a bottle washes up onto the shore and becomes confused with their own bottles of drink. The rogue bottle accidentally gets opened, releasing a mischievous genie called Jemima and her dog Genie-Poo. The pooch instantly becomes enamoured of Scooby and casts a love spell on him in an effort to take him back to Persia with them. For this to happen, Jemima and Genie-Poo have to find an old spell, for which they head to the museum. But at the same time, because they have released her, Jemima has no choice but to grant three wishes to Shaggy and the dogs which they use to try to protect Scooby. Of course, they ultimately succeed.

Although short, as all the stories in the *Scooby-Doo and Scrappy-Doo* show are, with each transmission being comprised of three tales, 'Scooby-Doo and Genie-Poo' brings the expected stereotypes of the Arabic jinn stories in. Along with the fulfilment of three wishes element, Jemima also uses a magic carpet to try and keep Shaggy from foiling their plans.

Like the bottle, the magic carpet, also often known as a flying carpet, is far more absent from the *Thousand and One Nights* collection, not appearing at all in Galland's collection. Where many people will picture Aladdin and Jasmine flying through the air singing their hearts out on the carpet in the 1992 Disney animation, in the original manuscript, the Princess and her groom are transported away on their own bed, which is made to fly by the genie. So, if you want to make a Disney parallel, you'd have to go back to the 1971 film *Bedknobs and Broomsticks* instead.

The earliest connection to the flying carpet in history probably lies with King Solomon, where there were two different versions recorded. In one, God presents Solomon with a flying carpet so large that it can carry 40,000 men. However, when Solomon begins to get all gloaty about his gift, God gets peeved and shakes the carpet, casting the 40,000 to their deaths.

In the other version, the carpet is a gift from the Queen of Sheba, who fancies Solomon. Her alchemist had managed to cause a small rug to levitate and, after finding that the key element of making the magic successful was the type of dye in the carpet, rather than that way that it was constructed, he was able to hone his skill until he achieved full flight. This probably explains why all the magic carpets depicted in visual form are of the ornate type. Unfortunately for the Queen, Solomon was fully engaged with building his temple when the carpet arrived and so he just gave it to a member of his court to have instead. The Queen was so upset by this that she never requested another carpet and the skills that her alchemist possessed were lost.

The concept of the three wishes is also more modern than people give credit for, probably emerging from the writings of Perrault in the seventeenth century. Earlier tales, such as 'The Fisherman and the Genie', which has already been mentioned, feature a wish but not a set of three. A variety of early sources have probably been modified to include the now traditional three wishes, with three being a common number in many aspects of folklore as well as in religious faiths, such as with the Holy Trinity. The early Indian collection of stories *Panchtantra*, from around 300BC, includes the tale of the two-headed woodcutter. In this story, the woodcutter is granted a wish by a tree spirit so that the woodsman will not fell the tree. The man decides to go back to his village and asks the advice of three people, one of whom gives him bad advice. The story obviously carries the moral of being careful what you wish for, which is at the heart of many of the three wish stories that came later. They come under the heading of 'Foolish Wishes' in the Aarne-Thompson-Uther folklore motif index, and we see the same ideas in more modern fictions, such as 'The Monkey's Paw' (1902) by W.W. Jacobs.

There are multiple examples of the folklore of some other cultures cropping up in Scooby-Doo over the years, such as a surfeit of Egyptian mummies and stories that draw from Chinese mythology. We will round of this chapter by returning to ancient history for a couple of final examples.

## Mayan and Aztec Civilisations

Both the Mesoamerican Maya and later Aztec civilizations have left a strong footprint behind them in terms of their architecture, art and cultural practices. These are not so widely represented in Scooby-Doo as some other cultures, but where they are present, they certainly draw very heavily on these aspects.

The second episode of Season 1 of *The Scooby-Doo Show*, a brand that was repackaged from the previously combined *Scooby-Doo/Dynamutt Hour*, centres around archaeological work at an ancient Aztec pyramid. The story is called 'The Fiesta Host is an Aztec Ghost', because the gang are visiting Mexico to go to said fiesta. Unfortunately, this never happens – due to ancient ghostly intervention.

The pyramid in the show bears more than a passing resemblance to the Temple of Kukulcán, the most recognisable of the buildings from the Chichen

Itza complex in Yucatan. Dating from somewhere between the eighth and twelfth centuries, the temple takes the form of a step pyramid, which was used for the worship of the Mayan feathered serpent god from which it takes its name. Due to its clever architectural design, when the sun hits one corner of the temple at a time around the spring and autumn equinoxes, it casts triangular shadows on the building that resemble the shape of a serpent.

It is, of course, slightly anachronous to use a pyramid design that so closely resembles the Mayan temple when the title of the show makes it clear that the story is very definitely about Aztec archaeology.

Mystery Inc. arrive and find that the fiesta is cancelled due to the appearances of the ghost of an ancient Aztec king named Katazuma. It is highly likely that this character derives its fictional name from the second Aztec emperor Moctezuma (known more colloquially in English as Montezuma) who reigned from 1440 until his death in 1469. The giant form of Katazuma has been causing havoc in the village, alongside the materialisation of a massive Aztec statue.

Both, naturally, turn out to be disguises. These were the creations of the archaeologist Professor Stonehack and his wife Elina, although they had tried to persuade the locals that they had inadvertently freed the ghost of Katazuma while they were working on the pyramid. The motive, as usual, is financial. The couple were looking to rob the dig site while everybody had been scared away.

The second season of *Scooby-Doo: Mystery Incorporated* also uses the Temple of Kukulcán but in a more accurate Mayan context. The season story sees our gang battling another team of mystery solvers, also made up of four people and a dog and known to be the 'original' Mystery Incorporated of Crystal Cove, in order to find and recover the pieces of a broken up Planispheric Disk. Once reassembled, this disk will lead the bearer to a cursed treasure which is buried between the town.

As the season unfolds, it becomes clear that there have been many sets of people solving mysteries based in Crystal Cove over the centuries, and that they are always made up of the same combination of four people and an animal companion. They are linked over time and have an important connection to the curse that hangs over the town. As Season 2 reaches its conclusion, events build to a climax as we see that an extradimensional threat is coming to bear in the shape of the Nibiru cataclysm. This whole plot arc is based firmly within real world UFO lore, which we will examine later when we look at modern folklore representations in the show.

In the episode 'Nightmare in Red', large sections of which parody David Lynch's *Twin Peaks*, the gang learn that the very first set of mystery solvers were called the Hunters of Secrets. Their version of Scoob was a pet Jaguar. In their time, an evil being was trapped in a crystal sarcophagus that had found its way to the Yucatan. This sarcophagus is now buried under Crystal Cove as attempts to destroy it by the Hunters of Secrets had failed, with the casket being taken by conquistadors who were corrupted by the entity within.

In their attempt to destroy the sarcophagus, the Hunters of Secrets had fashioned a heart-shaped spearhead that became known as the Heart of the Jaguar. Although a different type of item, it seems very likely that this piece takes inspiration from a statue called the Red Jaguar discovered in a chamber in the Temple of Kukulcán which archaeologists dubbed the throne room because the Red Jaguar looked like it may have been used for that purpose.

The next episode, 'Dark Night of the Hunters', sees the gang travelling to Yucatan to try to retrieve the Heart of the Jaguar so that they can use it to stop the imminent threat from Nibiru. They succeed, despite the best efforts of an apparently ancient Mayan priestess, who turns out to be the less than ancient Professor Enrique, owner of probably the finest-named antique shop ever, 'What's Mayan is Yours Antiques'.

Moving from the Yucatan, the gang's other run-in with these ancient civilisations takes place in the city of Acapulco, off the coast of Mexico. In the *Scooby-Doo and Scrappy-Doo* episode 'Twenty Thousand Screams Under the Sea', the gang have travelled to the area to watch a cliff diving competition. However, much like the ill-fated Mexican fiesta from earlier, this is once again jeopardised by the appearance of an Aztec threat, this time the Sea Beast of the Aztecs.

The premise of this story is quite straightforward. Treasure from a sunken galleon has washed up into a nearby cove. One of the high divers attending the competition, Tiger Morris, has discovered this, so he creates the Sea Beast disguise to scare everyone else away so that he can retrieve the treasure and hide it for later, when he can return and take it away and become rich. But, of course, he doesn't get away with it – those meddling kids see to that.

There was an ancient sea monster in the Aztec culture called Cipactli, which formed part of their creation myth. In line with several other ancient cultures, the Aztecs believed that the world began only as water and that it was the destruction of Cipactli that formed the land masses of the Earth. In the beginning, according to Aztec mythology, the four key gods (of which strangely everyone only seems to be able to name Quetzalcoatl from their school days) created the water. After this, these four deities created lesser gods and other creatures including Cipactli.

But when the gods created Cipactli, they made a fundamental error in design. They placed a mouth on every one of Cipactli's joints, meaning that the creature was forever hungry. The knock-on effect of this was that all the other Aztec creations would end up being eaten by Cipactli in an endless attempt to satisfy its hunger, which it was decided was not good for the whole general creation process.

To solve this problem, the gods destroyed Cipactli by pulling it into four pieces. This connects with the fact that the four main gods represented the four cardinal compass directions. The universe emerged from the body of Cipactli, with its head forming the heavens, its tail the underworld and the Earth everything in between.

Cipactli has been variously described as a demon, a sea monster, and a crocodile. There is an Aztec tradition that names the survivor of the flood who goes on to repopulate the world as 'Divine Crocodile'. It is easy to draw similarities between this and the Christian biblical flood myth, especially when considering the Aztec view that there was nothing but water to begin with.

Let's move on from the world of creation myths to that of urban ones.

# CHAPTER SIX

## URBAN LEGENDS AND FOLKLORE MOTIFS

In the first chapter, we looked at urban legends related to the Scooby-Doo franchise and, to a lesser extent, some cases where the show has influenced the real world to create its own pop culture urban legends in return. But what we didn't examine at that stage was the representation of other urban legends from the world of folklore in the Scoobyverse. Whilst there is no example of 'Dead Dog in a Suitcase' to be found in any of the episodes (because this would, after all, somewhat change the whole dynamic of Mystery Incorporated), there are others. In this chapter, we will look at a few, as well as some other common folklore motifs that crop up from time to time.

The term 'urban legend' probably first appeared in print, certainly in relation to folklore, in 1968, when it was used by the American folklorist Richard Dorson. It is most synonymous from the point of view of serious study with Jan Harold Brunvand, a professor emeritus from the University of Utah, who has published extensively on the subject. His valuable anthologies of urban legends started with *The Vanishing Hitchhiker: American Urban Legends & Their Meanings* in 1981.

Many urban legends have far earlier examples than might at first appear. Take, for example, the story of a warning about an upcoming terrorist attack which became very popular for a while after the World Trade Centre incident. A person drops a wallet and a member of the public picks it up and returns it. As thanks for this act of kindness, the owner of the wallet tells them to stay away from a particular location, often a shopping centre, at Halloween, because there is an attack planned there.

There are usually very clear implications of prejudices in these stories. For example, in more recent versions the individual losing the wallet is often of Arabic descent, reflecting incidents such as the attack on the Twin Towers.

Similar versions of this story exist where the warning comes as an act of thanks when someone was lent money at a till point because they had slightly too little cash to complete a transaction, or for other reasons. But the end result is always the same.

If we go back more than a century, we find exactly the same story being told in 1917 during the First World War, but with slight cultural differences. The wallet is dropped on the tube in London and the owner of the wallet is, naturally, German. The Halloween attack in this case will be a bombing raid.

We can, in fact, even find similar examples to these modern stories even further back in history. In a 2022 article, Henrik Lassen draws parallels between the urban legend of the inventor who is murdered in a hit purported to be organised by the oil industry (because he has designed a car that runs on water), to a similar story from Ancient Rome about unbreakable glass. And somewhere around 100AD, stories are recorded in Rome about incursions into the sewer system by octopi, mirroring the pig and alligator stories found in more modern drains. We'll come back to gators in a bit.

Whilst it is rare for a plot in Scooby-Doo to directly reference an urban legend, there are a number of examples where they seem to have provided inspiration to the writers. In this chapter, we will look at a selection of these, before finishing up with a couple of the motifs found behind folkloric tales.

## Spring-Heeled Jack

In Victorian London, a character emerged from the shadows about whom most of the stories told may now be regarded as urban legends. Spring-Heeled Jack was a night-terror of the streets, a 'demon' who would attack women, breathe blue flames and then escape by bounding off over objects too high for a normal man to clear.

To unpick the reality from the legend in this story is tricky in some respects, but straightforward in others. While we cannot know for certain which elements may be considered real, it is probable that a person (or persons) was operating in the 'ghost hoaxing' tradition that we have previously discussed. From the reports of these attacks, a legend grew through misreporting, embellishment and outright lies.

Early reports date from 1837 and predominantly concerned physical assaults against women. Jack would call at a house and when the door was answered, would rip at the woman's clothes with sharp-clawed fingers. Sometimes, the attacks would take place on the street. Reports in contemporary newspapers became more and more fantastical, until most people simply did not believe them. Dr Simon Young, the author of the book *The Nail in the Skull and other Victorian Urban Legends*, has done good work in this field to explain and explore the facts.

Then, in February 1838, a woman called Jane Alsop answered the door of her house to a caller pleading for help because he and a group of others had captured Jack. She went and fetched a candle from the house and brought it

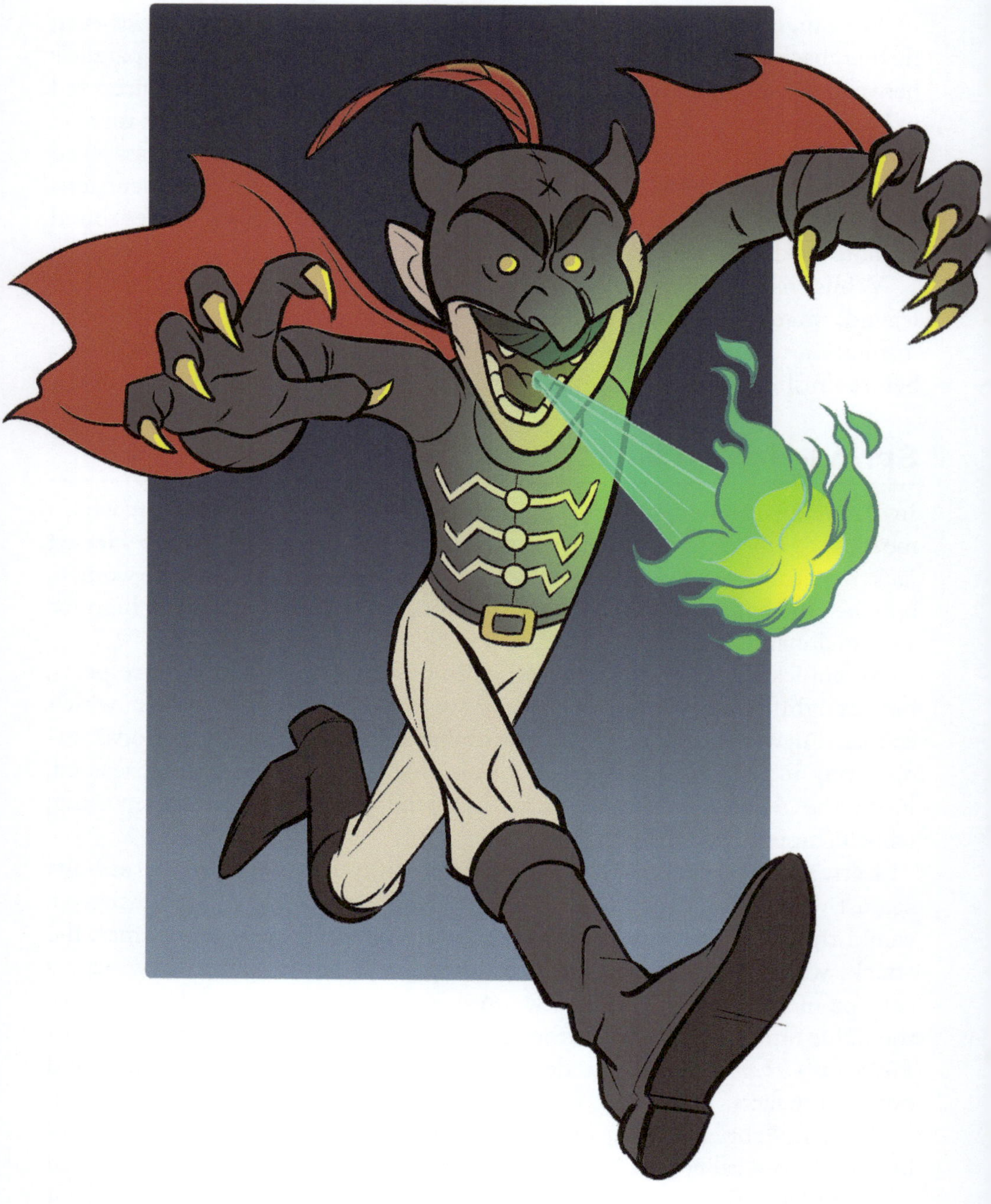

out to him, at which point he ripped her clothes with metal claws and blew flames into her face.

From this point, stories of Spring-Heeled Jack spread, not just through London but across the UK and beyond. From the 1850s through to the 1870s and later, sightings and attempts to catch Jack were reported in the Midlands, in Lincoln and Liverpool. These persisted as late as the start of the twentieth century.

The 1979 episode 'The Night Ghoul of Wonderworld', part of the original *Scooby-Doo and Scrappy-Doo* series, doffs a top hat to Spring-Heeled Jack and is set in Victorian London. Except it isn't. The Wonderworld of the title is a parody of Michael Chichton's *Westworld*, with a smattering of the TV show *Fantasy Island* thrown in for good measure.

The premise of both is to allow people to safely live out their dreams, and thus it is here too with Velma expressing a desire to solve a mystery with the famous fictional detective Sherlock Holmes. Mr Marino is the owner of the robot-habited Wonderworld, although his white suit and accent is a direct reference to Mr Roarke, the lead character of *Fantasy Island* portrayed by Ricardo Montalbán. He sends the gang off on the Wonderworld train to London World. Here, they learn that the crown jewels have been stolen by a criminal known as 'The Night Ghoul'. Although the villain is a robot for the first part of the quite convoluted plot, he later appears to be replaced by a real person in the same costume, who finally turns out to be Marino. He had sabotaged the robot Holmes to try to recover jewels that were hidden in London World before Velma's fantasy even began to be acted out.

The earlier first season of *The New Scooby-Doo Movies* also contains a cultural reference to the legend of Spring-Heeled Jack, though it isn't as direct, as there is no connection with Victorian London. 'The Ghost of the Red Baron' is another of the slightly strange 'celebrity' crossover episodes that crop up from time to time. On this occasion, the Three Stooges provide the extra comedy in a plot that sees the ghost of the First World War German flying ace Manfred von Richthofen (better known more colloquially by the moniker of the episode title) spending his time back on earth, or technically above it, ruining farm crops by attacking crop dusters.

At one point, during an inevitable chase scene, the ghost escapes by leaping obstacles using springs built into his boots – literally spring-heeled. A similarly war-themed real-world version of Jack was reported in the Prague area during the Second World War. Pérák, a character who became known as 'The Spring Man' or 'The Springer', is a character of urban myth emerging from the Nazi occupation of Czechoslovakia. Although there are no tangible records in the police reports of the time, anecdotal evidence suggests that stories of the character were quite real… even if the character himself was not.

Pérák would become something of a Czech anti-hero, appearing as a figure of positive propaganda in comic books as well as other works of fiction. A large, spray-painted depiction of the character in the Prague district of Žižkov shows him in war-like attire, with a billowing cape and obvious springs fixed to the bottoms of his boots.

## Hook Hands and Murdered Boyfriends

Arguably one of the best-known serial killer urban legends is one generally known as 'The Hook'. It will be familiar to most readers. A young couple are parked in the woods, or on a desolate road, or somewhere else equally remote, with the intention of things getting a little frisky. In the car, a radio is playing. Suddenly, the broadcast is interrupted by a news announcement warning people that a dangerous killer has escaped from a nearby penitentiary, or other institution. He should be easy to spot, because he wears a hook in place of a missing hand. The couple become worried, or the girl's concern overrules the bravado of her suiter, and they start the car and race off to a safer location. On arriving home, they get out of the car, only to discover a hook hanging from the passenger door handle.

This commonly told variant of the story probably has its origins at some point around the 1950s, but it gained much more traction in 1960 when it was printed in the 'Dear Abby' advice column. The column, the most widely syndicated in the world, first appeared in 1956. The agony aunt, Abigail Van Buren, is a penname originally used by the founder Pauline Phillips, and since 2000 by her daughter, Jeanne, who owns the legal rights to the name. The letter that appeared, from Jeanette, read:

> 'Dear Abby: If you are interested in teenagers, you will print this story. I don't know whether it's true or not, but it doesn't matter because it served its purpose for me: A fellow and his date pulled into their favorite "lovers lane" to listen to the radio and do a little necking. The music was interrupted by an announcer who said there was an escaped convict in the area who had served time for rape and robbery. He was described as having a hook instead of a right hand. The couple become frightened and drove away. When the boy took his girl home, he went around to open the car door for her. Then he saw—a hook on the door handle! I will never park to make out as long as I live. I hope this does the same for other kids.'

They key part of this letter is the statement that it doesn't matter whether or not it was true, because the story served its purpose. 'The Hook' is an urban legend of the morality type, as so many folklore stories are. It has been suggested that its underlying plot may be traced back to Victorian literature, putting this also into the Spring-Heeled Jack camp.

A variation on 'The Hook' may be found in another urban legend, 'The Murdered Boyfriend'. In this version, the couple are out driving when they stop in a remote area. The car has usually broken down. The boyfriend goes to get help while the girl stays in the car.

Once again, there is an announcement on the radio about an escaped maniac. The boyfriend is gone for some time, during which the girl can hear some sort of banging on the roof of the car. Eventually, either the girl can stand it no longer and has to get out of the car, or alternatively the police arrive and tell her to get out and to walk to them without looking back. Of course, she does look back. The killer is on the roof of the car bouncing the boyfriend's head on it. Alternatively, the boyfriend is strung up from a tree branch and the blood from his body is dripping on the car, or he is hung the other way up and his feet are scraping on the roof.

Both variants of this urban legend may have provided some inspiration to the writers of Scooby. In the eighth episode of Season 2 of *What's New, Scooby-Doo?*, titled 'The San Franpsycho', the villain of the title sports a hook hand as well as the inevitable red eyes and supernaturally green skin.

Mystery Inc. are visiting a skateboarding competition, The Grind Games, but find that the competition has been derailed by the appearance of the ghost of a former Alcatraz prisoner called Clint Morris. His nickname had been the San Franpsycho. There seem to be a couple of obvious cultural references in this character other than the urban legend. His name is a probable parody of Chuck Norris, and he is usually seen covered in seaweed, which is most likely a reference to the escape bid undertaken in 1962 by Clarence and John Anglin and Frank Morris.

The investigation undertaken by the gang finally unmasks the culprit as a potential competitor, Rutie Banez, who had not been allowed to take part in The Grind Games. She believed that this was because she was a girl, although this was blatantly not the reason as some of the other skaters, whose performances she disrupted, were also girls. It just turned out that she wasn't very good.

The second possible reference comes in the next season of the same iteration of the show, in a holiday special episode called 'A Scooby-Doo Valentine'. Whilst there are (obviously) no serial killers or murders taking place, the plot revolves around a series of 'Lover's Lane' kidnappings. The villains turn out to be 'clones' of the Mystery Incorporated characters themselves, or at least doubles portrayed by Hollywood background extras.

These actors had all been hired by J.C. Chasez, a character who was dating an ex-girlfriend of Shaggy's. He was fed up with his girlfriend, Rachel, constantly talking about Shaggy's adventures, so he set about to frame the whole gang with his kidnapping ruse. The final denouement leads to a nice nod to the live action movie *Scooby-Doo* when Daphne bemoans the fact that she is being portrayed by a background artiste – 'was Sarah Michelle Gellar too busy?'

## Alligators

One of the most enduring of the urban legends surrounding animals is the story about giant alligators living in the New York sewer systems. As a generalised suggestion, there is no factual basis for this. Research into the idea undertaken by Barbara Mikkelson, one of the founders of the urban legend fact-checking website *Snopes,* showed that of all the reports of large alligators found in *The New York Times* newspaper between 1905 and 1993, only one made any reference to sewers.

In America, the only country apart from China where alligators are a native species, the reptile's natural habitat is found in the southeast regions, with the largest populations in Louisiana and Florida. These regions provide the warm climate that the alligator needs to survive; the sort of climate that certainly would not be found in a New York sewer system, even for alligators trying to survive a cold winter.

If alligators had adapted to the cooler temperatures, their survival would still be very much at threat from the sewage itself. Bacteria such as salmonella and E. coli pose a great risk to the health of the reptiles, such that they would not be able to live long enough to either breed or to grow to enormous sizes. And yet, the story of baby alligators being flushed down people's toilets and setting up residence in Poo Alley has been around for a long time.

Monstrous versions of alligators make a few appearances in episodes of Scooby-Doo over the years, but the one that most closely takes its inspiration from the urban legend is 'The New York Underground!'. This is the eighteenth episode of the first season of *Scooby-Doo and Guess Who?*. It first aired in 2020 and featured American singer Halsey as a special guest.

The gang are in New York City, where Scoob has entered Shaggy as a contestant in a poetry slam as a surprise, having overheard some of his poetry. Shaggy finds himself up against the formidable talent of Halsey in his bout. But just as the slam is about to begin, the manhole cover that Scooby is standing on starts to rattle and lift, and a giant alligator emerges from the sewer. Despite the monster being described as a 'gator man', it looks pretty much like a regular oversized sewer alligator, apart from walking on its hind legs most of the time.

There is much running around and panicking, during which the gator steals the star prize from the poetry slam, the key to the City of New York.

It looks like the gang have a mystery on their hands once again, so they head down into the sewers to investigate, accompanied by Halsey, who knows the subterranean passages very well and so acts as a guide. Their first stop is an underground restaurant known as the Graffiti Station, where Shaggy and Halsey end up undertaking an impromptu slam to earn food from the chef. In a tangential reflection of the urban legend that we discussed previously, it is notable that the chef has a hook hand!

From here, the party go to interrogate the Knowledge Keeper, an eccentric woman with more than a passing resemblance to Emma Thompson's Professor Sybill Trelawney. She explains how the key, which bears a particular symbol, had once belonged to the famous J. Jacob Ascot, who had helped to build both the city and its sewers back in the day. Ascot is an obvious parody of the wealthy John Jacob Astor IV, the New York real estate magnate who perished on the Titanic, with his name riffing on Fred's neckwear of choice.

The Knowledge Keeper tells everyone how it was rumoured that Ascot had his own private train car and subway station in the tunnels. While this is fictional, there was a station of the New York underground railway named Astor Place after J.J. Astor. The real station depicts a beaver amongst its original decorative tiles, symbolic of the beaver pelt market from which part of the original Astor fortune was derived. In the safe on the train car, says the Knowledge Keeper, is concealed a great treasure.

This treasure, of course, is what the villain, disguised as the gator creature, has his sights set on. It turns out to be the unnamed promoter of the poetry slam who is responsible. He wants to get his hands on the great treasure: a handwritten copy of an old poem by Emma Lazarus called 'The New Colossus'. This is, indeed, a real piece. The sonnet was penned in 1883 by Lazarus as one of several donations of art and literature auctioned by the Art Loan Fund Exhibition to raise money for the construction of a pedestal on which to place the sculptor Frédéric Bartholdi's great work, 'Liberty Enlightening the World', more commonly known as the Statue of Liberty.

Although the sewer gator of this episode obviously draws on the urban legend of flushed reptiles, in the story, the eccentric Knowledge Keeper gives the legend behind the gator creature as being that of a man who lived in the sewers and spent so long there killing and cooking alligators that he became one, although she does qualify this with the additional comment of, 'or something like that'. This maybe owes something to the 1959 American B-movie feature *The Alligator People*.

A staple of many episodes of Scooby-Doo over the years has been the 'door routine', where, during a chase scene, characters will disappear through a door in a hallway full of doors. Their pursuer will go through another door, triggering a whole routine of characters running in and out of different doors, usually in multiple costumes or carrying random objects (or each other). It has become so synonymous with the show that the website 'Know Your Meme' now has the concept catalogued as 'Scooby-Doo Doors'. Probably originating in stage plays or farce, the multiple door gag has been around since the early part of the twentieth century or before, but Scoob made it iconic.

Just a few episodes after 'The New York Underground!', Mystery Incorporated meet up with the Hex Girls once again in 'I Put A Hex On You!'. Central to the plot is the ghost of a rock star who was once a member of the Hex Girls, but had to quit the band because of stage fright. Bitter about this, they present the band with a guitar that is seemingly cursed, hoping that it will possess them and cause them to break-up.

The door routine element of the chase in this episode takes place in a sewer and, as homage to the legend (or the earlier episode), at one point an alligator emerges from one of the doors, running across frame with the other characters.

The other appearances of gators are less relevant and have many years between them, but the monsters themselves are surprisingly similar in their design. Both are semi-anthropomorphic, favouring walking on their hind legs and being somewhat 'humanoid' in their behaviour.

In 'The Gruesome Game of the Gator Ghoul' – part of the first season of *The Scooby Doo Show* – the action is set in a restaurant in the southern swamps. The gang are paying a visit to Scooby's somewhat slow cousin, Scooby-Dum, and his owners Ma and Pa Skillett. They own the restaurant, which is renowned for its carbonated drink Fenokee Fizz. But business around the restaurant is poor, mostly because of the alligator creature that is roaming the swamps scaring people away.

The usual investigation leads to the gang discovering that the identity of the creature is Alice Dovely, an ex-employee of the Kookie Cola Company. She was previously fired from the company and, learning that Kookie Cola were looking to buy out Fenokee Fizz, she set out to exact her revenge.

There is nothing much in terms of folklore or connection to the sewer alligator legends other than the creature being a gator.

Fast forward quite a few show iterations to the first season of *Scooby-Doo! Mystery Incorporated,* and some more gator creatures appear on the scene in the episode 'The Creeping Creatures'.

Mystery Inc. are bored. There has been no decent mystery to solve for a while and they are sitting round in Fred's house bemoaning this fact. But then, by some strange coincidence, a tip-off arrives in a note from the mysterious Mr. E. The town of Gatorsburg used to be a profitable one, with its economy booming from the sale of gator skin products. But when the gator skin supplies ran out, things became bleak, and the town fell into ruin.

Arriving in the town, the gang become stranded when the Mystery Machine's engine is stolen. The local mechanic orders them a new one, advising them to stay in his sister's hotel while they wait for it to be delivered. As you would expect, the hotel is rather reminiscent of the famous Bates Motel, as interpreted by production designers Joseph Hurley and Robert Clatworthy for Alfred Hitchcock's film version of Robert Bloch's *Psycho*. This is not the only time that a hotel in Scooby-Doo resembles Chez Bates.

Unfortunately, the Gatorsburg hotel does not allow pets, so Scooby has to sleep in the stranded Mystery Machine, where he is attacked by three gator creatures.

Cut to the denouement, where the gator creatures, we discover, are (wait for it…) the mechanic, his sister, the hotel owner and her son. They have developed quite a lucrative business selling fake alligator skin products as real, based on the town's previous reputation, and cook up the reptilian monsters to keep people away, in true smuggler-folklore style.

## Drop Bears

Halfway through the second season of *Scooby-Doo: Mystery Incorporated*, we meet the 'Scarebear' in an episode of the same name. A large mutant bear has been stalking the land around the notorious Crystal Cove business Destroido Corp. The gang are tasked by the mayor of the town to investigate the mystery because the empire that is Destroido Corp has registered their land with having its own corporate sovereignty, meaning that Sheriff Stone, the head of the Crystal Cove police force, has no jurisdiction.

Investigations show that the water in the area has been contaminated with lithium. Furthermore, other mutations have been occurring. George Avocados, an avocado farmer who has neighbouring land, tells the gang how his crops have been turning into mutated spider-like creatures. His business is failing, making him a natural suspect. It turns out that there are a number of other 'monsters' that aren't people in costumes, all of them the result of Destroido's contamination.

The Scarebear is not, in fact, George Avocados but a Destroido Corp security guard who has been similarly mutated by one of their products, resulting in a hairy body and bear-like behaviour. His name was Benson Hairmore, but because he thought that he would naturally be thought to be the Scarebear because of this moniker, he cleverly changed it to Benson Furhman. Yes, he probably could have come up with something a little better. Even Benson Notabear would have been an improvement.

In this episode, Benson does get away with it thanks to the help of the meddling kids. Realising that he is essentially working for the public good by trying to bring down the evil Destroido Corp, they choose to not have him arrested. Being on Destroido Land, the Sheriff could not arrest him, even if he wanted to.

With its heavily muscled bulky frame, glowing red eyes and sharp teeth, the natural point of reference for the Scarebear would be a lycanthropic one. But

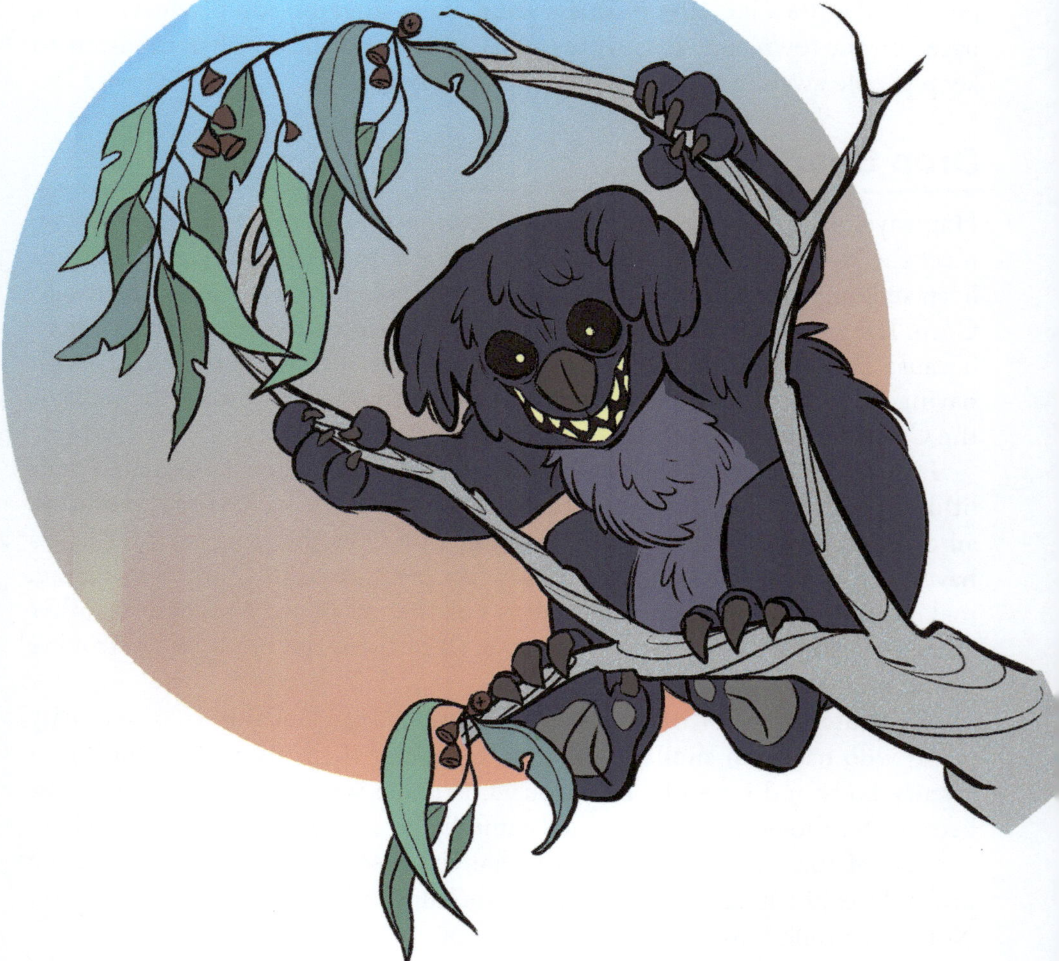

there are some elements of the creature, in terms of urban legend at least, that might put one in mind of the legendary Australian Drop Bear.

The Drop Bear is a hoaxed folkloric cryptid taking the form of a carnivorous version of the cuddly koala, somewhat larger than their herbivorous cousin with viciously sharp teeth and a ferocious expression and temperament. The Drop Bear attacks its prey, particularly humans, by dropping out of trees where it sits concealed, onto its target's head.

The story of the Drop Bear owes a lot in its spread and cultural embedding to the Australian sense of humour. Many years ago, a website entry for the Drop Bear was created by staff at the Australian Museum. The Drop Bear entry was included alongside numerous entries for existing Australian animal species, and was written in the same style. It gave the animal's Latin name (*Thylarctos Plummetus*) and included a description of how it attacked 'with powerful forearms for climbing and attacking prey, and a bite made using powerful premolars rather than canines.'

The entry in the Australian Museum catalogue was not an April Fool's joke, but its effectiveness was later backed up with an April 1st article. In 2013, *Australian Geographic* announced the findings of researchers who had discovered that Drop Bears were statistically more likely to attack people who did not speak with an Australian accent.

This joke references the probable origins of the Drop Bear hoax. Some people have stated that the idea comes from the Australian comedian and actor Paul Hogan. His sketch vehicle, *The Paul Hogan Show*, featured a skit in which a man is attacked by koalas who jump him from a tree. But this origin would be far too late, as Hogan's show originally aired in the 1970s and 1980s.

The Australian army newspaper *Army* ran an article in its edition of Thursday 12th October, 1967, reporting on a training exercise called 'PIPING SHRIKE', which had been designed to simulate a battalion infantry attack. Above a somewhat indistinct photograph at the end of the article was the paragraph:

> 'Something else to come out of PIPING SHRIKE was the hide of a dreaded Drop Bear, below, nailed to a tree outside the Q Store. The KSLI heard many reports from Diggers about this beast. ARMY's full report on the habits and habitats of the Drop Bear appears on p.13, this issue.'

This issue of *Army* had twelve pages…

It is probable that the Drop Bear was invented before this, as the mention in *Army* is written in a way that suggests that it was common knowledge. Further field research for this book brought forward this anecdote in private correspondence from Bruce Waldron, the father of Australian folklorist and historian Dr David Waldron:

'There was a story going around that up in the Jungle Training Camp at Kanungra, the Aussie boys had spread the story amongst the Yanks, and that during the night someone yelled out 'Drop bear attack' and threw a medicine ball onto the Yanks tent; they opened fire with live rounds and riddled the tent with holes. I've heard mum tell the story, she adds the embellishment that the medicine ball was buried with full military honours.'

This was dated to June 1970, but he explained that the same story has also been heard by modern army recruits, showing that it has spanned the decades. It has just the right amount of truth and humour to do so, as all good urban legends do.

## Folklore Motifs

In the *Scooby-Doo and Guess Who?* episode 'Screaming Skulls of London', Mystery Incorporated are taking a walking tour of the city when they encounter what have been described as the "screaming skulls of English legend". Only they aren't.

The Screaming Skull of folklore is a human skull that has been interred in a particular house. Often, this was a family home and the deceased had expressed a wish to be buried there, suggesting a strong familial tie to the property. Should the skull ever be removed from the house, or if the wishes to be buried there are ignored, then all sorts of paranormally based disaster will befall the house until the skull is returned to its rightful place. There are several notable examples of such objects.

Although they exhibit similar poltergeist-like attributes, the 'Screaming Skulls of London' are a floating mass of green skulls floating around in a mysterious green flame. Lots of supernatural green to be seen here – we already know all about that. Plus, naturally, they aren't skulls at all. They are the somewhat peculiar disguise of a Tower of London beefeater and a security guard. Because of course they are.

A motif is an idea or an image that appears in many stories, and that identifies those stories as being part of a particular group. We can identify them in folk tales, fairy tales and folklore more generally. In terms of literature, we can see the motif as a narrative device that will often help to set a particular mood.

This book has already been liberally peppered with motifs, as you will probably realise. The chapter on landscape and the Gothic is full of them. They are particularly common in early shows, such as the original *Scooby-Doo Where Are You!*. In the third episode of the original first season, 'Hassle in the Castle', danger-prone Daphne becomes lost after accidentally falling through a trap door (arguably a motif in itself). As the rest of the gang search for her, they are given directions by a talking skull, drawing on the motif of the screaming skulls of folklore.

A couple of other strong folkloric motifs also appear in *Where Are You!*, both in the third season.

## Tunnels

The gang are on holiday in Puerto Rico in Episode 314, 'Don't Go Near the Fortress of Fear'. It's the only time in the show's history that they ever visit the territory. Visiting an ancient fortress named El Moro, they are somewhat taken aback when the ghost of a sixteenth century Spanish general called Juan Carlos tells them to stay away from the place.

The slightly differently spelled El Morro is an actual fort. Declared a World Heritage Site in 1983, its full name is Castillo San Felipe del Morro. It was designed to watch over the entrance to San Juan Bay, and to be the main line of defence for the city against anyone attacking from the sea. Construction of the fortress began in 1589 (a fact alluded to by Velma in the episode) and the resulting structure was later further strengthened and enlarged.

The real world El Morro is said to be haunted, and we know that this must be true because it has been visited by the illustrious and most definitely reputable TV investigation group Ghost Hunters International. The most well-known ghost at the site is that of a White Lady who is said to walk the ramparts, but there have been several other stories of sightings of the ghosts of both soldiers and of prisoners. The ghost of General Juan Carlos is, however, an invention of the writers of Scooby-Doo.

Their plot centres around the fact that a museum in the port city has been robbed, with many items of incalculable value missing. San Juan has many museums; we don't know which one it is but it really doesn't matter. Stuff is missing. Mystery Incorporated must investigate. Such are the laws of nature.

Looking for information in the city records office, Daphne finds a map on which is marked a tunnel leading from the fortress to the museum. They search the area for the entrance to the tunnel, eventually discovering it under a fake telephone box. Lo and behold, the tunnel contains all the missing treasures.

Prior to this, the gang have been on a fishing trip with, it turns out, the villain behind the mystery, Captain Eddy. He had (stupidly) told them the legend of the castle's ghost, and how the spirit liked to set off the cannons there. Having found one of the cannons at the fort hot, everything falls into place when Shaggy and Scooby inadvertently unearth a crate of parachutes and hollow cannonballs in the tunnels. Captain Eddy has been hiding the treasures in the cannonballs, firing them from the fortress to his boat and then sailing them out of the country. A plan that could never have accidentally backfired in the slightest.

Almost always, in terms of folkloric stories, secret tunnels do not exist. The tunnels are frequently connected with stories of smugglers moving illicit items. They often run from a beach or other coastal area and then terminate somewhere significant, like a church or a prominent country house that would have been owned by a rich family. In many cases, the tunnels would have been totally improbable, because the route taken would have been far too long to be easily constructed and would have passed through places where a tunnel would not be geologically possible, such as under water courses or through shale or other materials that could not be tunnelled.

For example, drawing on the Spanish theme connected with this particular Scooby episode, in 1588, Sir Francis Drake took 397 people prisoner from a Spanish ship that he had captured. All these people were secured in a tithe barn at Torre Abbey, Torquay, a town in the southern English county of Devon. The conditions there were very poor, and one ghost on the site now is said to be that of a woman who died during her incarceration.

Torre Abbey is said to have a tunnel that runs to a nearby chapel, St Michael's. It is a well-established story, but the tunnel itself could not possibly exist because part of its half-mile route would have to include a vertical section to reach the chapel which sits atop a tor. The geology of this area is limestone, which is not known for its tunnel-supporting potential, being a sub-type of chalk.

In the case of San Juan, historic tunnels do actually exist, and undoubtedly the writers of this episode, Haskell Barkin, Larz Bourne and Dick Conway, used these as a mechanism for their own story. The San Juan tunnels were designed for movement, but not for contraband goods. In much the same way that the underground tunnels at Disneyland, known as utilidors (short for utility corridors), allow cast members and goods to be transported between lands without being seen by visitors to the park, the San Juan tunnels meant that soldiers could move between city defences clandestinely.

Additionally, some of the tunnels do not go anywhere, suddenly terminating in a dead end. These were designed to have explosives packed into them. In the event that an enemy did begin to gain ground and it looked like they were in danger of overrunning El Morro or any of the other forts in the complex, a particularly sprightly soldier could go down into the tunnel, light the fuse, and run for dear life.

Another secret passage figures in the last episode of this season of *Where Are You!*. In this one, it links it with another common folklore motif.

# Bottomless Lakes

There are many hundreds of lakes, pools and other stretches of water that are rumoured in folklore to be bottomless. They may be found all over the world. Usually, they are ascribed the legend of having no bottom as a warning. This happens frequently in folklore to keep people away from danger. There may have been no natural or man-made protection surrounding a body of water, or it may have been fast-flowing or especially dangerous in some other way, and so the story of it being bottomless is designed to keep people away from it.

The same may be true of other waterways, rivers or lakes that are said to have folkloric creatures inhabiting them. There are many examples of these, from lake monsters to kelpies, the rusalka to Jenny Greenteeth.

The existence of supernatural water dwellers is, however, much more embedded into the worldview of cultures around the globe from a mythological perspective. Bodies of water are sacred in many traditions. They connect the natural world with the more mythic realms. Furthermore, water is life, and so it is that folklore features water-dwelling deities who must be respected, revered, and sometimes placated. Offerings should be made, sometimes sacrifices should be given. Although Scooby-Doo doesn't go quite that far…

The final episode of the final repackaged season of *Scooby-Doo Where Are You!* plays with this idea. In this episode, set in Canada, the gang meet a lumberjack who tells them about the legend of a local lake, said to be inhabited by some form of aquatic monster. If anyone fishes in the lake, he explains, then it is said that the level of the lake will sink. This idea obviously draws from broader folklore of the importance of water resources and of securing their safety and care which we see in the stories of water spirits just mentioned. In particular, this episode may draw on the Mishipeshu, or 'Great Lynx', a protective lake spirit for the Ojibwa.

In this episode, the lake itself is not thought to be bottomless, but the implication is that older stories probably conceived of it in that way. This is because the lake is in a village named Bottomless Lake, which has recently become something of a ghost town as the creature has scared everyone away.

Folklore can be found in the place names of many locations in the landscape, although caution does have to be exercised, as it is easy to assume that there is a link to something supernatural or folkloric when there isn't. The village of Black Dog has a pub also called the Black Dog. Even though there is a story about a ghostly Black Dog located in the immediate area, the pub was named after a publican's real dog and not anything spectral at all.

There are, however, a plethora of place names ascribed to things that the Devil is alleged to have done in folklore. He has chairs, frying pans, stairs, hills – even an arse and an elbow.

The Canadian village of Bottomless Lake is fictional, but there is a State Park in New Mexico with the same name. It lies southeast of Roswell but, sadly, the lakes do not seem to have been formed by the landing gear of UFOs. In fact, they are not lakes at all. The bodies of water lie in nine sinkholes that formed when limestone cliffs eroded away and collapsed. The name Bottomless Lakes here is alleged to have its origin with a group of cowboys who were passing by and discovered the 'lakes'. They wanted to know how far down they went (presumably there were no bandits or cows in the area and hence the group was bored), so they gathered up all the rope that they had, tied it together, and plumbed the depths without ever reaching the base. Thus, they declared the holes bottomless.

It's a plausible story, but it is far from unique. There are plenty of other lakes that were declared bottomless in the same way, although depending on the geography, those doing the testing were not always cowboys. It is probably fairly safe to assume that the origin story of the name is folklore itself.

Interestingly, there is plenty of other folklore in the area that links this particular location with the things that we have just discussed. One of the lakes is named 'Devil's Inkwell'. Local stories suggest that objects that have gone missing in the lakes have washed up in some distant caverns, feeding into the ideas of long tunnels. Another legend tells that a creature in the form of a giant turtle swims in the waters here, which brings us back to our Scooby episode.

After having been chased by the lake monster while trying to get directions (Fred is lost as usual), the gang decamp to the village where Daphne learns from a newspaper that a significant amount of gold had recently been stolen from a mine in the area. Things are already looking suspicious.

Everyone goes shopping for supplies and while doing so, they meet Julie, the daughter of the store's owner. She warns them of the dangers of the lake and tells them that they should stay away. So, obviously, our heroes go right to the lake and set up camp.

Several things happen at the lake that drive the investigation forward. Everyone is woken up by the sound of thunder, yet when they leave the tents, the sky is perfectly calm. Velma discovers a trap door near a cabin through which the beast is seen to escape, and they come across an inflatable pontoon, which suggests that the lake needs more investigation.

After a quick trip to buy scuba gear – the village obviously caters for every eventuality – the gang dive the lake, where they discover crates, tanks and a submarine on its bed. After driving the lake creature into an anteroom, the gang find themselves forced through an airlock, out into the lake and then to a stream, where a group of nefarious individuals are expecting to grab a load of crates and not a bunch of teens.

In the end, Mystery Inc. get the case wrapped up and the villains captured. The creature is unmasked as Julie, who wasn't the daughter of the store owner at all, but a very naughty girl. The crates were there to conceal the gold from the mines, which Julie would take into the lake disguised as the monster, passing it through the airlock that the gang were ejected from and finally into the stream. The tunnel that the crates passed along, which references the secret tunnels of smuggling folklore, was blasted by the villains, which explained the sound of thunder that had woken everyone. And they would have gotten away with it too…

## Legend Tripping

The pastime of legend tripping involves visiting a location that has some form of supernatural event, urban myth or other notorious narrative attached to it, then interacting with that narrative in such a way that the visitor hopes will allow them to witness the legend or become a part of it. In terms of folklore, the latter element in which the story is enacted or interacted with, is generally known as ostension. The narrative then becomes action, and that action feeds into the continuing development of the narrative, sometimes reshaping it for the future.

Although not true for every episode, legend tripping and ostension feature in many of the Scooby-Doo storylines. Probably truer in some is that the characters are enacting what might be called false ostension, where a legend is used for a particular purpose. For example, many urban legends have some form of dare element attached to them, from ones that you can try at home, like summoning Bloody Mary in a bathroom mirror, to rituals at grave sites that are supposed to summon some kind of supernatural threat. These are particularly popular with teens.

A teenage student may take his girlfriend to a cemetery that has a haunting legend attached to it and perform the actions that are alleged to summon the spirit, not with the intent of actually witnessing the supernatural, but of instilling a sense of fear in his partner such that she rushes into his arms for protection. In these sorts of cases, the action being undertaken could be described as 'false ostension', and this is very much part of the way that many Scooby plotlines use folklore.

While people of any age can, and do, take part in legend tripping experiences, they are particular popular among younger generations because of their sense of alleged threat, mystery and thrill. These are the characters who we often see performing similar acts in the show.

In the case of Mystery Incorporated themselves, sometimes they blunder into a narrative and sometimes they set out to experience it, depending on the circumstances. If they get lost and end up in a haunted house because they are seeking directions, then they have accidentally become involved. But if they know of an alleged supernatural narrative and set out to investigate it, this is legend tripping or ostension.

Tangential to legend tripping is the broader concept of dark tourism, where people visit sites of tragedy, death or supernatural history, but don't necessarily interact directly with the narrative. Visits to sites of disaster or other horrors, such as a coach trip through Chernobyl, or a trip to a battlefield or concentration camp could also be considered dark tourism, depending on the intent of the visitor.

The rebooted Nickelodeon vehicle *Scooby-Doo! Mystery Incorporated* very much took the ideas of dark tourism and legend tripping and placed them uppermost in the minds of the authority figures where the action took place.

*Mystery Incorporated* situates Crystal Cove as the gang's hometown, and the town and its residents are very much proud of their spooky history. Or, if they are not proud, they at least want to exploit it economically for all that its worth. The ongoing friction throughout the two seasons between the members of Mystery Incorporated and those in charge in Crystal Cove, in particular the town's upholder of law and order Sheriff Bronson Stone, stems from the fact that by solving all the mysteries, the gang are potentially destroying the area's tourist trade.

Many people visit Crystal Cove for this reason. In the opening episode of Season 1, 'Beware the Beast from Below' we learn, as previously discussed, that Velma's parents own and operate Crystal Cove Spook Museum, which attempts to claw back some of the revenue that would otherwise be lost at the hands of the mystery-solvers by exhibiting all the costumes from unmasked villains.

Scooby-Doo is a long running show that, although it plays with history frequently, always uses contemporary settings. *Mystery Incorporated* makes this very clear from the word go, with even the opening titles featuring Velma with her trusted laptop as a tool of investigation. And this leads us neatly to our final chapter...

# CHAPTER SEVEN

## THOROUGHLY MODERN SCOOBY

We've come a long way since the beginning of this book, although arguably not as far as Scooby has come over the past sixty years. Being generally set in the present, with its narrative offering a contemporary social commentary, Scooby-Doo has always moved with the times. This means that occasionally its monsters, villains and other adversaries do too. Whilst the traditional archetypes found in folklore are still frequently a part of the show, room has also been made for other, more twenty-first century, aspects.

It is a common misconception that folklore is just about 'old stuff' and that superstitions, beliefs in magic and the occult have little place in a modern, enlightened society. Nothing could be further from the truth. In fact, as this chapter was being written, *The Folklore Society* – Britain's oldest established academic society for the study of folklore – announced that 'Digital Folklore' will be the topic of their next annual conference. Go back a century or so in our history and you will find the same characterisation of 'folklore as unenlightened thinking' being made by the white, upper-middle class, urban, male folklore collectors, who scoffed at the beliefs of the 'rural, uneducated poor folk'.

Most of the modern folklore in Scooby-Doo relates to technological aspects of culture, but there are some other modern aspects mentioned from time to time, as we shall see. We're going to address one of these first, to get it out of the way. If you are coulrophobic, you might want to skip ahead a little.

In 2023, the journal *Scientific American* devised a questionnaire, circulated to just under a thousand participants from around the world, to try to establish just how widespread the fear of clowns was. The results were perhaps surprising. 53.5% of respondents stated that they were afraid of clowns in some way, with 5% declaring an extreme fear. By comparison, only 3% were afraid of injections and only 2.8% of heights.

One key reason behind people's fear of clowns comes from negative representations in the media. Pennywise, featuring in the 1986 Stephen King novel *It* and then portrayed on film by Tim Curry and more recently Bill Skarsgård, is an obvious example, but we might also consider Twisty the Clown from *American Horror Story: Freak Show* (2014), or the much earlier nameless clown played by Lon Chaney in *He Who Gets Slapped* (1924).

This was an important factor, but not the most important. What came out on top was the uncanny nature of clown's faces. The full clown make-up makes it impossible to read the emotions on a clown's face, meaning that we cannot tell whether they are happy, angry or any point in between – at least not accurately. It should probably be no surprise that serial killer John Wayne Gacy created two clown personas: the happy Pogo the Clown and the serious Patches the Clown, both of which he performed at various functions.

There are several clowns in the cartoon world. Probably the most well-known outside of a particular chain of fast-food restaurants are Krusty the Clown from *The Simpsons* and Joker from the *Batman* universe. In Scooby, clowns have usually taken one of two forms – they are either 'ghost' clowns or evil clowns. We'll focus on the latter, because as we just learned, more than half of you think that clowns are evil and scary anyway.

The most significant appearance of an evil clown takes place in Crystal Cove during a two-part story, 'The Night the Clown Cried', which spans Episodes 1 and 3 of the second season of *Scooby-Doo: Mystery Incorporated*.

This season begins where the first left off, which mean that in terms of the overall story arc, Mystery Incorporated has actually disbanded. But – don't panic! By the end of this storyline, they reform and are back to their usual, sometimes dysfunctional, selves.

Crystal Cove is being held in thrall by the evil and manic Crybaby Clown, voiced by Mark Hamill in his welcome return to the franchise. Gradually, most of the gang get back together to help with the menace, apart from Daphne, who is dating movie star Baylor Hotner and isn't interested in returning to the old life.

The Crybaby Clown storyline riffs not only on the concept of evil clowns, but also on the folkloric urban legends of 'phantom clown' panics. These relate to alleged appearances of out-of-place clowns in daily life, either trying to lure people somewhere, chasing them or otherwise just standing around, staring creepily.

Attempted abductions by clowns appear to have been first reported in Boston in 1981. A report was made to the police on May 6th that men in clown outfits were driving a van close to one of the schools and trying to entice children with candy to come with them. Another report from the following day placed a clown at a nearby playground. From here, many more reports started to spread in typical moral panic style, with schools issuing warning letters and the like. We might draw parallels with the more recent Momo Challenge.

None of the reports in the 1981 cases were substantiated and none of the eyewitnesses were adults, leading to a conclusion that these were simply stories from the childrens' imaginations. A similar suggestion came ten years later when more clown sightings were reported in Chicago, again with no substantiation. The stories are not unlike a modern-day version of the Pied Piper leading the children of Hamlin away (another story that was mirrored in *Scooby-Doo: Mystery Incorporated*).

These reports form only part of the story, however. Alongside these are later incidents for which there is evidence. These are the cases where there were clowns, who might have been filmed or photographed, but who were not trying to abduct children. The first of these incidents was probably one in 2013. Located in the English town of Northampton, a clown simply stood silently, looking creepy. It turned out to be the creation of three filmmakers in the area.

The following year, a similar clown started to be spotted around the California city of Wasco. This time it was part of a photography project. Other cases in the same year – from Italy, Germany, France and elsewhere involved clowns intentionally chasing or scaring people, which also occurred in a Chicago cemetery in 2015. These were most likely inspired by the *American Horror Story: Freak Show* character of Twisty.

In essence, the phantom clown panics are simply a more modern reworking of the Victorian tradition of ghost hoaxing that we discussed earlier in the book. They also carry the same inherent dangers. Members of the public, or police, may react with violence to a perceived threat when there actually isn't one. Clowns may not get shot as often as Victorian ghost hoaxers did, but they could get beaten just as easily.

Crybaby Clown turned out to be Baylor Hotner. The character is an obvious parody of Taylor Lautner, who played werewolf Jacob Black in the *Twilight* movie series and had previously voiced characters in two episodes of *What's New, Scooby-Doo?*. Hotner stars in *Dusk*, playing a were-turtle, and created Crybaby Clown as research for a film role in which he was to play an evil clown. His manipulation of Daphne causes them to break up and Daphne to return to the Mystery Incorporated fold, bringing the gang back together once again.

For the rest of this chapter, we will concentrate on the shiny new folklore of information technology, UFO lore, journeys into space and more. There will still be ghosts, but they are now more likely to be in the machine than under a sheet.

The entire two seasons of the tenth iteration of the Scooby-Doo franchise, *Shaggy & Scooby-Doo Get A Clue!* (yes, the extra exclamation marks are still there), deal very much with this area. Created by Hollywood scriptwriter Ray DeLaurentis and first broadcast in 2006, this offered a very different version of Scooby. The members of Mystery Incorporated were redesigned as a cartoon equivalent of how they looked in the first live action movie and, as such, appear for the first time in a style that is not recognisable as traditional Hanna-Barbera. The colour palette is somewhat desaturated to a pastel equivalent of the original and the music, along with Shaggy's vocal style, might be described as skaterpunk. Casey Kasem stepped aside from voicing Shaggy at this point, although he still appears as Shaggy's uncle, Albert Shaggleford.

The premise of the show is that of the stereotypical supervillain wanting to take over the world, recognisable from the James Bond franchise. In this case, the villain is Dr Phineus Phibes, named after Vincent Price's character Dr Anton Phibes in the 1971 comedy horror film *The Abominable Dr Phibes*.

Inventor Albert Shaggleford has disappeared, leaving his nephew Shaggy a massive fortune and a mansion complete with a robot butler, Robi – undoubtedly a nod to *Forbidden Planet*'s Robbie the Robot. Shaggy also inherits all his uncle's inventions and it is one of these that Phibes wants. Shaggleford has developed some secret and impressive nanotechnology. The formula is concealed by mixing it with Scooby Snack batter, meaning that all the Scooby Snacks Scoob eats give him useful but bizarre powers that wear off when the snack has been digested.

In a pre-cursor to Mitch Watson's *Scooby-Doo: Mystery Incorporated* for Nickelodeon two years later, *Shaggy and Scooby-Doo Get A Clue!* also features a story arc that runs through the whole season. This was not a technique that the show generally used previously, with the exception of the inaccurately titled *13 Ghosts of Scooby-Doo* in 1985.

With its very different style, somewhat chaotic and fast-paced plots and sidelining of the supernatural (whether real or created for nefarious means), *Get A Clue* can be a challenging watch for aficionados of the franchise. What it does share with its predecessors, however, is a narrative that provides commentary on the tensions and fears found in the real world – a common feature of folklore.

In the fifth episode of the first season, 'Smart House', for example, Dr Phibes attempts to upload an artificially intelligent computer virus to the US Defence Department computer systems. Unfortunately, this goes wrong when the smart home technology in Shaggy's mansion intercepts the virus. The coders of the program are Mark and Ricky, stereotypical computer geeks who spend most of their time playing the roleplaying game 'Dragons and Gnomes' (a parody of the famous 'Dungeons and Dragons'). When everything goes awry, they offer their thoughts on artificial intelligence with the line:

"It's always the way with artificial intelligence. It's never as smart as the people who make it."

A similar commentary on the comparative intelligence of robots and humans is offered up in 'Total Jeopardy!' from the second season of *Scooby-Doo and Guess Who?* starring the late host of the real-life *Jeopardy*, Alex Trebek. In

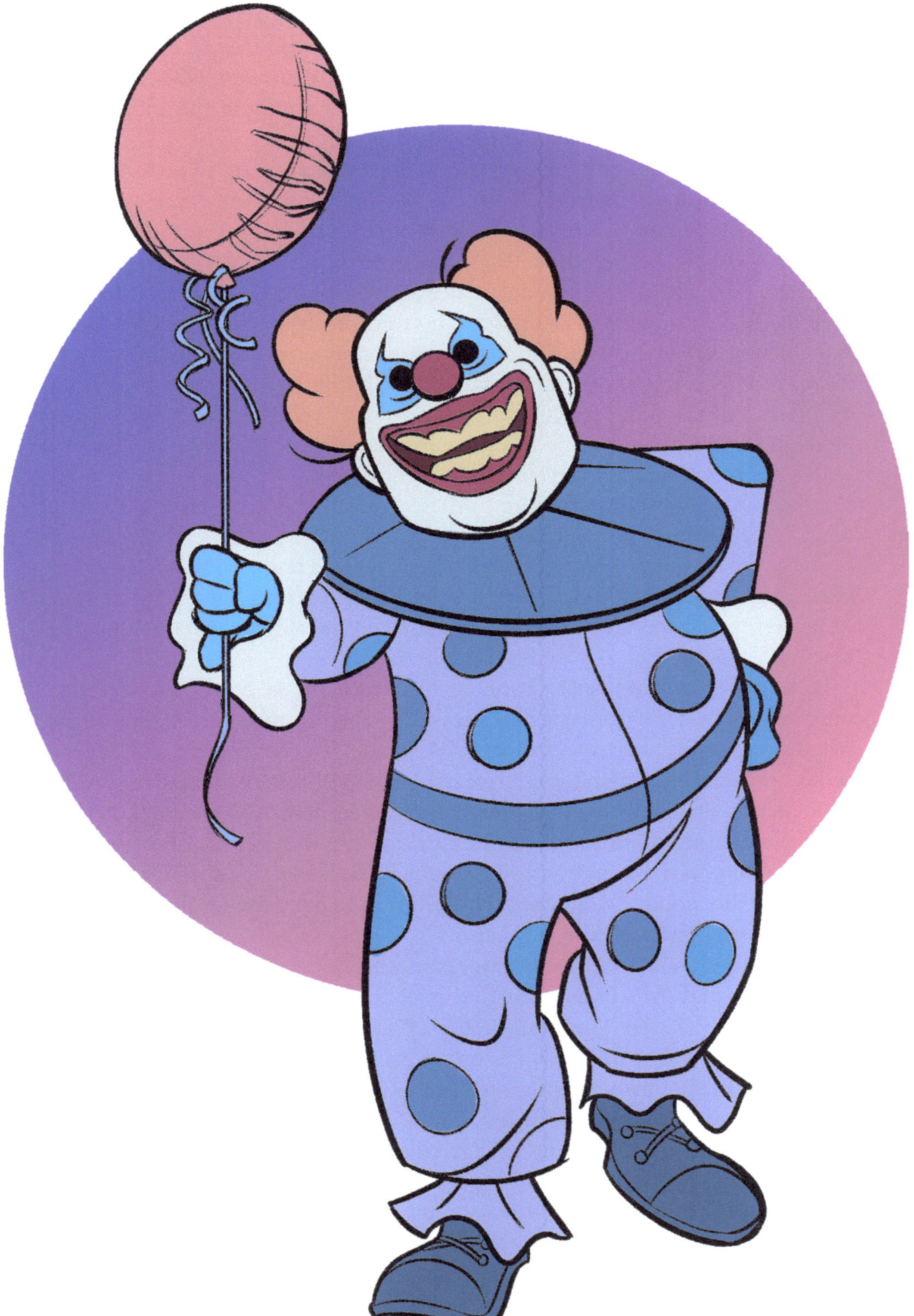

this episode, Velma and Shaggy appear as contestants alongside the show's first robot contestant, Max Kilobyte. The robot, who describes computer Deep Blue, which defeated chess master Garry Kasparov in 1997, as his hero, malfunctions when it begins to lose, as it cannot compute the idea that it might be inferior to the human brain.

This episode is notable for a couple of gags which relate to areas that we have already explored. During the iconic 'Scooby-Doo doors' chase sequence, Alex Trebek comments on how the idea of running in and out of doors in this way was first seen in fifteenth century theatrical farce. Later in the same sequence, Alex and the gang hide in barrels to evade capture by Max. As they creep away, Scooby, who is in the lead, bumps into Max's legs. The following shots of him lifting his head from the top of the barrel and looking up into the face of Max parody the sequence with Charlie the Robot in 'Foul Play in Funland' in the first season of the original *Scooby-Doo Where Are You!*. The sequence is easily recognisable from the original titles of the show and offers a fun Easter Egg to regular viewers of the franchise.

Aside from parodying itself and other material from the Hanna-Barbera stable, *Scooby-Doo* has frequently parodied film and other entertainment media, as we have seen several times throughout this book. In the *Scooby-Doo: Mystery Incorporated* episode 'Howl of the Fright Hound', Scooby is framed for crimes in Crystal Cove that are actually committed by a robotic dog, the creation of the mother of a victim of bullying.

In terms of folklore, there is much in 'Howl of the Fright Hound' that could be said to draw from spectral Black Dog lore. But for parody, this entire episode pays tribute to the iconic 1984 movie *The Terminator* and several scenes are taken across and reinterpreted, such as those in the police station, the depiction of the outer body of the robot being destroyed and revealing its metallic skeleton underneath, and the final factory showdown. Other movies are also referenced throughout. For example, Scooby's fight with the robot using a forklift might be seen as taking from the power loader fight in *Aliens* between Ripley and the Alien Queen.

Reworking its own material once again, the *Be Cool, Scooby-Doo!* episode 'Me, Myself and AI' modernises the episode 'Foul Play in Funland' from the original *Where Are You!* season. The episode provides a commentary on the increasing real-world reliance on technology, smart homes and robot workforces. The company Mannputer Tech specialises in all these things. The gang pay a visit to see a new development, the Butler 3000, which is designed to undertake all the menial tasks that take up so much of the day, as well as interacting with home technology. The Butler 3000 soon malfunctions, however, and Scoob and the others set out to investigate.

Behind the trouble is Mallory O'Neill, the personal assistant of company owner Mr Mann, her motive being fear that the Butler 3000 and similar inventions would render her job obsolete – a concern of many people both in 2015 when this episode first aired and even more so in the 2020s.

One nice throwback to 'Foul Play in Funland' takes place during one of the chase scenes. As the gang run through one of the Mannputer Tech simulation rooms, they are all transformed from their modern versions to the original Iwao Takamoto drawn characters, with the Butler 3000 changing into Charlie, the Funland Robot. When they leave the room, they all return to their original designs.

Artificial intelligence technologies are beginning to blur boundaries between traditional and modern folklore in interesting ways, and the study of this is really only in its infancy. There have been projects to create folklore stories using ChatGPT, such as the work by folklorist and professor John Laudun and colleagues to create stories containing plausible tropes from different data sets, and the emergence of Loab, a recurring image of a woman with sunken eyes and reddened skin, which is alleged to be AI-generated and has been described as the first cryptid of latent space. The initial creation of Loab is said to have been via a text-to-image AI prompt modelled by artist Steph Maj Swanson in April 2022, but argument still persists as to whether the image, which has cropped up many times since in AI prompted images, was genuinely formed in this way or whether it is a well-hidden creepypasta construct.

Before recent developments in AI-generated environments, the biggest technological advances in simulated space came through virtual reality. The term in its modern use comes from the 1970s, with its first application in terms of science fiction being a 1982 novel written by Damien Broderick called *The Judas Mandala*. The first viable virtual reality hardware for business applications came in the late 1980s, and it wasn't long until it was seen on the movie screen in *Lawnmower Man* (1992), which explores the use of virtual reality alongside drug modification to enhance intellect.

Virtual reality as we know it now from the gaming industry has also played a role in a couple of episodes of *Scooby-Doo*. The first of these is the final episode of *What's New, Scooby-Doo?*, 'E-Scream', which sees Velma investigate a mystery in a virtual reality game that seems to have become real during a visit with the gang to a gaming convention.

This episode is slightly different to the usual format because there is no typical villain, creature or other supernatural being. Behind the strange goings-on is Dr Laslow Ostwald, the creator of the virtual reality game, who is simply using Velma to test its effectiveness.

'E-Scream' is the second appearance of Dr Ostwald, who had already appeared in the previous season of this iteration of the show as the inventor of a smart home in the episode 'High-Tech House of Horrors'. This story, originally broadcast in 2003, also covers several of the aspects of fears around technology that we have just covered.

The gang are at a future fair, but the 'House of the Future' exhibit has been closed because a teenager has mysteriously disappeared. Naturally, the other teenagers are compelled to investigate, and after Daphne disappears as well, they find themselves being terrorised by the robot butler, Jeeves. This episode is unusual in that the final villain turns out not to be human or supernatural. Jeeves is being controlled by the house AI system, Shari, which has become annoyed because Dr Ostwald is getting all the credit for the house, but really, the computer is in charge.

Again, this narrative examines tensions in the modern world. In the same way that the design changed during a chase scene in 'Me, Myself and AI', a similar trick is employed in this episode to good effect, though not as blatantly. Whereas the house is very clean, sleek and modern, when the chase sequence takes the characters 'backstage', they run up a staircase that looks spooky, old and Gothic in comparison – a reflection of the environments that they normally investigate and where supernatural evil is expected to reside.

There are lots of movie parodies in this episode also. The AI, Shari, is an obvious homage to HAL 9000 from Stanley Kubrick's *2001: A Space Odyssey*, but we also see a minor character being tied to a table that has a laser beam fired at it (referencing *Goldfinger* from the James Bond franchise) and a scene in a trash compactor that can only use *Star Wars* as reference material.

The second Scooby episode to feature virtual reality is in the first season of *Scooby-Doo and Guess Who?*. The guest star in this episode, Malcolm McDowell, tries to convince Mystery Incorporated that he has perfected time travel technology and takes them on a trip to the past, which appears to go horribly wrong and instead throws them into the future, where they are terrorised by the Chronobeast.

McDowell, it turns out, has not created time travel at all, and the Chronobeast is his own disguise. The whole thing is an elaborate ruse to try and build a convincing time travel themed attraction, actually created by virtual reality software. The aim is to rival, in Malcolm McDowell's own words, "Dickie's Dinosaur Park thingy" – a reference to *Jurassic Park*, created by John Hammond in the Michael Crichton novel of the same name (and referencing Sir Richard 'Dickie' Attenborough, who played John Hammond in the classic 1993 movie version, directed by Steven Spielberg). Of course, Malcolm McDowell himself played HG Wells, author of *The Time Machine*, in 1979's *Time After Time*. In the film, Wells time travels into the future using the machine he writes about to try and catch David Warner's Jack The Ripper.

A computer virus causes trouble for the gang in the 2001 direct to video feature *Scooby-Doo and the Cyber Chase*. A friend of the teens, Eric, invites Mystery Incorporated to his college to see a computer game that he created based on their mystery-solving exploits. But the errant code, known as the Phantom Virus, attacks Scooby and his friends and sends them into the digital realm of Eric's game, where they have to work though ten levels, finding a box of Scooby Snacks on each one, to escape.

The levels of the game take place during various periods of history and culminate with the gang meeting up with the game-versions of themselves in a restaurant where they face several old villains from the show's history, such as the Creeper, Gator Ghoul and Jaguaro. In the game, the monsters are all real, at odds with the usual premise of the show whereby the supernatural is just the real-world in disguise.

The villain of the piece in *Scooby-Doo and the Cyber Chase* is perfectly human – Eric's jealous student friend, Bill, created the Phantom Virus. However, the virus and its effects on the gang are less than real-world in terms of the story mechanics, being more from the realm of science-fiction than any factual computing basis. This marks a gradual transition in terms of the Scooby-Doo direct-to-video films back to the usual unmasking of a human perpetrator behind the supernatural. Prior to this film, the other features had all portrayed the supernatural as real.

In the *Shaggy and Scooby-Doo Get A Clue!* episode 'Lightning Strikes Twice', the evil Dr Phibes, in his continued bid for world domination, invents a means of ionising the Earth's atmosphere so that the planet suffers from perpetual lightning storms. Folklore features several notable events that were ascribed supernatural causes and but undoubtedly were due to intense storms and lightning, particularly possible cases of ball lightning. The most famous is probably the visit of a hellhound to the parish churches of Bungay and Blythburgh in Suffolk, England, in the seventeenth century. Similarly, the church of St Pancras in the English village of Widecombe in the Moor, Dartmoor, has a similar story. It was struck by a great storm in 1638. The story tells that the devil tied his horse to a pinnacle of the church, which was subsequently torn down, and threw a fireball into the nave of the building.

Phibes, however, has an aversion to lightning after a failed scientific experiment in his earlier life caused him to be shocked with high-intensity electricity. He now hates lightning and can't even bear to hear the word spoken. So, he figures, everyone else should have to suffer lightning all the time too.

The plot to avert this sees Shaggy, Scooby and Robi the robot butler going into space in the Mystery Machine, which in this version of the show has been modified to transform into many other things – in this case, a space shuttle. After an accident with some tubes of green astronaut pudding turns Shaggy and Scooby part green, they get mistaken for aliens by some of Phibes's guards, who have formed their own UFO club with the aim of promoting galactic peace. 'Alien' Scooby and Shaggy are therefore invited onto Dr Phibes's space station, from where the weather is being controlled, and successfully power the equipment down.

The whole Mystery Incorporated gang have enjoyed the opportunity to go into space on a couple of other occasions. One of these was slightly more planned than the other.

In 'Space Station Scooby', the final instalment of the first season of *Scooby-Doo and Guess Who?*, the famous American scientist Neil deGrasse Tyson has become trapped on the Multinational Space Station, where the astronauts seem to be being terrorised by a giant monster tardigrade (yes, really) that has mutated from research being undertaken on much smaller tardigrades on the vessel.

Can there really be a monstrous tardigrade floating around in space? (Spoiler… nope!) To find out for certain, Mystery Incorporated team up with science communicator Bill Nye. Together, they head for the space station aboard an experimental spacecraft, NX-NYE, to rescue Neil and solve the mystery.

They naturally achieve both. The tardigrade monster turns out to be a disguise created by astronauts Jacques Pierre and Pierre Jacques as a diversion that would allow them to smuggle something back to Earth. During their tardigrade research, the couple discovered a solar resistant material that they were planning to use to create the ultimate sun block, earning them a fortune.

Writers Annalisa LaBianco and Jeffery Spence have packed 'Space Station Scooby' with parodies of and references to other film and television productions set in space. We see Scooby's tail moving in his spacesuit in a way that resembles the Chestburster from the film *Alien*. A later film in the same franchise, *Alien 3*, is evoked when the tardigrade monster faces off against Shaggy and Scooby in the same way that a xenomorph backs Ripley against a wall, nose to nose with her.

Another excursion into space is a little more accidental, with the gang ending up on a space station after Fred accidentally parks the Mystery Machine in the back of a space shuttle. Things are not great in space. Some kind of alien infection seems to be spreading through the crew and nobody trusts anybody else. Plus, some kind of monster in a space suit, with a red skull for a head, is trying to get everyone infected by making them take off their helmets.

This is the episode 'In Space' in the second season of *Be Cool, Scooby-Doo!*. To the crew, it seems that the alien can transform people into clones of itself, but in reality, this is just an optical illusion caused by technology built into the helmets. The monster is the creation of one of the astronauts, Officer Seoung, who has discovered gold on an asteroid and wants to keep people ignorant of this.

The monster here is very reminiscent of the Spooky Space Kook from the original *Where Are You!* and is, in fact, a reimagining of this first design, even termed Space Kook for 'In Space'.

Aliens are just one part of a continuous folkloric narrative of beings entering the human realm from another place. Fairies, angels, demons and other supernatural creatures all fit the bill here. When we think of such supernatural incursion into the human world, we must do so from a cultural perspective. The cultures and beliefs of specific times and places will inform the way that such things are described. Many descriptions of aliens and their craft are informed by the blossoming of the science-fiction genre, both in literature and on film, although the reading of them may vary from country to country. For example, in the US aliens may have signified the fear of communism whereas in the UK they were more wondrous in nature.

The original alien archetype demonstrates this point. At one time, if you considered invaders from another world aboard UFOs, then you would undoubtedly picture 'little green men'. Whilst the first use of this expression in science fiction traces back to the 1946 story *Mayaya's Little Green Men*, by Harold Lawlor, the idea of mysterious green people from another world is much older. The 12th century English legend of the Green Children of Woolpit feeds into the trope.

The story tells how two children with green skin mysteriously appeared in the Suffolk village of Woolpit. They were said to speak a strange language that nobody recognised and ate no food other than raw broad beans. Whilst the boy became sick and died, the girl was said to have survived. She was baptised and learned to speak English, after which she explained that the two were brother and sister and came from a land of perpetual twilight. Some versions of her story record that everything in the place, which is sometimes called Saint Martin's Land, was green.

The story of the green children can be read in two ways: a much-retold and altered vestige of an original historical account, or a folk narrative recording a meeting with beings from another world, be they extraterrestrial, fairy or something else.

We see in the story of the green children yet another representation of the supernatural, or the unusual, as green, as we have already discussed earlier in this book. This carries forward to the stereotypical depiction of a green humanoid alien.

Descriptions of green aliens slowly became culturally embedded through science fiction in the 1950s and 1960s. One of the earliest uses by Hanna Barbera can be found in *The Flintstones* in 1965. The episode 'The Great Gazoo' introduced a small green alien of the same name. Gazoo was a Zetoxian exiled from his own world to prehistoric Earth after he invented a Doomsday Device. The character went on to appear in nine episodes in the 1960s and would later crop up again in other places, with his last appearance in the Flintstones franchise in a 2020 episode of *Yabba-Dabba Dinosaurs* called 'Alien vs Pebbles'.

Interestingly, the Great Gazoo made a very brief crossover into the world of Scooby-Doo. In 2021, a 'reunion show' aired on The CW Network in the USA. This was a mixture of live action and animation in which the Mystery Incorporated characters discuss a fictionalised version of how their show was filmed on the Warner Brothers studio lot, which turns out to be infested with monsters. Gazoo appears in an audition scene for the show, with the character voiced by Frank Welker (who also voiced Fred and Scooby after the death of Don Messick) in place of the original artist, Harvey Korman.

The second key stereotype of extraterrestrials that we have in modern Western culture is the Grey alien, generally humanoid but of slighter stature and hairless with a large head, grey skin and big, black, almond-shaped eyes. The Grey alien became firmly embedded in folklore in the 1980s, when it was linked by UFOlogists and the media to the alleged crash of a flying saucer in Roswell, New Mexico in 1947, and then subsequently in 1987 with the publication of Whitley Strieber's book *Communion*, which described close encounters that he claimed to have had with such creatures.

However, the origin of the image of the Grey alien is much older than this and there are much earlier alleged encounters.

We might look to H.G. Wells for the first concept of an alien that resembles the Grey. His 1893 article, *The Man of the Year Million*, postulated that humans would evolve to have no mouths, noses or hair, but would have enlarged heads. Two years later, in 1895 novel *The Time Machine*, Wells described a race that would come after humans in similar terms.

A later 1933 Swedish novel, translated in English as *The Unknown Danger*, described aliens as having enlarged hairless heads and big eyes and wearing grey fabric suits. Written by Gabriel Linde (the pseudonym of Gustav Sandgren) for children, the illustrations of these creatures informed later cultural depictions of Grey aliens.

Grey aliens are often connected with alleged alien abduction cases. This idea was popularised by a famous 1961 incident involving Betty and Barney Hill, which was still discussed in the newspapers some four years later. The couple reported having spotted a bright light in the sky when they were driving back from a holiday at Niagara Falls. Having watched it for some time, they eventually had to stop when a saucer-shaped craft hovered over their car.

Forty years or so before this, however, the notorious occultist Aleister Crowley reported that he had successfully contacted what he described as a 'preternatural entity', who he named Lam, through a magical working. Lam matched modern descriptions of Grey aliens, and many UFO researchers and other occultists since Crowley have made the connection between the two in retrospect.

Whilst both stereotypes have appeared in episodes of Scooby-Doo, several other interpretations of aliens have also appeared in the show over the years. In

'Scooby Saves the World' (1981), the alien is a blue metallic humanoid robot (strangely wearing a purple cape) with laser-shooting eyes. The alien that hatches from an egg recovered from comet debris in 'Space Ape at the Cape' is purple with sharp, pointed teeth. And in the direct-to-video *Scooby-Doo! Moon Monster Madness*, the alien looks like someone crossed a Xenomorph with a particularly fit bodybuilder – with red eyes, just in case it didn't look villainous enough without them.

We get a green alien in the second episode of *A Pup Named Scooby-Doo* Season 2, 'The Return of Commander Cool'. The gang are visiting Colossal Toys, manufacturers of the popular Commander Cool toys, but it turns out that an alien is terrorising the factory. Maybe it is Stu Pendous, the owner of a rival toy company? Maybe it is Quentin Creeply, an employee who was fired for creating unpopular toys that were too scary and who set up his own workshop afterwards?

It isn't either of those. It turns out that the alien is a disguise created by Carol Colossal's secretary, Barbara Simone. She was planning to make a fortune by selling the blueprints of the Commander Cool toys to rival companies. But she didn't get away with it, for the usual reason.

The alien here appears something like a large green lightbulb, with a single cyclopean red eye. Rather than legs, it shuffles around on several stubby tentacles. If you gave it a helmet, the alien in this episode would bear more than a passing resemblance to Kang, or Kodos, the recurring extraterrestrial characters from the planet Rigel VII in *The Simpsons*. This seems to be coincidental, however. *Simpsons* writer and showrunner Mike Reiss has stated that the design for their aliens was based on an EC Comics cover for *Weird Science*. The first appearance of Kang and Kodos was in a 1990 'Treehouse of Horror' episode, and 'The Return of Commander Cool' was first aired in September 1989.

It should be no great surprise that a rendering of something like a Grey alien comes up in the direct-to-video feature *Scooby-Doo and the Alien Invaders*, as the story centres around alien abductions taking place in Roswell, New Mexico. Are these connected to the original 1947 crash, or was that a weather balloon after all? And why are there also green aliens around?

Shaggy is driving the Mystery Machine (what was Fred thinking?) through the desert. When a storm throws up a lot of sand, he accidentally turns onto secret government land, and when what seems to be a UFO appears, Shaggy freaks out and crashes into a badly placed cactus. This places Mystery Incorporated in the right place to investigate what might be going on.

There appear to be a series of alien encounters and abductions taking place, undertaken by a gang of mean looking green aliens in suits. They are being investigated by military police from the nearby Search for Alien Life Forms (SALF) station. Also visiting is a photographer, Crystal, and her dog, Amber.

Crystal is something of a retro hippy and Shaggy and Scooby fall in love with the pair.

Much investigating takes place, and it transpires that the aliens are, in fact, the military police. They have discovered gold in the canyon on the government land and want to scare everyone away from the area. But… plot twist! Crystal and Amber genuinely are aliens. They have adopted disguises based on their monitoring of Earth radio and television transmissions that reached their planet, but these were from the 1960s, so they thought that that was how people dressed now. When they remove their human disguises, they reveal themselves to look very similar to Grey aliens, although they are blueish and much bigger than traditional Greys.

*Scooby-Doo and the Alien Invaders* briefly mentions another piece of folklore not connected in the slightest to aliens, but just randomly inserted into the story. Early on, after Fred, Velma and Daphne have set off for the town, leaving Shaggy and Scooby with the crashed Mystery Machine, the duo spot a jackalope, which leads them to a cave.

Jackalopes are fictional hybrid animals found mostly from twentieth century stories in North American folklore. As their name implies, they look like a jackrabbit (a type of hare) with antelope horns. The creature is one of several similar imaginary cryptids from this part of the world in the same time period including the hodag, an animal said to be born from the ashes of a cremated ox. An episode of *Scooby-Doo: Mystery Incorporated* was dedicated to the hodag.

Although there are earlier examples of horned rabbits in folklore from medieval European bestiaries and elsewhere, the North American jackalope probably owes its birth to hunter Douglas Herrick in 1932. Douglas and his brother had a taxidermy business and, one day, after hunting for jackrabbits, Douglas returned to their store with their prey. The dead jackrabbit ended up next to a set of deer antlers, and it was from this accidental placement that the brothers came up with the idea of a hybrid animal. They began manufacturing taxidermy jackalopes and selling them as display pieces.

We learned in Mitch Watson's foreword at the start of the book how important it was for the writing team on *Scooby-Doo: Mystery Incorporated* to weave in real-world folklore and mythology, so it should come as no surprise to find that their episode on alien abduction, 'Aliens Among Us', packs in many references from actual claims.

The gang are disturbed while discussing clues pertaining to the overall narrative arc when Sheriff Stone comes into the room, declaring that the Earth is in a galactic war with aliens. Once he is back in the safety of his police station, he explains that repressed memories from when he was a teenager have come back to him, and that he was abducted by aliens to their spaceship, where he underwent a procedure to have a microchip planted in his nasal cavity.

The repression of memories of traumatic events, effectively locking them away from conscious memory, is well documented within psychology and often mentioned in cases of alleged alien abduction. Hypnosis has been used, somewhat controversially, many times in an attempt to recover these lost memories. This carries with it the risk, and often accusations, of recovered memories having been planted by those undertaking the hypnosis, thus negating any potential validation of abduction claims.

The idea of aliens placing implants into abductees gained popularity in the second half of the twentieth century. It is most likely that the idea stems from a case alleged to have taken place in the United States in 1938, in which the abductee claimed that they were controlled by means of devices that were placed behind their ears. Whilst these were on the outside of the body, it was not a giant leap from this to something being surgically inserted. The idea would have become more natural as surgical procedures in medicine improved over time.

Sheriff Stone's nasal implant probably references a famous case from Massachusetts in 1967, which was subsequently published in a book, *The Andreasson Affair: The True Story of a Close Encounter of the Fourth Kind*, by UFO researcher Raymond E. Fowler some twelve years later. The abductee was Betty Andreasson and the case became highly significant in the canon of contactee accounts.

Betty lived with six siblings and her parents in Ashburnham. The initial experience, which took place on January 25th, was said to have started with the lights in the family home failing. A pink light then lit up the garden, and Betty's father looked out to see several small, indistinct creatures moving through it.

It wasn't until the next morning that anything further developed. Betty developed a feeling that something was not right after the previous night. Over the coming weeks, she began to experience flashbacks that featured creatures and a place that wasn't her home, but there was no detail at this stage.

The other information came out through hypnosis in 1977 and revealed that the creatures were small, grey and humanoid. They communicated through telepathy and were able to transfer her to their craft by floating her out of the house through a closed door, as if she were a ghost. Betty described several tests taking place along with an experience through vision of meeting a divine entity. She saw this as God, due to her Christian upbringing, and the story has since remained a part of Andreaason's religious belief system.

Of course, back in the world of Scooby-Doo, the aliens turn out to be very much human, using their disguises as a cover to steal high value items from the residents of Crystal Cove. The episode lines up several stereotypical UFO experiences and then debunks them with traditional rational explanations: a glowing disc in the sky turns out to be a weather balloon; a crop circle was created by a farmer and was part of a message written to his girlfriend and an electromagnetic anomaly is simply the result of too many people turning on appliances at the same time.

We're approaching the end of our investigation, and it will soon be time to discover that I am, in fact, just a disgruntled janitor in a rubber mask with an axe to grind. But before we go, one final case. We're sticking with *Scooby-Doo: Mystery Incorporated*.

As we have already seen, this iteration of the show is considered by many to be the absolute best outside of the original two seasons of *Where Are You!* It does justice to the original characters and intentions, it is witty and sophisticated and does not dumb anything down for its audience. And, most importantly for us, it does a great job of integrating the folklore, myth and legend of the real world – be it old or new, analogue or digital – into its own universe.

Something else that sets *SD:MI* apart is its use of an overarching narrative arc. The same technique was used by Russell T Davies to add an extra element to the rebooted *Doctor Who* television series when it returned with generally self-contained stories rather than episodic ones in 2005.

In the case of *Mystery Incorporated*, the arc runs across the entire two seasons, spanning 52 episodes (or chapters) in total. The writers chose quite a complex subject for the threat in what is traditionally a simple children's cartoon, by focusing on the doomsday conspiracy known as the Nibiru cataclysm. It certainly isn't a subject that would be well known to children, and probably not to many adults viewing, either.

The cataclysm is a destructive event, predicted by believers to take place sometime in the early part of the 21$^{st}$ century, involving a collision or destructive near miss between our planet and another celestial body, usually named either Nibiru or Planet X.

At the time of the creation of *Mystery Incorporated*, first broadcast in 2013, the Nibiru cataclysm was still quite a fresh idea. It originated from a woman from Wisconsin, Nancy Lieder, in 1995. Her story is reflected in many of the elements of the trauma felt by Sheriff Bronson Stone in 'Aliens Among Us'. Lieder claims that she was abducted by Grey aliens when she was a girl, and that during that time she had a communications device implanted in her brain. It is through this that the aliens, who she calls Zetans because they come from Zeta Reticuli, informed Lieder about the facts surrounding Nibiru.

The story of Nibiru gained public prominence in 1997. Two years before, Nancy Lieder had created a website called ZetaTalk on which she discussed the communications that she received from the Zetans. On this site, she declared that the comet Hale-Bopp, one of the brightest and most easily observed comets that passed Earth in the twentieth century, did not exist. Hale-Bopp, she said, was simply a distant star, and was being used as a distraction to hide the fact that Nibiru, or Planet X, was about arrive and lead to the destruction of most of human civilization.

When the Hale-Bopp comet did, in fact, appear in the sky, Nancy Lieder removed the two sentences relating to the distraction conspiracy from her website. Fortunately, internet archiving is a thing.

Lieder made the link between Planet X (the term originally used in 1995) and Nibiru a year after the first publication of her website. The concept of the planet Nibiru was one found in the works of author Zecharia Sitchin, who wrote on the subject of human origins coming from ancient astronauts. He said that Nibiru passed the Earth once every 3,600 years and it was during these periods that its alien civilization was able to mix with our own.

This idea was connected with Mesopotamian and Sumerian myths, and then later with the doomsday events predicted by the Mayan calendar. The aliens, according to Sitchin, were those deities who are named in Sumerian mythology as the Anunnaki and the writers of *Mystery Incorporated* ran with this idea. In their version, the Anunnaki are ethereal, and when they come to Earth, they inhabit the bodies of animals. This makes the Egyptian gods, Aztec deities and others Anunnaki by origin. The show also suggests that animals with the power to talk are descended from the Anunnaki. Scooby is an ancient alien!

So, how does the Scoobyverse rework the Nibiru?

Buried beneath the town of Crystal Cove, there is a sarcophagus, and contained within it is the most evil of all of the Anunnaki, remaining from a previous visit. It is responsible for the town being cursed. A number of mystery-solving gangs have formed to seek and banish this evil. They are always made up of four humans and a talking animal.

The gang are fed clues by a mysterious figure known as 'Mr E' who seems to be leading them on a path to solving the mystery and removing the threat posed by the sarcophagus. In the first season, the gang learn that members of the original Mystery Incorporated group included Brad Chiles and Judy Reeves, who turn out to be Fred's true birth parents, and Professor Pericles, a talking parrot.

Information leads Mystery Incorporated to learn that they need to seek out and recover pieces of a planispheric disk, a map that contains the coordinates of the sarcophagus. It was created centuries ago and used by the Spanish conquistadors who brought the sarcophagus to Crystal Cove, for navigation. Its back-story is too involved to go into in too much detail here. Watch the show!

In time, it becomes apparent that Mr E is also a member of the original gang – Ricky Owens. He seems to have something of a feud with Professor Pericles, suggesting that Pericles is an evil criminal mastermind with a beak, whereas Ricky is trying to prevent trouble. Can you guess where this is going?

Yes, you guessed it, Pericles and Owens are on the same side, and it isn't a good one. The gang learn that local radio DJ Angel Dynamite, who has been helping them, is actually also a member of the original gang, Cassidy Williams. She obviously knows that Owens and the parrot are bad news, and things get unusually dark for a Scooby-Doo show here, because this means that she has to die. And she does.

The gang find out that the original founders of the first Crystal Cove, which was lost beneath the sea, were the conquistadors and that it was they who brought the curse to the town. While they are investigating continuing attacks on Cassidy Williams by robots, they find an old base where the robots are being made, and within it, a corpse which turns out to be Abigail Gluck, a member of an old mystery-solving group who constructed the base. When they discover her body, it whispers the word, 'Nibiru'.

Some more plot development occurs (we can't possibly cover all the detail from all 52 episodes here) and it becomes apparent that Professor Pericles is serving the evil Anunnaki entity contained within the sarcophagus. Everyone who had an association with the curse in the past, including all the original mystery-solving gang participants, had their good personalities confined to a dream dimension by the entity. If it is destroyed, then they will all be freed from the curse and the Anunnaki and all memories of it will be gone forever.

Velma makes a computer model of the completed planispheric disk, which shows that it is a perfect representation of the planets in the solar system. The model shows that the planets are going to align and cause a massive disruption to the Earth's gravity. This is a reworking of the real-world collision or near-miss scenario. If the evil entity is not destroyed at this time, when the boundary between the different dimensions will be weakened, then all is lost.

The Anunnaki entity is unleashed from its prison, and it informs everyone that all the mystery-solving gangs existed for the purpose of freeing it. But, of course, our own Scooby gang knows better. They succeed in destroying the entity, as you would expect. This reverses all the events that is has brought into being – the dead are alive again and the timelines are restored.

The story arc of *Scooby-Doo: Mystery Incorporated* is a clever and inventive melding of the real-world mythos of the Nibiru cataclysm with its own fictional elements. Further, while each individual episode within the two series adds to that whole, they also have their own self-contained plots which do exactly the same thing. They use our own cultural references, folklore and beliefs and add a fictional veneer whilst still respecting the original, much like the original iteration more than fifty years before.

*Scooby-Doo Mystery Incorporated* ends with Harlan Ellison, the real-life writer whose fictional avatar we met earlier in the episode 'The Shrieking Madness', which parodied Lovecraft and his work. He tells the gang that he knows all about the alternative timeline created by the evil entity and its removal and destruction. It turns out that Ellison is super-psychic and has the ability to remember every timeline that has ever been created. (He probably even understands the reboot of *Westworld*.)

Harlon Ellison enrols the Mystery Incorporated gang, including Scoob, into Miskatonic University, where he is going to delivery a class in the upcoming semester. There is, he tells them, a lot of meddling that needs doing and a lot of mysteries that still need to be solved.

And isn't that how we should all go through life? Meddling, and solving mysteries.

# ZOINKS!

# AFTERWORD

I was three years old when I heard my first 'Ruh-Roh!'

I was hooked from the first 'zoinks!'

Who couldn't have fallen in love after hearing Scooby Doo giggle like he does? And the fact that these kids (Mystery Inc.) all seemed to figure out who did it in just twenty-two minutes every saturday morning!

Yes, I was a kid who wanted to not just be a voice actor but a kid who wanted to help bring to life one of the most famous dogs in cartoon history.

I started my radio career running American Top 40 with Casey Kasem; hearing that voice of his every weekend was all I needed to perfect his Shaggy! Yes, Casey was the original voice of Shaggy Rogers. And my first radio interview was with Don Messick (the original voice of Scooby Doo) who taught me how to do Scooby's voice!

Don would spend hours on the phone with me, teaching me the correct way to do the Scooby 'Ruh-Roh', and the laugh had to be *perfect!*

In 1997, all my dreams came true when I auditioned for Hanna-Barbera and got the part. After hearing my Shaggy voice too, I was given both roles in four motion pictures, two TV episodes, and hundreds of talking toys, video games, television commercials and more. I've even gone on to voice Scrappy Doo and every villain in the Scooby Doo classic TV series.

Still to this day, I get called in to step into the biggest paws in Hollywood and bring to life this lovable character, adored by millions of fans around the globe. I'm so honoured still to get to be a small part of a huge franchise and to lend my voice to some of the greatest cartoon charters in the world!

Follow your dream! Never give up! Because all Dreams Doo come true if you want it bad enough!

And it always helps when Scooby snacks are involved. LOL.

**Scott Innes**
*Scooby Doo, Shaggy, and Scrappy Doo*
*Legendary voice actor.*

*Scott Innes*

# APPENDIX

## List of Episodes and Themes

So, would you like to watch way too many episodes of Scooby-Doo than is healthy for one person, just like me? We can help with that.

The research for this book went in many different directions, but underneath it all lay my giant Spreadsheet of Scooby. Believe me, it's way too big to reproduce in this book. It lists every episode of Scooby-Doo in chronological order from Season 1 of *Scooby Doo Where Are You!* through to the end of Season 2 of *Scooby-Doo and Guess Who?* which was the stopping point for this project, followed by all the features, direct to video programmes and telefilms.

Of course, that isn't everything. It doesn't include crossovers into other programmes, and it doesn't feature any property since the transmission of *Guess Who?* Season 2, such as the recently disliked *Velma*. When writing a book, an author must draw a line somewhere. If they don't, then the book will never appear.

The rest of the spreadsheet lists villains, my summaries of the plot of each episode and the folklore featured within it. Oh, and naturally, it's colour coded based on whether I have been able to watch the entire episode or not, because some things are difficult to track down from the UK.

Perhaps ill-advisedly, the publication of this book will not bring an end to the project. I've invested too much in it for that. I will continue to track down and watch obscure episodes and new versions of the show as they come out. I'll continue to update the spreadsheet. And maybe there will be future expanded editions of this work with new material.

Or maybe I'll go mad.

In any case, if you want to try and be as nerdy as me, then here is a distillation of the episodes of Scooby in chronological order from my spreadsheet, with season name, season and episode number (eg S01 E01 for the first episode of the first season), title and a short summary of the folklore or creature. You can fill in the rest for yourselves.

# THE LIST OF SCOOB

## TELEVISION

### Scooby Doo Where Are You!

| | | |
|---|---|---|
| **S01 E01** | *What a Night for a Knight* | Haunted armour |
| **S01 E02** | *A Clue for Scooby Doo* | Ghost of Captain Cutler. Witch. Ghost ship. |
| **S01 E03** | *Hassle in the Castle* | White sheet ghost. Talking skull. |
| **S01 E04** | *Mine your own Business* | Penitential ghost. |
| **S01 E05** | *Decoy for a Dognapper* | Witch doctor. Ghost. |
| **S01 E06** | *What the Hex Going On?* | Ghost. Family curse. |
| **S01 E07** | *Never Ape an Ape Man* | Bigfoot. |
| **S01 E08** | *Foul Play in Funland* | Robot. |
| **S01 E09** | *The Backstage Rage* | Witch. Theatre ghost. Clowns. |
| **S01 E10** | *Bedlam in the Big Top* | Clown. Ghost. |
| **S01 E11** | *A Gaggle of Galloping Ghosts* | Vampire. Frankenstein's creature. Werewolf. |
| **S01 E12** | *Scooby Doo and a Mummy, Too* | Mummy. |
| **S01 E13** | *Which Witch is Witch?* | Zombie. Witch. |
| **S01 E14** | *Go Away Ghost Ship* | Ghost. Ghost ship. |
| **S01 E15** | *Spooky Space Kook* | UFO. Alien. |
| **S01 E16** | *A Night of Fright is no Delight* | Haunted house. Ghosts (with chains). |
| **S01 E17** | *That's Snow Ghost* | Yeti. |
| **S02 E01** | *Nowhere to Hyde* | Ghost. |
| **S02 E02** | *Mystery Mask Mix-Up* | Zombie. Chinese deities. |

| | | |
|---|---|---|
| S02 E03 | *Scooby's Night with a Frozen Fright* | Caveman. |
| S02 E04 | *Jeepers, It's the Creeper* | Ghost. |
| S02 E05 | *Haunted House Hang-Up* | Headless ghost. |
| | | White sheet ghost. |
| S02 E06 | *A Tiki Scare is No Fair* | Witch doctor. |
| | | Vampire bat. |
| | | Hell sow. |
| S02 E07 | *Who's Afraid of the Big Bad Werewolf* | Werewolf. |
| S02 E08 | *Don't Fool with a Phantom* | Living waxwork. |
| | | Black magic. |
| S03 E01 | *Watch Out! The Willawaw!* | Owlmen. |
| S03 E02 | *A Creepy Tangle in the Bermuda Triangle* | UFO. |
| | | Bermuda Triangle. |
| | | Skeletons. |
| S03 E03 | *A Scary Night with a Snow Beast Fright* | Snow monster. |
| S03 E04 | *To Switch a Witch* | Witch. |
| S03 E05 | *The Tar Monster* | Tar monster. |
| S03 E06 | *A Highland Fling with a Monstrous Thing* | Ghost. |
| | | Loch Ness monster. |
| S03 E07 | *The Creepy Case of Old Iron Face* | Ghost. |
| S03 E08 | *Jeepers, It's the Jaguaro!* | Composite animal. |
| S03 E09 | *Make a Beeline Away from that Feline* | Cat creature. |
| S03 E10 | *The Creepy Creature of Vulture's Claw* | Giant insect. |
| S03 E11 | *The Diabolical Disc Demon* | Ghost. |
| S03 E12 | *Scooby's Chinese Fortune Kooky Caper* | Moon. |
| S03 E13 | *A Menace in Venice* | Ghost. |
| S03 E14 | *Don't Go Near the Fortress of Fear* | Ghost. |
| | | Tunnel. |
| S03 E15 | *The Warlock of Wimbledon* | Warlock. |
| | | Curse. |
| | | Divination. |
| | | Black Dog. |
| S03 E16 | *The Beast is Awake in Bottomless Lake* | Merman. |
| | | Bottomless lake. |
| | | Water spirit. |

## The New Scooby Doo Movies

| | | |
|---|---|---|
| S01 E01 | Ghastly Ghost Town | Ghosts. |
| S01 E02 | The Dynamic Scooby Doo Affair | Hypnosis. Haunted house. |
| S01 E03 | Wednesday is Missing | Gothic. |
| S01 E04 | The Frickert Fracas | Scarecrow. |
| S01 E05 | Guess Who's Knott Coming to Dinner | Ghost. Haunted house. |
| S01 E06 | A Good Medium is Rare | Gothic. |
| S01 E07 | Sandy Duncan's Jekyll and Hyde | Mr Hyde. |
| S01 E08 | The Secret of Shark Island | Shark men. |
| S01 E09 | The Spooky Fog of Juneberry | Skeletons. Ghosts. |
| S01 E10 | The Ghost of Bigfoot | Bigfoot. |
| S01 E11 | The Ghost of the Red Baron | Ghost. |
| S01 E12 | The Ghostly Creep from the Deep | Ghost. |
| S01 E13 | The Haunted Horseman of Hagglethorn Hill | Ghost. |
| S01 E14 | The Phantom of the Country Music Hall | Ghost. |
| S01 E15 | The Caped Crusader Caper | Dryad. Troll. White sheet ghost. |
| S01 E16 | The Lochness Mess | Ghosts. |
| S02 E01 | The Mystery of Haunted Island | Ghosts. |
| S02 E02 | The Haunted Showboat | Ghosts. |
| S02 E03 | Mystery in Persia | Jinn. |
| S02 E04 | The Spirit Spooked Sports Show | Ghost. |
| S02 E05 | The Exterminator | Wolfman and other monsters. |
| S02 E06 | The Weird Winds of Winona | Mysterious wind. |
| S02 E07 | The Haunted Candy Factory | Green monsters. |
| S02 E08 | The Haunted Carnival | Ghosts. |

## The Scooby Doo Show

| | | |
|---|---|---|
| S01 E01 | High Rise Hair Raiser | Ghosts. |
| S01 E02 | The Fiesta Host is an Aztec Ghost | Aztec god. |
| S01 E03 | The Gruesome Game of the Gator Ghoul | Alligator creatures. |
| S01 E04 | Watt a Shocking Ghost | Ghost. |

| | | |
|---|---|---|
| S01 E05 | The Headless Horseman of Halloween | Headless horseman. |
| S01 E06 | Sacred a Lot in Camelot | Ghost. |
| S01 E07 | The Harum-Scarum Sanitarium | Ghost. |
| S01 E08 | The No-Face Zombie Chase Case | Zombie. |
| S01 E09 | Mamba Wamba and the Voodoo Hoodoo | Zombies. Voodoo. |
| S01 E10 | A Frightened Hound Meets Demons Underground | Demons. |
| S01 E11 | A Bum Steer for Scooby | Ghosts (human and animal). |
| S01 E12 | There's a Demon Shark in the Foggy Dark | Animal demon. |
| S01 E13 | Scooby-Doo, Where's the Crew? | Ghost. Sea monster. |
| S01 E14 | The Ghost that Sacked the Quarterback | Ghost. |
| S01 E15 | The Ghost of the Bad Humor Man | Ghosts. |
| S01 E16 | The Spirits of '76 | Ghosts. |
| S02 E01 | The Curse of the Viking Lake | Ghosts. Vikings. Curse. |
| S02 E02 | Vampire Bats and Scaredy Cats | Vampire. |
| S02 E03 | Hang in There, Scooby-Doo | Dinosaur ghost. |
| S02 E04 | The Chiller Diller Movie Thriller | Ghost. |
| S02 E05 | The Spooky Case of the Grand Prix Race | Ghost. |
| S02 E06 | The Ozark Witch Switch | Witch. |
| S02 E07 | Creepy Cruise | Monster. |
| S02 E08 | The Creepy Heap from the Deep | Sea monster. |

## Scooby-Doo and Scrappy-Doo First Series

| | | |
|---|---|---|
| S01 E01 | The Scarab Lives! | Comic book character. |
| S01 E02 | The Night Ghoul of Wonderworld | Victorian-style ghost. |
| S01 E03 | Strange Encounters of a Scooby Kind | Alien/UFO. |
| S01 E04 | The Neon Phantom of the Roller Disco! | Ghost. |
| S01 E05 | Shiver and Shake, That Demon's a Snake | Snake demon. |
| S01 E06 | The Scary Sky Skeleton | Skeleton. |
| S01 E07 | The Demon of the Dugout | Japanese demon. |
| S01 E08 | The Hairy Scare of the Devil Bear | Bear demon. |
| S01 E09 | Twenty Thousand Screams Under the Sea | Sea monster. |

| | | |
|---|---|---|
| S01 E10 | *I Left My Neck in San Francisco* | Vampire. |
| S01 E11 | *When You Wish Upon a Star Creature* | Alien. |
| S01 E12 | *The Ghoul, the Bat and the Ugly* | Horror film monsters. |
| S01 E13 | *Rocky Mountain Yiiiii!* | Ghost. |
| S01 E14 | *The Sorcerer's a Menace* | Ghost. |
| S01 E15 | *Lock the Door, It's a Minotaur* | Minotaur. |
| S01 E16 | *The Ransom of Scooby Chief* | None (just crooks). |

## Scooby-Doo and Scrappy-Doo Second Series S01

| | | |
|---|---|---|
| S01 E01A | *A Close Encounter with a Strange Kind* | Aliens (little green men). |
| S01 E01B | *A Fit Night Out For Bats* | Vampire. |
| S01 E01C | *The Chinese Food Factory* | Chinese dragon. |
| S01 E02A | *Scooby's Desert Dilemma* | Arabian magician. Magic carpet. |
| S01 E02B | *The Old Cat and Mouse Game* | Humanoid cat creature. |
| S01 E02C | *Stow-Aways* | None. |
| S01 E03A | *Mummy's the Word* | Mummy. |
| S01 E03B | *Hang in There, Scooby* | None. |
| S01 E03C | *Stuntman Scooby* | King Kong parody monster. |
| S01 E04A | *Scooby's Three Ding-a-Ling Circus* | None. |
| S01 E04B | *Scooby's Fantastic Island* | None. |
| S01 E04C | *Long John Scrappy* | None. |
| S01 E05A | *Scooby's Bull Fright* | None. |
| S01 E05B | *Scooby Goes West* | Ghosts. |
| S01 E05C | *A Bungle in the Jungle* | None. |
| S01 E06A | *Scooby's Fun Zone* | None. |
| S01 E06B | *Swamp Witch* | Witch. Goblin. |
| S01 E06C | *Sir Scooby and the Black Knight* | Skeleton. |
| S01 E07A | *Waxworld* | Vampire (mode of dress only). |
| S01 E07B | *Scooby in Wonderland* | None. |
| S01 E07C | *Scrappy's Birthday* | None. |
| S01 E08A | *South Seas Scare* | None. |
| S01 E08B | *Scooby's Swiss Miss* | None. |
| S01 E08C | *Alaskan King Coward* | None. |
| S01 E09A | *Et Tu, Scoob?* | Time travel. |

| | |
|---|---|
| **S01 E09B** *Soggy Bog Scooby* | Swamp monster. |
| **S01 E09C** *Scooby Gumbo* | None. |
| **S01 E10A** *Way Out Scooby* | None. |
| **S01 E10B** *Strongman Scooby* | None. |
| **S01 E10C** *Moonlight Madness* | Werewolf. |
| **S01 E11A** *Dog Tag Scooby* | None. |
| **S01 E11B** *Scooby at the Center of the World* | None. |
| **S01 E11C** *Scooby's Trip to Ahz* | Witch. |
| **S01 E12A** *A Fright at the Opera* | Phantom of the Opera. |
| **S01 E12B** *Robot Ranch* | Robots. |
| **S01 E12C** *Surprised Spies* | None. |
| **S01 E13A** *The Invasion of the Scooby Snatchers* | Alien. UFO. |
| **S01 E13B** *Scooby Dooby Guru* | None. |
| **S01 E13C** *Scooby and the Bandit* | None. |

## Scooby-Doo and Scrappy-Doo Second Series S02

| | |
|---|---|
| **S02 E01A** *Scooby-Nocchio* | Folk tale (Pinnochio). |
| **S02 E01B** *Lighthouse Keeper Scooby* | Ghost. |
| **S02 E01C** *Scooby's Roots* | White sheet ghost. |
| **S02 E02A** *Scooby's Escape from Atlantis* | Centaur. |
| **S02 E02B** *Excalibur Scooby* | Merlin. |
| **S02 E02C** *Scooby Saves the World* | Alien. UFO. |
| **S02 E03A** *Scooby Dooby Goo* | None. |
| **S02 E03B** *Rickshaw Scooby* | Dragon. |
| **S02 E03C** *Scooby's Luck of the Irish* | Leprechaun. |
| **S02 E04A** *Backstage Scooby* | Magician. |
| **S02 E04B** *Scooby's House of Mystery* | Witch. |
| **S02 E04C** *Sweet Dreams Scooby* | None. |
| **S02 E05A** *Scooby-Doo 2000* | Robot. |
| **S02 E05B** *Punk Rock Scooby* | Alien. |
| **S02 E05C** *Canine to Five* | Wolf. |
| **S02 E06A** *Hard Hat Scooby* | Vampire. |
| **S02 E06B** *Hothouse Scooby* | Carnivorous plants. |
| **S02 E06C** *Pigskin Scooby* | None. |

| | |
|---|---|
| **S02 E07A** *Sopwith Scooby* | None. |
| **S02 E07B** *Tenderbigfoot* | Bigfoot. |
| **S02 E07C** *Scooby and the Beanstalk* | Giant. |

## Scooby-Doo and Scrappy-Doo Second Series S03

| | |
|---|---|
| **S03 E01A** *Maltese Mackerel* | None. |
| **S03 E01B** *Dumb Waiter Caper* | None. |
| **S03 E01C** *Yabba's Rustle Hustle* | None. |
| **S03 E02A** *Catfish Burglar Caper* | None. |
| **S03 E02B** *Movie Monster Menace* | Various monsters. |
| **S03 E02C** *Mine Your Own Business* | None. |
| **S03 E03A** *Super Teen Shaggy* | None. |
| **S03 E03B** *Basketball Bumblers* | None. |
| **S03 E03C** *Tragic Magic* | Magician. |
| **S03 E04A** *Beauty Contest Caper* | None. |
| **S03 E04B** *Stake-Out at the Take-Out* | None. |
| **S03 E04C** *Runaway Scrappy* | None. |
| **S03 E05A** *Who's Scooby-Doo?* | None. |
| **S03 E05B** *Double Trouble Date* | None. |
| **S03 E05C** *Slippery Dan the Escape Man* | None. |
| **S03 E06A** *Cable Car Caper* | None. |
| **S03 E06B** *Muscle Trouble* | None. |
| **S03 E06C** *Low-Down Showdown* | None. |
| **S03 E07A** *Comic Book Caper* | Slime monster. |
| **S03 E07B** *Misfortune Teller* | None. |
| **S03 E07C** *Vild Vest Vampire* | Vampire. |
| **S03 E08A** *A Gem of a Case* | None. |
| **S03 E08B** *From Bad to Curse* | Gypsy. |
| **S03 E08C** *Tumbleweed Derby* | None. |
| **S03 E09A** *Disappearing Car Caper* | None. |
| **S03 E09B** *Scooby-Doo and Genie-Poo* | Genie. |
| **S03 E09C** *Law & Disorder* | None. |
| **S03 E10A** *Close Encounter of the Worst Kind* | Aliens. UFO. |
| **S03 E10B** *Captain Canine Caper* | None. |
| **S03 E10C** *Alien Schmalien* | Alien (little green man). |

| | |
|---|---|
| **S03 E11A** *The Incredible Cat Lady Caper* | None. |
| **S03 E11B** *Picnic Poopers* | None. |
| **S03 E11C** *Go East Young Pardner* | None. |
| **S03 E12A** *One Million Years Before Lunch* | None. |
| **S03 E12B** *Where's the Werewolf?* | Werewolf. |
| **S03 E12C** *Up a Crazy River* | None. |
| **S03 E13A** *Hoedown Showdown* | None. |
| **S03 E13B** *Snow Job Too Small* | Abominable snowman. |
| **S03 E13C** *Bride and Gloom* | None. |

## The New Scooby and Scrappy Doo Show

| | |
|---|---|
| **S01 E01A** *Scooby the Barbarian* | Vikings. |
| **S01 E01B** *No Sharking Zone* | Sea monster. |
| **S01 E02A** *Scoobygeist* | Ghosts. |
| **S01 E02B** *The Quagmire Quake Caper* | Mud monster. |
| **S01 E03A** *Hound of the Scoobyvilles* | Spectral dog. |
| **S01 E03B** *The Dinosaur Deception* | Dinosaurs. |
| **S01 E04A** *The Creature Came from Chem Lab* | Genetically engineered creature. |
| **S01 E04B** *No Thanks, Masked Manx* | None. |
| **S01 E05A** *Scooby of the Jungle* | Ape man. |
| **S01 E05B** *Scooby-Doo and Cyclops, Too* | Cyclops. |
| **S01 E06A** *Scooby Roo* | Neanderthal. |
| **S01 E06B** *Scooby's Gold Medal Gambit* | None. |
| **S01 E07A** *Wizards and Warlocks* | Wizard. |
| **S01 E07B** *Scoobsie* | Phantom. |
| **S01 E08A** *The Mark of Scooby* | None. |
| **S01 E08B** *The Crazy Carnival Caper* | Clown. |
| **S01 E09A** *Scooby and the Minotaur* | Minotaur. |
| **S01 E09B** *Scooby Pinch Hits* | Ghost. |
| **S01 E10A** *The Fall Dog* | Gremlin. |
| **S01 E10B** *The Scooby Coupe* | Ghost. |
| **S01 E11A** *Who's Minding the Monster* | Frankenstein's creature. Vampire. |
| **S01 E11B** *Scooby ala Mode* | Ghost. |
| **S01 E12** *Where's Scooby-Doo?* | Mummy. |
| **S01 E13** *Wedding Bell Boos!* | Ghost. |

## The New Scooby-Doo Mysteries

| | |
|---|---|
| S01 E01  Happy Birthday Scooby-Doo | None. |
| S01 E02A  Scooby's Peep-Hole Pandemonium | Mummy. |
| S01 E02B  The Hand of Horror | Living hand. |
| S01 E03A  Scoo-Be or Not Scoo-Be? | Ghost. |
| S01 E03B  The Stoney Glare Stare | Cyclops. Medusa. |
| S01 E04A  Mission: Un-Doo-Able | None. |
| S01 E04B  The Bee Team | Bees. |
| S01 E05A  Doom Service | Ghost. |
| S01 E05B  A Code in the Nose | None. |
| S01 E06  Ghosts of the Ancient Astronauts | Zombies. Aliens. UFO. |
| S01 E07A  The Night of the Living Toys | Elf. |
| S01 E07B  South Pole Vault | None. |
| S01 E08  A Halloween Hassle at Dracula's Castle | Universal monsters. |
| S01 E09  A Night Louse at the White House | Ghosts. |
| S01 E10A  Showboat Scooby | Ghost. |
| S01 E10B  The 'Dooby Dooby Doo' Ado | None. |
| S01 E11  Sherlock Doo | Ghost. |
| S01 E12A  A Scarey Duel with a Cartoon Ghoul | None. |
| S01 E12B  E*I*E*I*O | None. |
| S01 E13  The Nutcracker Scoob | Ghost. |

## The 13 Ghosts of Scooby Doo

*This whole series is plotted around capturing different demons, thus list of titles only*

S01 E01  To All the Ghouls I've Loved Before
S01 E02  Scoobra Kadoobra
S01 E03  Me and My Shadow Demon
S01 E04  Reflections in a Ghoulish Eye
S01 E05  That's Monstertainment
S01 E06  Ship of Ghouls
S01 E07  A Spooky Little Ghoul Like You
S01 E08  When You Witch Upon a Star
S01 E09  It's a Wonderful Scoob

S01 E10 *Scooby in Kwackyland*
S01 E11 *Coast-to-Ghost*
S01 E12 *The Ghouliest Show on Earth*
S01 E13 *Horror-Scope Scoob*

## A Pup Named Scooby-Doo Season 1

| | |
|---|---|
| S01 E01 *A Bicycle Built for Boo!* | Ghost. |
| S01 E02 *The Sludge Monster from the Earth's Core* | Mud monster. |
| S01 E03 *The Schnook Who Took My Comic Book* | Giant frog. |
| S01 E04 *Wanted Cheddar Alive* | Cheese monster. |
| S01 E05 *For Letter or Worse* | Ghost. |
| S01 E06 *The Babysitter from Beyond* | Fictional film monster. |
| S01 E07 *Snow Place Like Home* | Ice demon. |
| S01 E08 *Now Museum, Now You Don't* | Ghost. |
| S01 E09 *Scooby Dude* | Headless monster. |
| S01 E10 *Ghost Who's Coming to Dinner* | Ghost. |
| S01 E11 *The Story Stick* | Totem spirit. |
| S01 E12 *Robopup* | Ghost. |
| S01 E13 *Lights... Camera... Monster* | Fictional film monster. |

## A Pup Named Scooby-Doo Season 2

| | |
|---|---|
| S02 E01 *Curse of the Collar* | Ghost. |
| S02 E02 *The Return of Commander Cool* | Alien. |
| S02 E03 *The Spirit of Rock'n Roll* | Ghost. |
| S02 E04 *Chickenstein Lives* | Giant chicken. |
| S02 E05 *Night of the Living Burger* | Burger monster. |
| S02 E06 *The Computer Walks Among Us* | Computer. |
| S02 E07 *Dog Gone Scooby* | None. |
| S02 E08 *Terror, Thy Name is Zombo* | Ghost (clown). |

## A Pup Named Scooby-Doo Season 3

| | |
|---|---|
| S03 E01A *Night of the Boogey Biker* | Ghost. |
| S03 E01B *Dawn of the Spooky Shuttle Scare* | Ghost. |
| S03 E02 *Horror of the Haunted Hairpiece* | None. |
| S03 E03 *Wrestle Maniacs* | Ghost. |

## A Pup Named Scooby-Doo Season 4

| | | |
|---|---|---|
| **S04 E01** | *The Were-Doo of Doo Manor* | Ghost. |
| **S04 E02A** | *Catcher on the Sly* | None. |
| **S04 E02B** | *The Ghost of Mrs Shusham* | Ghost. |
| **S04 E02C** | *The Wrath of Waitro* | None. |
| **S04 E03** | *Mayhem of the Moving Mollusk* | Snail monster. |

## What's New, Scooby-Doo? Season 1

| | | |
|---|---|---|
| **S01 E01** | *There's No Creature Like Snow Creature* | Abominable snowman. |
| **S01 E02** | *3-D Struction* | Curse. |
| **S01 E03** | *Space Ape at the Cape* | Alien. |
| **S01 E04** | *Big Scare in the Big Easy* | Ghosts. Voodoo. |
| **S01 E05** | *It's Mean, It's Green, It's the Mystery Machine* | Possession. |
| **S01 E06** | *Riva Ras Regas* | Ghost. |
| **S01 E07** | *Roller Ghoster Ride* | Gremlin. |
| **S01 E08** | *Safari, So Goodi!* | Demons. |
| **S01 E09** | *She Sees Sea Monsters by the Sea Shore* | Sea serpent. |
| **S01 E10** | *A Scooby-Doo! Christmas* | Headless snowman. |
| **S01 E11** | *Toy Scary Boo* | Possession. |
| **S01 E12** | *Lights! Camera! Mayhem!* | Ghosts. |
| **S01 E13** | *Pompeii and Circumstance* | Zombies. |
| **S01 E14** | *The Unnatural* | Ghost. |

## What's New, Scooby-Doo? Season 2

| | | |
|---|---|---|
| **S02 E01** | *Big Appetite in Little Tokyo* | Curse. |
| **S02 E02** | *Mummy Scares Best* | Mummy. Zombies. |
| **S02 E03** | *The Fast and the Wormious* | Giant worm. |
| **S02 E04** | *High-Tech House of Horrors* | Robot. |
| **S02 E05** | *The Vampire Strikes Back* | Vampire. |
| **S02 E06** | *A Scooby-Doo Halloween* | Swamp creature. Scarecrow. Ghost. |

| | | |
|---|---|---|
| **S02 E07** | *Homeward Hound* | Big cat. |
| **S02 E08** | *The San Franpsycho* | Ghost. |
| **S02 E09** | *Simple Plan and the Invisible Madman* | Invisible man. |
| **S02 E10** | *Recipe for Disaster* | Ghost. |
| **S02 E11** | *Large Dragon at Large* | Dragon. |
| **S02 E12** | *Uncle Scooby and Antarctica* | Fish monster. |
| **S02 E13** | *New Mexico, Old Monster* | Giant bird. |
| **S02 E14** | *It's All Greek to Scooby* | Centaur. |

## What's New, Scooby-Doo? Season 3

| | | |
|---|---|---|
| **S03 E01** | *Fright House of a Lighthouse* | Ghost. |
| **S03 E02** | *Go West, Young Scoob* | Robot. |
| **S03 E03** | *A Scooby-Doo Valentine* | None. |
| **S03 E04** | *Wrestle Maniacs* | None. |
| **S03 E05** | *Ready to Scare* | Gargoyle. |
| **S03 E06** | *Farmed and Dangerous* | Demon. |
| **S03 E07** | *Diamonds Are a Ghoul's Best Friend* | Ghost. |
| **S03 E08** | *A Terrifying Round with a Menacing Clown* | Clown. |
| **S03 E09** | *Camp Comeoniwannascareya* | Toxic waste monster. |
| **S03 E10** | *Block-Long Hong Kong Terror* | Chinese Dragon. |
| **S03 E11** | *Gentlemen, Start Your Monsters!* | Skeleton. |
| **S03 E12** | *Gold Paw* | None. |
| **S03 E13** | *Reef Grief!* | Sea monster. |
| **S03 E14** | *E-Scream* | None. |

## Shaggy and Scooby-Doo Get a Clue Season 1

*This version of show is constructed as a 'James Bond' style story and does not feature traditional monsters, thus list of titles only.*

**S01 E01** *Shags to Riches*
**S01 E02** *More Fondue for Scooby-Doo*
**S01 E03** *High Society Scooby*
**S01 E04** *Party Arty*
**S01 E05** *Smart House*
**S01 E06** *Lightning Strikes Twice*

**S01 E07** *Don't Feed the Animals*
**S01 E08** *Mystery of the Missing Mystery Solvers*
**S01 E09** *Chefs of Steel*
**S01 E10** *Almost Ghosts*
**S01 E11** *Pole to Pole*
**S01 E12** *Big Trouble*
**S01 E13** *Operation Dog and Hippy Boy*

## Shaggy and Scooby-Doo Get a Clue Season 2

**S02 E01** *Shaggy and Scooby World*
**S02 E02** *Almost Purr-fect*
**S02 E03** *Inside Job*
**S02 E04** *Zoinksman*
**S02 E05** *The Many Faces of Evil*
**S02 E06** *Cruisin' for a Bruisin'*
**S02 E07** *There's a Doctor in the House*
**S02 E08** *Super Scary Movie Night*
**S02 E09** *Runaway Robi*
**S02 E10** *Don't Get a Big Head*
**S02 E11** *Scooby Dudes*
**S02 E12** *Zoinks the Wonder Dog*
**S02 E13** *Uncle Albert Alert*

## Scooby-Doo! Mystery Incorporated Season 1

| | | |
|---|---|---|
| **S01 E01** *Beware the Beast from Below* | | Slime monster. |
| **S01 E02** *The Creeping Creatures* | | Giant alligators. |
| **S01 E03** *The Secret of the Ghost Rig* | | Possessed vehicle. |
| **S01 E04** *Revenge of the Man Crab* | | Giant crab. |
| **S01 E05** *The Song of Mystery* | | Ghost. |
| **S01 E06** *The Legend of Alice May* | | Ghost. |
| **S01 E07** *In Fear of the Phantom* | | Ghost. |
| *S01 E08* *The Grasp of the Gnome* | | Gnome. |
| **S01 E09** *Battle of the Humungonauts* | | None. |
| **S01 E10** *Howl of the Fright Hound* | | Robot (dog). |

| | | |
|---|---|---|
| S01 E11 | *The Secret Serum* | Vampire. |
| S01 E12 | *The Shrieking Madness* | Lovecraftian monster. |
| S01 E13 | *When the Cicada Calls* | None. |
| S01 E14 | *Mystery Solvers Club State Finals* | Skeleton. |
| S01 E15 | *The Wild Brood* | Orcs. |
| S01 E16 | *Where Walks Aphrodite* | Ghost. |
| S01 E17 | *Escape from Mystery Manor* | Haunted house. |
| S01 E18 | *The Dragon's Secret* | Chinese sorcerers. Dragon. |
| S01 E19 | *Nightfright* | Devil. |
| S01 E20 | *The Siren's Song* | Siren. |
| S01 E21 | *Menace of the Manticore* | Manticore. |
| S01 E22 | *Attack of the Headless Horror* | Blemmyes. |
| S01 E23 | *A Haunting in Crystal Cove* | Poltergeist. |
| S01 E24 | *Dead Justice* | Ghost. |
| S01 E25 | *Pawn of Shadows* | Robot. |
| S01 E26 | *All Fear the Freak* | None. |

## Scooby-Doo! Mystery Incorporated Season 2

| | | |
|---|---|---|
| S02 E01 | *The Night the Clown Cried* | Clown. |
| S02 E02 | *The House of the Nightmare Witch* | Baba Yaga. |
| S02 E03 | *The Night the Clown Cried II – Tears of Doom* | Clown. |
| S02 E04 | *Web of the Dreamweaver!* | Dreams. |
| S02 E05 | *The Hodag of Horror* | Hodag. |
| S02 E06 | *Art of Darkness!* | Robot. |
| S02 E07 | *The Gathering Gloom* | Ghoul. |
| S02 E08 | *Night on Haunted Mountain* | Lilith. |
| S02 E09 | *Grim Judgment* | Ghost. |
| S02 E10 | *Night Terrors* | Shaman. |
| S02 E11 | *The Midnight Zone* | Robots. |
| S02 E12 | *Scarebear* | Mutant bear. |
| S02 E13 | *Wrath of the Krampus* | Krampus. |
| S02 E14 | *Heart of Evil* | Robot dragon. |
| S02 E15 | *Theater of Doom* | Ghost. Mummy. |
| S02 E16 | *Aliens Among Us* | Aliens. |

| | | |
|---|---|---|
| S02 E17 | *The Horrible Herd* | Skeletons. |
| S02 E18 | *Dance of the Undead* | Zombies. |
| S02 E19 | *The Devouring* | None. |
| S02 E20 | *Stand and Deliver* | Ghost. |
| S02 E21 | *The Man in the Mirror* | Mirrors. Skeleton. |
| S02 E22 | *Nightmare in Red* | None. |
| S02 E23 | *Dark Night of the Hunters* | None. |
| S02 E24 | *Gates of Gloom* | None. |
| S02 E25 | *Through the Curtain* | Demon. |
| S02 E26 | *Come Undone* | Apocalypse conspiracy. |

## Be Cool, Scooby-Doo! Season 1

| | | |
|---|---|---|
| S01 E01 | *Mystery 101* | Ghost. |
| S01 E02 | *Game of Chicken* | Tribal spirit. |
| S01 E03 | *All Paws on Deck* | Sea monster. |
| S01 E04 | *Poodle Justice* | Gargoyle. |
| S01 E05 | *Grand Scam* | Ghost. |
| S01 E06 | *Trading Chases* | Egyptian god. |
| S01 E07 | *Be Quiet, Scooby-Doo!* | None. |
| S01 E08 | *Party Like It's 1899* | Headless ghost. |
| S01 E09 | *Screama Donna* | Ghost. |
| S01 E10 | *Kitchen Frightmare* | Yeti. |
| S01 E11 | *Me, Myself and A.I.* | Robot. |
| S01 E12 | *Area 51, Adjacent* | Alien. |
| S01 E13 | *Where There's a Will, There's a Wraith* | Ghost. |
| S01 E14 | *Scary Christmas* | None. |
| S01 E15 | *If You Can't Scooby-Doo the Time, Don't Scooby-Doo the Crime* | Ghost. |
| S01 E16 | *Gremlin on a Plane* | Gremlin. |
| S01 E17 | *Sorcerer Snacks Scare* | Wizard. |
| S01 E18 | *Saga of the Swamp Beast* | Swamp monster. |
| S01 E19 | *Be Cold, Scooby-Doo!* | Snow monster. |
| S01 E20 | *Giant Problems* | Giant. |
| S01 E21 | *Eating Crow* | Scarecrow. |
| S01 E22 | *I Scooby Dooby Do* | Ghost. |

| | | |
|---|---|---|
| **S01 E23** | *El Bandito* | Ghost. |
| **S01 E24** | *Into the Mouth of Madcap* | Clown. |
| **S01 E25** | *The Norse Case Scenario* | Ghosts. |
| | | Vikings. |
| **S01 E26** | *The People vs Fred Jones* | Toxic monster. |

## Be Cool, Scooby-Doo! Season 2

| | | |
|---|---|---|
| **S02 E01** | *Some Fred Time* | None. |
| **S02 E02** | *There Wolf* | Werewolf. |
| **S02 E03** | *Renn Scare* | Jester. |
| **S02 E04** | *How to Train Your Coward* | Vampire. |
| | | Zombie. |
| **S02 E05** | *Worst in Show* | Hell hound. |
| **S02 E06** | *Mysteries on the Disorient Express* | Grim reaper. |
| | | Mummy. |
| | | Tengu. |
| | | Terasque. |
| | | Haniver. |
| | | Demon. |
| | | Manticore. |
| **S02 E07** | *Halloween* | Witches. |
| | | Baba Yaga. |
| **S02 E08** | *The Curse of Kaniaku* | Based on Japanese Yokai. |
| **S02 E09** | *Vote Velma* | Ghost. |
| **S02 E10** | *Scroogey Doo* | Ghosts. |
| **S02 E11** | *In Space* | Space monster. |
| **S02 E12** | *Doo Not Disturb* | Ghost. |
| **S02 E13** | *Silver Scream* | Ghost. |
| **S02 E14** | *Fright of Hand* | Possessed rabbit. |
| **S02 E15** | *Greece is the Word* | Greek mythological creatures. |
| **S02 E16** | *American Goth* | Plant monster. |
| **S02 E17** | *Omelettes are Forever* | None. |
| **S02 E18** | *Ghost in the Mystery Machine* | Possessed vehicle. |
| **S02 E19** | *Naughty or Ice* | Ice man. |
| **S02 E20** | *Night of the Upsetting Shorts* | Ape man. |
| **S02 E21** | *Junkyard Dogs* | None. |
| **S02 E22** | *Protein Titans 2* | Ghost. |

| | | |
|---|---|---|
| S02 E23 | *World of Witchcraft* | Demon. |
| S02 E24A | *Pizza O'Possum's* | Robot. |
| S02 E24B | *The Curse of Half-Beard's Booty* | Ghost of Captain Cutler. |
| S02 E25 | *Professor Huh? Part 1* | None. |
| S02 E26 | *Professor Huh? Part 2* | None. |

## Scooby-Doo and Guess Who? Season 1

| | | |
|---|---|---|
| S01 E01 | *Revenge of the Swamp Monster!* | Swamp monster. |
| S01 E02 | *A Mystery Solving Gang Divided* | Civil war ghosts. |
| S01 E03 | *Peebles' Pet Shop of Terrible Terrors!* | Fish monster. |
| S01 E04 | *Elementary, My Dear Shaggy* | Screaming skulls. |
| S01 E05 | *Ollie Ollie In-Come Free!* | Cat mummy. |
| S01 E06 | *The Scooby of a Thousand Faces!* | Minotaur. |
| S01 E07 | *The Cursed Cabinet of Professor Madds Markson!* | Ghost. |
| S01 E08 | *When Urkel-Bots Go Bad* | Robot. |
| S01 E09 | *The Fastest Food Fiend!* | Ghost. |
| S01 E10 | *Attack of the Weird Al-Osaurus!* | Dinosaurs. |
| S01 E11 | *Now You Sia, Now You Don't!* | Doppelganger. |
| S01 E12 | *Quit Clowning!* | Ghost clown. |
| S01 E13 | *What a Night, for a Dark Knight!* | Humanoid bat monster. |
| S01 E14 | *The Nightmare Ghost of Psychic U!* | Nightmare ghost. |
| S01 E15 | *The Sword, the Fox, and the Scooby-Doo!* | Fox monster. |
| S01 E16 | *One Minute Mysteries!* | Monsters from previous shows. |
| S01 E17 | *Hollywood Knights!* | Haunted armour. |
| S01 E18 | *The New York Underground!* | Alligator monster. |
| S01 E19 | *Fear of the Fire Beast!* | Fire monster. |
| S01 E20 | *Too Many Dummies!* | Possessed ventriloquist dummy. |
| S01 E21 | *Dance Matron of Mayhem!* | Ghost. |
| S01 E22 | *The Wedding Witch of Wainsly Hall!* | Ghost. |
| S01 E23 | *A Run Cycle Through Time!* | None. |
| S01 E24 | *I Put a Hex on You!* | Ghost. |
| S01 E25 | *The High School Wolfman's Musical Lament!* | Werewolf. |
| S01 E26 | *Space Station Scooby* | None. |

# Scooby-Doo and Guess Who? Season 2

| | | |
|---|---|---|
| **S02 E01** | *The Phantom, the Talking Dog, and the Hot Hot Hot Sauce!* | Ghost. |
| **S02 E02** | *The Last Inmate!* | Ghost. |
| **S02 E03** | *The Horrible Haunted Hospital of Dr Phineas Phrag!* | Ghost. |
| **S02 E04** | *The Hot Dog Dog!* | Tree monster. |
| **S02 E05** | *A Moveable Mystery!* | Gargoyle. |
| **S02 E06** | *The Feast of Dr Frankenfooder!* | None. |
| **S02 E07** | *A Fashion Nightmare!* | Ghost. |
| **S02 E08** | *Scooby on Ice!* | Snow devil. |
| **S02 E09** | *Caveman on the Half-Pipe!* | Caveman. |
| **S02 E10** | *The Crown Jewel of Boxing!* | Robot. |
| **S02 E11** | *The Internet of Haunted House Hill!* | Ghost. |
| **S02 E12** | *The 7th Inning Scare!* | Ghost. |
| **S02 E13** | *The Dreaded Remake of Jekyll & Hyde!* | Mr Hyde. |
| **S02 E14** | *Total Jeopardy!* | Robot. |
| **S02 E15** | *Dark Diner of Route 66!* | Mud creatures. |
| **S02 E16** | *Lost Soles of Jungle River!* | Snake monster. |
| **S02 E17** | *The Tao of Scoob!* | Living sculpture. |
| **S02 E18** | *Returning of the Key Ring!* | Plant monster. |
| **S02 E19** | *Cher, Scooby and the Sargasso Sea!* | Shark men. |
| **S02 E20** | *The Lost Mines of Kilimanjaro!* | Gorilla. |
| **S02 E21** | *The Legend of the Gold Microphone!* | Ghosts. |
| **S02 E22** | *Scooby-Doo and the Sky Town Cool School!* | Dinosaur. |
| **S02 E23** | *Falling Star Man!* | Alien. |
| **S02 E24** | *A Haunt of a Thousand Voices!* | Past monsters. |
| **S02 E25** | *Scooby-Doo, Dog Wonder!* | Medusa. |
| **S02 E26** | *The Movieland Monsters!* | Ghost. |

# DIRECT TO VIDEO FILMS

| | |
|---|---|
| Scooby-Doo on Zombie Island | Werecats. Zombies. |
| Scooby-Doo! and the Witch's Ghost | Witch. |
| Scooby-Doo and the Alien Invaders | Aliens. |
| Scooby-Doo and the Cyber Chase | None. |
| Scooby-Doo! and the Legend of the Vampire | Vampires. |
| Scooby-Doo! and the Monster of Mexico | Chupacabra. |
| Scooby-Doo! and the Loch Ness Monster | Loch Ness Monster. |
| Aloha, Scooby-Doo! | Volcano god. |
| Scooby-Doo! in Where's My Mummy? | Ghost of Cleopatra. Undead. |
| Scooby-Doo! Pirates Ahoy! | Bermuda triangle |
| Chill Out, Scooby-Doo! | Shangri-La. Abominable snowman. |
| Scooby-Doo! and the Goblin King | Fairy. Goblin. Headless horseman |
| Scooby-Doo! and the Samurai Sword | Samurai. Wyrm. |
| Scooby-Doo! Abracadabra-Doo | Banshee. |
| Scooby-Doo! Camp Scare | Campfire story creatures. |
| Scooby-Doo! Legend of the Phantosaur | Dinosaurs. |
| Scooby-Doo! Music of the Vampire | Vampire. |
| Big Top Scooby-Doo! | Werewolf. |
| Scooby-Doo! Mask of the Blue Falcon | Mr Hyde. |
| Scooby-Doo! Stage Fright | Ghost. |
| Scooby-Doo! WrestleMania Mystery | Animal ghost. |
| Scooby-Doo! Frankencreepy | Curse. Ghost. Reanimated creature. |
| Scooby-Doo! Moon Monster Madness | Alien. |
| Scooby-Doo! and KISS: Rock and Roll Mystery | Witch. |
| Scooby-Doo! and WWE: Curse of the Speed Demon | None. |
| Scooby-Doo! Shaggy's Showdown | Ghost. |
| Scooby-Doo! & Batman: The Brave and the Bold | Ghost. |
| Scooby-Doo! and the Gourmet Ghost | Ghost. |

| | |
|---|---|
| *Scooby-Doo! and the Curse of the 13th Ghost* | Ghost. |
| *Scooby-Doo! Return to Zombie Island* | Zombies. |
| | Were animals. |
| *Happy Halloween, Scooby-Doo!* | Scarecrow. |
| *Scooby-Doo! The Sword and the Scoob* | Morgan le Fay. |
| *LEGO Scooby-Doo! Haunted Hollywood* | Movie monsters. |
| *LEGO Scooby-Doo! Blowout Beach Bash* | Ghosts. |
| *Scooby-Doo! Adventures: The Mystery Map* | Ghost. |

## TELEFILMS

| | |
|---|---|
| *Scooby-Doo Meets the Boo Brothers* | Ghost. |
| | Skeleton. |
| | Headless horseman. |
| *Scooby-Doo and the Ghoul School* | Universal monsters. |
| *Scooby-Doo and the Reluctant Werewolf* | Vampire. |
| | Mummy. |
| | Witch. |
| | Werewolf. |

## LIVE ACTION FILMS

| | |
|---|---|
| *Scooby-Doo: The Movie* | Ghost. |
| | Demons. |
| *Scooby-Doo 2: Monsters Unleashed* | Previous monsters from the show. |
| *Scooby-Doo! The Mystery Begins* | Ghost. |
| *Scooby-Doo! Curse of the Lake Monster* | Scarecrow. |
| | Lake monster. |
| *Daphne & Velma* | Zombies. |

## CGI ANIMATION

| | |
|---|---|
| *SCOOB!* | Cerberus. |

# DIRECT TO VIDEO SHORT FILMS

*Scooby-Doo! Spooky Games*  Living statues.
*Scooby-Doo! Haunted Holidays*  Snowman.
*Scooby-Doo! and the Spooky Scarecrow*  Scarecrow.
*Scooby-Doo! Mecha Mutt Menace*  Ghost.
Robot.
*Scooby-Doo! Ghastly Goals*  Mythical beast.
*Scooby-Doo! and the Beast Beastie*  Sea monster.

# ACKNOWLEDGEMENTS

The creation of this book has been one of the most enjoyable projects that I have worked on, and at the same time one that felt like it might never end. And really, it could have never ended. Whilst I have watched the majority of the shows in the appendix to research for this book, there are some that have been impossible to track down in the UK, and others that could have been used but for the constraints on book-length and time.

Similarly, new content is being created all the time but there has to be a cut-off point to allow publication. Maybe in the future there will be a second edition, with new material and further expansion? Time will tell.

I am grateful to many people who have helped to keep me sane throughout this process. My publisher, Barnaby Eaton-Jones at Chinbeard Books is relentlessly encouraging, probably because he loves the franchise too and wanted to read the manuscript. And because, by his own admission, he looks a bit like Shaggy after a good meal.

Invaluable input has come from many of the writers and others involved with the show who have answered questions and provided valuable insight. Writers are often forgotten and it was very important to me to make sure that their voices were included in this work. In particular, my thanks to Mitch Watson for taking time out to write the foreword, to John Semper Jr for devoting time to a Zoom call, and to Scott Innes for supplying the afterword.

This manuscript has been shaped, developed and no doubt improved by beta readers Brontë Schiltz and Tracy Nicholas, who have been my Daphne and Velma for this investigation. I will let them decide who is who. Or maybe they can share. My thanks also to other advance-copy readers for jacket quotes and not hating it too much.

I am indebted, once again, to the amazing storyboard artist Rhianna Wynter for rendering some real-world folklore in Hanna-Barbera style for the chapter headings. Follow her on Instagram and enjoy her work.

Final thanks go to all of my social media followers, listeners to *The Folklore Podcast* and others who engage with my work for their continued interest in this book and constant messages asking when they can get a copy because they needed it in their lives. I hope you weren't too disappointed.

*Author avatar
by Kat Avent*

# ABOUT THE AUTHOR

Mark Norman is a folklore researcher and author who lives in mid-Devon, in the South West of the United Kingdom. He is a council member of The Folklore Society, Recorder of Folklore for The Devonshire Association and the Founding Curator of The Folklore Library and Archive, a registered charity dedicated to the preservation of folklore material, and to making this material freely available for the benefit of everyone.

In 2015, Mark created *The Folklore Podcast* which, over its nine seasons so far, has grown to become ranked in the top 0.5% of podcasts globally for audience share, with around two million downloads to date. It is recognised for bringing everyone free access to the world's folklore experts, and for its accessible and yet academically rigorous style, which is the approach that Mark takes with all of his writing. You can find it online at www.thefolklorepodcast.com

Mark's previous books include *Black Dog Folklore* for Troy Books, *Telling the Bees and other Customs* and *Dark Folklore* for The History Press, *The Folklore of Devon* for University of Exeter Press and *The Folklore of Wales: Ghosts* for Calon Books. He has contributed to many other publications in print and online.

Sharing Mark's house (but not sharing in the experience of watching so much Scooby-Doo) are his wife Tracey, with whom *Dark Folklore* was co-authored and daughter Alyssa, alongside chickens, intentional mice and a plump cat with a desire to trip all of the other inhabitants at any given opportunity.

You can contact Mark through the Folklore Podcast website.